A Few Good Gays

A Few Good Gays

THE GENDERED COMPROMISES BEHIND MILITARY INCLUSION

Cati Connell

UNIVERSITY OF CALIFORNIA PRESS

University of California Press
Oakland, California

Library of Congress Cataloging-in-Publication Data

Names: Connell, Catherine, 1980- author.
Title: A few good gays : the gendered compromises behind military inclusion / Cati Connell.
Description: Oakland, California : University of California Press, [2023] | Includes bibliographical references and index.
Identifiers: LCCN 2022020943 (print) | LCCN 2022020944 (ebook) | ISBN 9780520382688 (cloth) | ISBN 9780520382695 (paperback) | ISBN 9780520382701 (epub)
Subjects: LCSH: Gay military personnel—United States. | Sexual minority military personnel—United States. | Transgender military personnel—United States. | United States—Armed Forces—Women. | United States—Armed Forces—Minorities.
Classification: LCC UB418.G38 C665 2023 (print) | LCC UB418.G38 (ebook) | DDC 355.0086/640973—dc23/eng/20220819
LC record available at https://lccn.loc.gov/2022020943
LC ebook record available at https://lccn.loc.gov/2022020944

Manufactured in the United States of America

32 31 30 29 28 27 26 25 24 23
10 9 8 7 6 5 4 3 2 1

For Taylor

Contents

Acknowledgments

In April 2020, as the world adjusted to the sudden isolation of pandemic life, a loose network of social scientists in desperate need of workplace camaraderie came together to write with each other on Zoom; thank you is far too insufficient a platitude to adequately convey the gratitude I feel for this incredible writing collective. As the days, months, and now years of working from home stretched on, that Zoom room became our new office. My writing partners quite literally *watched* this book get written while working on their own alongside me. They were there at midnight the night I turned in the first draft, making confetti out of scraps of scratch paper to celebrate as I hit submit. And they were there again the morning I first started revising. And then for the many days and rough patches and pep talks and tiny triumphs and minor breakdowns and major life events that followed. Most importantly, they were my entire social world through these years of living alone during a pandemic. Without them, I'm not sure I could have kept going at all. With them, I have written a book I feel proud of, and they have written brilliant articles, books, grant proposals, conference papers, job materials, tenure statements, and more! I am so lucky to have found family with Jess Simes, Dana Moss, Jackie Jahn, Merav Shohet, Sarah Miller, Paula Austin, Sultan Doughan, and the other occasional visitors who make this virtual office something truly special.

I am indebted to the cadets, servicemembers, and veterans who shared their life stories with me, and to the policy stakeholders who helped me find my way through a tangled thicket of policy changes, reversals, and double backs: Greg Brown, Fiona Dawson, Blake Dremann, Eric Fanning, Sue Fulton, Amanda Simpson, Brynn Tannehill, and Alex Wagner. Thank you to Aaron Belkin for meeting with me at the inception of this project and helping me get my bearings as I entered the unfamiliar territory of military policy. Aaron has been a tireless advocate for LGBTs, both in the service and well beyond. Under Aaron's leadership, the Palm Center produced a critical mass of interdisciplinary scholarship that helped to make the repeal and trans inclusion possible, including Aaron's own extensive body of work on the subject.

I was also fortunate to have sat down near Máel Embser-Herbert at a conference years back; from that chance encounter, I developed a friendship with someone whose early work was an inspiration for this project and whose current work is breaking new ground on the subject of transgender service. I was lucky to receive an advance copy of *With Honor & Integrity: Transgender Troops in Their Own Words* (with coauthor Bree Fram), which offers an essential oral history of the trans policy debates from those who feel its effects most keenly. In yet another happy coincidence, I'm so glad to have come across Steven Thrasher's delightfully colorful and smart 2013 *Gawker* article, "Haaay to the Chief: The Military-Industrial Complex Conquers the Homos" early in the writing of this book, which served as another point of inspiration. In a remarkable coincidence neither of us was aware of, it turns out Steven and I went to high school together over twenty years ago! Since then, my fellow Oxnard Yellowjacket has been such a friend and cheerleader to this project and the next.

I am beyond grateful to the colleagues who helped me find my way to the end with feedback on various drafts and iterations over the years. Thank you to Sara Crowley, Trevor Hoppe, CJ Pascoe, Brandon Robinson, Amy Stone, and the anonymous manuscript reviewers for your generous and brilliant suggestions! At Boston University, I'm indebted to Heather Mooney for research assistance, the Department of Sociology for helping to fund transcription and editorial costs, Nazli Kibria for her support as dean of the social sciences, and the faculty and students who gave feedback on ideas and drafts. I have learned so much from my sociology and WGS colleagues along the way, especially Japonica Brown-Saracino, Heba Gowayed, Max Greenberg, Saida Grundy, Lida Maxwell, Sandy McEvoy, Ashley Mears, Anthony Petro, Jess Simes, and Keith Vincent. Thank you also to Elliot Chudyk, who is an essential and trusted interlocutor and collaborator when it comes to feminist and queer theory building.

It is such a joy to have found a supportive academic and activist community online who offered generative ideas and inspirations at every step of this project. I'm kicking myself for not keeping notes over the years of everyone who has helped, but I hope y'all know who you are! I did have the presence of mind to jot down the names of everyone who chimed in with great ideas about title and cover design, and while this is only a small fraction of the larger whole, I'd like to thank Nicole Bedera, Tristan Bridges, Shantel Buggs, Kelsy Burke, Devon Goss, Trenton Haltom, Laura Heath-Stout, Krystale Littlejohn, Jeff Lockhart, Olivia McCargar, Greggor Mattson, Anthony Ocampo, Evren Savcı, Casey Stockstill, Amy Stone, and alithia zamintakis for your ideas. At the certain risk of forgetting many, I can't help but also send thanks to some of the sociologists whose work has offered joy and a creative spark over these years of writing: Joe Fischel, Clare Forstie, Patrick Grzanka, Angela Jones, Shannon Malone Gonzalez, Emily Mann, Mike Messner, Sanyu Majola, Mignon Moore, Ghassan Moussawi, CJ Pascoe, Jyoti Puri, Brandon Robinson, Evren Savcı, Paige Sweet, Salvador Vidal-Ortiz, Suzanna Walters, Laurel Westbrook, Jane Ward, and so many more! Y'all make this discipline a great place to live.

Thank you to the people who love and support me even at my most exhausting self: Paula Austin, Toshia and Jo Caravita, Connor Fitzmaurice, the Guthrie family (Emily, Chris, Miles, and Willa), Laura Heston, Bryan Kaufman, Steph Kinnear, Sarah Miller, Sarah Murray, Erika Nuñez, Rin Reczek, Megan Reid, Jess Simes, Sonya Sowerby, Susanne Sreedhar, Lisa Storer, and Stacy Wagner (it really takes a village to raise this child!). I feel incredibly lucky any time I get to be in the company of Travis Beaver, Emily Belanger, OJ Bushell, Courtney Cogburn, Sean Desilets, Dani Dirks, Georgiann Davis, Jessica Fields, Jen Gilbert, Samia Hesni, Ben Hine, Sarah Jackson, Jackie Jahn, Nate Jeffery, Anthony Lee, Dave McCabe,

Marie McDonough, Mark Ocegueda, Ranita Ray, Monse Segura, Merav Shohet, Helen Jeffery Simes, Rachel Westerfield, Caitlin Vanderbilt, and Keith Vincent.

The years go by, and I only become more stunned by the scope of the mentorship Christine Williams has bestowed upon me in the past twenty years. There is nothing about my research practice, my teaching, my mentoring, or my sense of purpose in this world that hasn't been shaped by her truly brilliant counsel. I'll never be able to repay the debt of gratitude I owe, but as she taught me to from the beginning, I try to do so by committing to becoming a better mentor, teacher, scholar, collaborator, and colleague to the incoming generations of feminist and queer sociologists who follow. I am also eternally grateful to the bad asses who made good trouble in the 2004 cohort at UT Austin; grad school was the best years of my life so far, largely thanks to Rin Reczek, Megan Reid, and Angela Stroud.

Thank you to Naomi Schneider, Letta Page, Sharon Langworthy, and Summer Farah for their invaluable editorial guidance. Thanks also to Lisa Storer for the crucial cover art assistance! Portions of this book's argument and/or the data it draws on appear in the journals *Social Problems* (2022), *Sexualities* (2017), *Sociology Compass* (2017), and the *Boston University Law Review* (2016). I thank the editors and anonymous reviewers for each article, whose feedback on these projects benefited this book as well.

Finally, thank you to my late brother Taylor, to whom this book is dedicated. I wish I'd had so many more years to learn from and with you. You were the first to introduce me to the dynamics of military life that would lead me to this project. I hope that despite our differences of opinion, including on the military itself, you would have been proud of your big sister's book that bears your name. I miss you every day.

Introduction

THE DAWNING OF A KINDER, GENTLER US MILITARY

> America is never wholly herself unless she is engaged in high moral principle. We as a people have such a purpose today. It is to make kinder the face of the nation and gentler the face of the world.
>
> President George H. W. Bush, 1989 inaugural speech

In contrast to the later aggressively hawkish rhetoric of post-9/11 politics, George H. W. Bush's inaugural vision of a kinder, gentler global governance seems quaint by comparison. Yet he would go on to launch the Gulf War, a decision that would directly and indirectly create the geopolitical conditions that gave rise to the interminable war on terror. This apparent mismatch is, in fact, emblematic of American politics. The national identity of the United States, defined by the ideals of freedom, liberty, and safety, have in fact *always* been constituted through violence, from its settler colonial origins onward.[1] And so, addressing the nation, the elder Bush announced the invasion of Iraq by framing it as an act of liberation. "Even as planes of the multinational forces attack Iraq," Bush said solemnly, "I prefer to think of peace, not war."[2] He lamented the inevitable casualties to come but pledged that "out of the horror of combat will come the recognition that no nation can stand against a world united"—a world with the United States at the helm. Thirty years later, that unrealized promise of world peace remains the carrot that justifies the stick of continued occupation in the Middle East.

What's more, the folding in of gay rights, women's rights, and trans rights to that national brand over recent decades has further legitimated war and militarism, now dressed up as mechanisms of gender and sexual equality. It is in this context that the US military has made extraordinary strides toward gender- and sexuality-inclusive personnel policies. With the repeal of Don't Ask, Don't Tell (DADT), the end of the combat exclusion rule for women, and the removal of medical regulations against transgender service, the military is now a kinder, gentler place for lesbian, gay, bisexual, and transgender people (LGBTs) and cisgender straight women—at least on paper. Still, these changes are not exactly the feminist and LGBT rights victories they purport to be. Just as Bush Sr. waged war in the name of world peace, the incorporation of LGBTs and cis straight women has served as an alibi for US globalism, shoring up US empire while shortchanging those it purports to protect.[3]

This accomplishment was aided and abetted by what I call the *homonormative bargain* of the gay rights movement, the purchase of inclusion (for some) at the expense of the antiwar, antiracist, and gender-expansive politics of gay liberation. Social movement tactics of visibility, normalcy, and assimilation in the late twentieth century made inclusion possible, but only through complicity with the racist, misogynist, and imperialist agenda of the US settler state. As I will demonstrate, even those who directly benefit from this attenuated inclusion are, in fact, harmed by the deal.

Curious about the reception of this policy sea change, I began interviewing Army ROTC cadets in 2015. I was eager to hear the perspectives of this cohort of future officers, the first to experience officer training under the new policy regime, to live, work, train, and serve where policy meets practice. One of my earliest interviews was with Cara, a cadet in her last year of ROTC training. A 22-year-old white cisgender straight woman, Cara was enthusiastic about the repeal of DADT. To her mind, the move better aligned the military with her generation's more live-and-let-live attitude about sexuality; in a few years, she predicted, DADT would be so thoroughly anachronistic that she and her fellow officers would barely remember it. Cara told me that in her ROTC program, "I haven't really met anyone who's been actively against any gay people or anything like that. . . . [Acceptance] is such a norm now, almost, at least in my experience." Still, she hedged, "I'm sure it would be, maybe, a little bit different in some of these more masculine type branches, such as infantry and armor, where it's all males." After a beat, she reversed course, recalling a story from her boyfriend, an Army infantry officer: "One of [his] classmates came out and said he was gay. It was kind of like, 'Okay.'" As she spoke, she shrugged her shoulders and held out her hands in a gesture that communicated indifference. She went on, "He did say there were some people who made comments, but that everyone else in their class [told those people], 'That's not okay.'" And so, Cara concluded, "I just really think our generation going into it is going to continue to shift that norm. It's going to be just like, accepted and like it always was there, you know?"

Given her welcoming attitude toward the DADT repeal, I expected Cara would be equally sanguine about the gender integration of combat. Yet on that topic, Cara's tone became cautious:

> I think it's very complicated. . . . My biggest concern with allowing it . . . is I think there is a huge discrepancy between physical strength, male and female, and I just don't think you can—we already do adjust standards for things like the PT [physical training] test and that sort of stuff, but if you're going to ask them to be in those roles, I think they have to rise up to the same standards as males and they need to be treated 100 percent the same. I do think *some* females can do it. But I think it's a very, very small percentage.

This tonal shift had me scratching my head. How could the same cadet regard the integration of lesbian, gay, and bisexual people (LGBs) as a much-needed corrective to old-fashioned attitudes, yet also maintain that the segregation of women from combat was a necessary evil? Similar gender-essentialist rationales also tempered Cara's enthusiasm for the third major policy change, transgender inclusion throughout the military:

> I understand [trans exclusion] from a military perspective with how many things you have to be male or female, especially with the physical stuff and the PT test. I don't know what the correct term is to use, but if you're saying you're female but you're actually male [*sic*], that could give you an extremely unfair advantage, just because your body is naturally built so much differently and you are naturally stronger than females. Something like that, I could understand why that would be an issue. So many things are male or female. You have to be one or the other.

It seemed that to Cara, the incorporation of sexual difference was only a problem to the extent that old guard military personnel held onto outdated homophobic beliefs. By contrast, the incorporation of gender difference was a dangerous proposition. The bodies of cisgender women are inadequate for combat missions, and the bodies of trans people, trans women in particular, introduce too much "unfair advantage" and logistical difficulty. If cisgender women were not enough and transgender women were too much, sexuality integration was the only policy shift that Cara found "just right."

Intrigued, I nonetheless regarded this dissonance as an idiosyncrasy in the moment. Surely other interviewees would be more consistent: pro- or anti-inclusion. Yet as interviewing went on, this splitting cropped up again and again. Cadets were simultaneously supportive of the DADT repeal and wary about (or even outright hostile toward) transgender inclusion and women in combat roles.[4] I wondered why, if sexuality integration was a "nonevent," as most of my interviewees claimed, respondents so often viewed increased gender integration as such a monumental—and perilous—disruption to the institution. After all, women had served informally and meritoriously on the front lines for decades, despite the formal ban on their participation.[5] And why would cadets who saw themselves as LGBT allies consider transgender service a bad idea?

Shortly thereafter, I expanded my inquiry to include military servicemembers and veterans.[6] Maybe this contradiction in the gender and sexuality beliefs of cadets could be chalked up to their relative inexperience with the institution itself. It could be the case that servicemembers and vets would be more skeptical about the DADT repeal or less concerned about the end of combat exclusion and trans regulations. Real-world military experience might bring their attitudes about gender versus sexuality integration into alignment. As I continued interviewing, though, the discordant pattern persisted, even intensified.

These mismatched attitudes toward gender, sexuality, and inclusion, I argue, are more than institutionally specific quirks; they illustrate a broader divergence in how we understand gender and sexuality in the twenty-first century. In short, the United States is in the midst of a historic uncoupling of gender and sexuality ideologies. To be sure, the history and structure of the military mattered for the ways research participants narrated exclusion and inclusion; in particular, the institution's aggressively heteromasculinist history and culture distinguish it from other contemporary organizational contexts in certain respects. However, as I show, the ideological uncoupling I found among respondents is also a consequence of the homonormative turn in gay rights organizing, the effects of which are felt well beyond the military. Decades of social movement strategy focused on dispelling myths of gender nonnormativity and minimizing the distance between hetero- and homosexualities has made LGB integration more palatable throughout society and its institutions.

Desexualization and the containment of the "effeminacy effect" that shaped the reimagining of homosexuality have made room for (some) expressions of LGB identity within the military's culture of hypermasculinity and within US society more generally.[7] The homonormative bargain carved out loopholes through which normatively gendered LGBs could slip. But it sidestepped the larger ideological forces of misogyny, transphobia, and femmephobia—the systematic devaluation of femininity—leaving them undisturbed. By choosing assimilation as its primary strategy for securing rights, the gay rights movement abandoned the gender deconstructionist tactics of its predecessor, gay liberation. On the one hand, this strategy tempered the harmful gender stereotyping of LGBs, gay and bisexual men in particular. On the other, it allowed biologically essentialist explanations of embodied gender difference—and gender deviance—to survive the mainstreaming of gay rights. This is why the end of the "gay ban" can be applauded by the same people who express significant anxiety about open trans service and women in combat.

Today, some gay and bisexual men can be repatriated by military service, while gender-nonconforming queers, cis women, and trans people remain gender outlaws by virtue of their "deficient" embodiment for military service. Further, this bargain remains a handshake deal; even the widespread support for open LGB service is highly conditional, revocable upon violation of the terms and conditions of homonormativity. Sexual harassment, jokes and teasing, and gender policing serve as mechanisms of what I call *queer social control* that enforce gender and sexual normativity for those who dare stray from it. Despite the promise of inclusivity, in practice, the military has made room only for a "few good gays," to the exclusion of all others.

Women's military service is largely understood through the frame I call *patriotic paternalism*: women are inherently in need of the protection of the patriot, symbolically figured as white, cisgender, heterosexual, male, and American. Patriotic paternalism legitimates the war on terror by claiming it is about "saving" women in the Middle East from the imagined brutality of Middle Eastern men while simultaneously positioning American women as in need of protection from the overestimation of their abilities that puts them in peril on the front lines.[8] The paternal patriot, an agent of what gender and sexuality studies scholar Inderpal Grewal calls the "security state," must now juggle the dual security threats of terrorism and women's integration.[9] A countervailing narrative, a subsect of liberal feminist discourse Grewal calls "security feminism," frames women's combat participation as a matter of empowerment but is dismissed by most cadets, servicemembers, and veterans, who see it as political correctness run amok, a progressive lie that erases the "truth" of sex difference and puts women (and by extension, the nation) in harm's way.

Finally, transgender service presents a unique conundrum. The military is an institution organized by birth-assigned sex segregation in facilities, physical fitness standards, uniforms, and so much else. The military personnel I interviewed tied themselves in knots as they talked through the transformation of the military's gendered organization into what I call a *transgendering organization*, engaged in the institutional work of actively incorporating transness into its foundational logics.[10] Open trans service was administratively unimaginable to many: *What criteria should be used to classify trans servicemembers as male or female? How are cis people disadvantaged or harmed by these classificatory accommodations? Will this unravel sex segregation entirely, leading the military into ungendered chaos?* Trans women's inclusion, in particular, incited gendered anxieties about cis women's safety, demonstrating the social power of transmisogyny, the simultaneous disadvantaging of trans women by virtue of their transness and their womanhood. Between open LGB service and gender integration, there is a liminal space to which trans people have been relegated, excluded by the frames of homonormativity, patriarchal paternalism, and feminist empowerment that define and delimit institutional belonging.

But is belonging even a goal worth pursuing? Incorporation into an apparatus of empire is a far cry from the aims of gay liberationists who held and fought for radically deconstructionist sexuality and gender politics.

Militarism and war were anathema to their organizing priorities and strategies. By analyzing inclusion's history and reception, I critically examine it as a social movement aspiration, ultimately arguing that its steep price is exacted through the continued abjection of queered Others both at home and abroad. The homonormative bargain squandered a great deal of liberatory potential. How did we get from there to here? And where do we go next?

SEX, GENDER, AND SEXUALITY IN THE HETEROSEXUAL MATRIX

In the Global North, gender and sexuality were socially and scientifically linked through the late nineteenth-century "invention" of the homosexual and heterosexual. In fact, sexologists and psychoanalysts first conceived of same-sex attraction not as a matter of sexual difference, as we might today, but rather as a symptom of gender inversion. Early medical models of homosexual behavior attributed homosexuality to gender confusion, thus tying together gender and sexual transgression through the figure of the "gender invert."[11]

Historian Margot Canaday has shown how the establishment of the US bureaucratic state relied heavily on the regulation of queerness (both gender inversion and sexual perversion).[12] State legitimacy was fostered through what Canaday calls the bureaucratization of homosexuality: the making, unmaking, and remaking of the gender/sexual deviant through legal and administrative mechanisms. Within the military, the evolving science of sexology shaped the management of potential threats to its authority. Medical screening practices in the early twentieth century scrutinized the bodies and minds of new recruits for evidence of gendered deviance that might contaminate and imperil the burgeoning dominance of the US military on the global stage. As homosexuality supplanted the concept of gender inversion, the military's surveilling gaze moved from its enactment of medical and psychological tests of gender abnormality to sodomy investigations and later to the prohibition of LGB identity as we now know it.

The homosexual and the transsexual, two newly distinct subjects, emerged from the transition away from the notion of gender inversion.

Homosexuality was no longer the by-product of gender confusion, but rather a sexual desire, quasi-autonomous from gender nonconformity, which was reconfigured and remedicalized as the medical/psychological "condition" of transsexuality.[13] Crucially, the knot between gender and sexuality was not entirely undone by this process, but positioned as a correlative rather than causal relationship. The coercive arrangement of bodies and desires into a coherent and naturalized sex/gender/sexuality system—what Judith Butler terms "the heterosexual matrix"—stabilized the shift away from the gender invert by providing two novel and well-defined replacement categories.[14] Within the heterosexual matrix, individuals are assigned a sex at birth, socialized into a corresponding gender identity, and expected to align their sexual desires by gender and into fixed and binary categories. The discursive power of the heterosexual matrix stabilized any potential uncertainty produced in the shift from the gender invert to the homosexual and transsexual.

By the late twentieth century, the destigmatization of LGBT subjectivities began to unsettle the matrix; the tie between gender transgression and homosexuality was loosened by increased visibility and acceptance. In fact, LGB people were proving to be just as capable of gender conformity as straight people. At the same time, increased transgender visibility introduced questions about the presumed naturalness of sexed bodies and their corresponding gender identities. This is a significant threat to the matrix; if the belief that assigned sex is immaterial to gender becomes too widely adopted, the entire system could be called into question. Sociologists Laurel Westbrook and Kristen Schilt deem the resulting hand-wringing a "gender panic," in which the dominant gender discourse "reacts to a challenge to the gender binary by frantically asserting its naturalness."[15] Gender panic has motivated, among other things, the recent rash of anti-trans legislative efforts adjudicating trans people's access to bathrooms, locker rooms, schools, and sports. Put differently, as the tie between gender and sexual identity undermined the heterosexual matrix and gender panic set in, the tie between sex and gender was reasserted as a counterbalancing and stabilizing force.

This heterosexual matrix is not only about gender and sex, but also race. It is embedded within and racialized through the history and legacy of European and US empire.[16] Colonization and enslavement were legitimated by dehumanization, which in turn relied on the "discovery" of sexed, gendered, and sexual deviance in its targets.[17] Practices of scientific racism identified the supposed inherent gender and sexual perversity of non-white people, thereby establishing their subhumanity in social, legal, and medical definitions that justified their subjugation. Through this process, indigenous people experiencing colonization and enslavement were defined by their embodiment rather than their enlightenment, the assumed purview of whiteness, and these taxonomic distinctions proved durable. Today, they underpin the continued preoccupation with the bodies and physicality of people of color. Consider the aforementioned war on terror, which racialized and targeted people from the Middle East and North Africa (MENA) en masse (while downplaying terrorist acts perpetrated by white actors in the United States and abroad).[18] This process has produced significant reinvigoration of colonial-Orientalist tropes of savagery, deceit, and embodied gender and sexual deviance.[19] It is crucial, then, that we bear in mind that revisions to the heterosexual matrix can benefit some Western LGBs while reinforcing the disciplinary power of that matrix elsewhere. Race, sex, and gender difference are evoked to define MENA people as always already terrorists, if not in action, in inherent constitution.[20]

To return to the subject of gender panic, Schilt and Westbrook find that sex-segregated institutions are especially likely sites for it. In the military, where facilities, uniforms, fitness standards, and specialization are strictly divided by sex, increased inclusivity calls into question these well-established classification systems, thereby evoking gender panic. When this happens, the process of determining sex/gender and revising related sorting practices is likely to default to biological or medical-based rationales rather than identity-based ones. This naturalization work tightens the normative connection between sex and gender that was loosened by transgender visibility. Because the connection between gender and sexual identity has been relaxed by contrast, I argue that gender panic and its effects are heightened in battles over women in combat and open trans service compared to open LGB service. As this book shows, biologized explanations of the psychological and physical unfitness of both groups pervade the narratives of combat desegregation and trans inclusion in a way that they do not in those of LGB integration.

FROM LIBERATION TO RIGHTS

Open LGBT service policies were made possible (and desirable) by the social movement shift from gay liberation to gay rights. Paradoxical though it may seem on its face, I argue that gay rights discourse tacitly cosigns transphobia, femmephobia, and even homophobia, insofar as it positions indistinguishability from norms of straightness and cisness as the end goal. As I will show, the compromise made by homonormative politics—the homonormative bargain—limits how much open service can bring about cultural change sufficient to disrupt patterns of bias in the military and elsewhere. This bargain also excised the more radical antiracist politics of the gay liberation movement that paved the way. Homonormativity has retroactively erased many of the threads gay liberationists identified as crucial sites of intervention: poverty, white supremacy, imperialism, misogyny, and transphobia. It has rewritten events like the Stonewall riots as single-issue responses to sexual oppression, rather than as an intersectional critique of and challenge to police repression and state violence across marginalized identities.[21]

In reality, gay liberation activists, especially gender nonconforming activists of color, were active in multiple projects of antiracist and anti-imperial resistance in the United States. Moreover, their contributions firmly planted gay liberation's fundamental tenets in a transgender epistemology: resistance to the disciplining power of gender, in addition to race and class, was understood as indivisible from resisting heterosexual hegemony. But this coalitional model did not survive the forces of social movement burnout, intergroup conflict, and Counter Intelligence Program (COINTELPRO) disinformation tactics, all successful in breaking solidarities between the gay liberation, Black liberation, Third World liberation, and feminist movements.[22] Over the 1970s and 1980s, the movement shifted toward the less aggressive tactical repertoires of persuasion and bargaining.[23] The goal of dismantling the institutions that gay liberation saw as oppressive was replaced with persuasive arguments and strategic bargaining to achieve inclusion within them. Liberation for all was supplanted by incremental gay rights advances for some.

As a package of collective benefits, a rights strategy pursues legal and cultural recognition and equal treatment. Access to rights was built on the ethos of homonormativity, a politic emphasizing sameness over difference, respectability over revolution.[24] Where gay liberation once resisted the state's encroachment on the sexual lives of queer and trans people, homonormativity seeks incorporation into the core institutions of liberal democracies. To garner attention and legitimacy in the highly competitive social problems marketplace, gay rights used sexual (and later gender) *identity* as the basis for its claims making. Adopting a quasi-ethnic conceptualization of sexual and gender identity made "LGBT" a legible legal category, thereby creating a pathway to seek remedy for discrimination and harm.[25]

This new tactical repertoire left aside the celebration of gender transgression in an effort to establish homosexual belonging within historically heterosexual institutions. Resistance to gender nonconformity, especially effeminacy, became a hallmark of the homonormative turn. Sociologist Peter Hennen defines effeminacy as "a historically varying concept deployed primarily as a means of stabilizing a given society's concept of masculinity and controlling the conduct of its men, based upon a repudiation of the feminine."[26] To pull homosexuality out of that state of repudiation, gay rights discourse severed the connection between effeminacy and homosexuality, moving gay and bisexual men to the other side of the masculine/feminine divide. Homosexuality, once conceptualized primarily as a manifestation of gender deviance, was politically transformed into a normalized and de-somatized identity.[27]

As I argue, this strategy was exceedingly successful in securing rights for some. Yet many queer and trans people are subjected to surveillance and sanction for gender transgression precisely *because* the gay rights movement so effectively excised them from the figure of the good LGBT citizen. The ways current, future, and former servicemembers narrate the DADT repeal compared to open trans service and gender desegregation of combat is the direct consequence of the homonormative bargain. Feminist scholar Deniz Kandiyoti coined the term "patriarchal bargain" to describe the strategies women use to succeed under the sexist and misogynist conditions of patriarchy; similarly, the homonormative bargain was struck to access success under the conditions of heterosexism.[28] As in any bargain, its gains have come with significant concessions: the homonormative bargain upholds and even exacerbates race, class, and gender inequality in the pursuit of sexual equality.

GENDERED MILITARISM AND THE SECURITY STATE

Militarism, the glorification of the military and militaristic modes of governance, is a deeply gendered ideological system. Political scientist Cynthia Enloe has argued that colonization and war are technologies of masculine dominance that feminize its subjects, thereby inscribing the gender binary and gender inequality onto geopolitical dynamics (that then trickle down to shape social practices like the gendered division of household labor).[29] The land we now call the United States was conquered and masculinized in such a manner, first through settler colonialism and later by maneuvers positioning it as a punishing and paternal force on the global stage. In the process, US militarism was gendered as masculine and racialized as white.

When social upheaval threatens to unseat that racialized masculine status, war reasserts and remasculinizes the national brand. Enloe uses the example of the Vietnam War (1954–75), a pivotal event for the development of gay liberation, as one such remasculinizing effort. The contemporary war on terror serves a similar purpose. The terrorist attacks on September 11, 2001 threatened to feminize the United States, whose defenses were so publicly "penetrated." By appointing itself to sovereign dominion over terror, the United States moved to recoup its gendered reputation, as even a cursory glance at 9/11 rhetoric and imagery amply demonstrates.[30] And unlike a specific nation like Vietnam, terror is a moving target. As a result, the pursuit of terror has authorized the United States to exercise incursion at will across the Middle East (and to surveil and indefinitely detain anyone in the name of homeland security).

In this endless war, the brown terrorist is positioned as the feminized, queered foil to the white American patriot.[31] Jasbir Puar and Amit Rai articulate this psychoanalytic formulation in which the gender invert is revived as the "monster-terrorist-fag."[32] The white gay American patriot is no longer monstrous, redoubling the threat of the brown Middle Eastern terrorist. The dual process of quarantining the racialized and sexualized Other (said monster-terrorist-fag) and selectively incorporating the acceptably raced, gendered, and sexualized homopatriot is the ground upon which open service made its home.[33] This dialectic is central to the production of what Puar calls homonationalism: the suturing together of homonormativity and nationalist zeal that queers the monster-terrorist-fag and *un*queers the homopatriot.[34]

The US military expressly inculcates martial masculinity, a variant within the gender system that sociologist Raewyn Connell calls "hegemonic masculinity": the "configuration of gender practice which embodies the currently accepted answer to the problem of the legitimacy of patriarchy."[35] Masculinity, per Connell, is fundamentally relational, established through the subjugation of women, femininities, subordinated gay masculinities, and marginalized non-white masculinities. Martial masculinity, specifically, valorizes the warrior, historically imagined as the stoic and lethal white, heterosexual, cisgender patriot. And it is a relational accomplishment, made possible through the formal and informal exclusion of cis straight women and LGBTs. As cis, (ostensibly) straight women were incorporated into the military over the twentieth century, the combat exclusion rule ensured the preservation of the most sacred stage on which martial masculinity was performed: the front lines. DADT and its predecessors also provided a mechanism to silence any LGBT servicemembers who managed to make their way in. Simultaneously, the cultural deployment of misogyny, homophobia, and transphobia reasserted martial masculinity through, among other things, venerated fraternal traditions that assuage gender panic by maintaining the symbolic exile of all things feminine. As documented by folklorist Carol Burke and others, these traditions include a plethora of sexually objectifying and sexually violent traditions (chants, ceremonies, hazing rituals) that use gendered and sexual humiliation as a bonding mechanism.[36]

Increasingly, however, these politics and practices are out of step with the US military's image as the great liberator, protecting the world from the illiberal brutality of Islamic extremism. Appeals to tolerance have been used as a political tool to justify that project. Political theorist Wendy Brown calls tolerance a "tactical political response" that legitimizes liberal universalism and thereby military intervention on its behalf.[37] Gender and sexual intolerance within the US military are a contradiction to this mission, thus motivating a rebranding project that includes the end of DADT, combat exclusion, and medical disqualifications of transgender servicemembers. For Brown, the frame of tolerance always implies a power relation between the tolerant and the tolerated. Thus the "pinkwashing" of the military through the incorporation of cis straight women and LGBTs technically fulfills a promise of tolerance while requiring the tolerated to twist and bend to fit the conditions of that tolerance.[38] This "tolerance trap," in the words of sociologist Suzanna Walters, forecloses possibilities for more radical social transformation.[39] In the case of the military, tolerance enables both inclusion and abjection simultaneously. As I will show, members of the military engage in a process of queer social control to contain the newly tolerated and the threat they represent to martial masculinity.

In the foundational essay "Can the Subaltern Speak?," postcolonial theorist Gayatri Chakravorty Spivak identified "white men saving brown women from brown men" as an authorizing logic that legitimated British colonial rule.[40] Today, the same rationale continues to obscure the era of US empire by hiding it "behind the veil of women's victimization."[41] Much of Western feminist discourse has done the same, only in this case, with white women intervening "on behalf of" their "Third World sisters" in an act of presumed universal womanhood.[42] The war on terror has given rise to a novel configuration of this saviorhood and "securitization," or the discourses shoring up the intrusion of security and surveillance apparatuses into all domains of social life. Inderpal Grewal calls this "security feminism."[43] It relies on the global sisterhood frame to justify interventionist policy and positions domestic national security as a feminist issue. The goal of "women's empowerment" is enacted through the active embrace of securitization. Feminist pacifism and resistance to militarism are obscured by security feminism as it is used to counter assumptions about women's physical or psychological unfitness for military service. To the extent that security feminism challenges patriotic paternalism, it is by "leaning in" to patriotism. This feminist variant, then, is not unlike homonationalist LGBT politics, yet it is less powerful as a rationale for inclusion because the LGB patriot has already doubled down on rejection of femininity and women by extension.

Gender and sexuality studies scholar Toby Beauchamp has documented how securitization also informs contemporary transgender politics. Beauchamp argues that in the security state, "surveillance is a central practice through which the category of transgender is produced, regulated, and contested."[44] Some trans subjects (white, gender conforming, productive citizens) are made legible and legitimate through surveillance; others are rendered security threats by their nonconformity. For example, when the Department of Homeland Security stoked fears of "male bombers [who] dress as females" to support the passage of the Real ID Act in 2005, trans advocacy organizations objected: not to the transmisogynist fearmongering, but to how the act would impede the freedom and privacy of the "good" trans citizen.[45] They called for increased access to gender marker changes so that trans US citizens might travel freely under the heightened scrutiny, a move that contributes to the emerging politics of transnormativity, which circumscribe transness to the surveilling gaze of medical and legal authority.[46] This does what legal scholar Dean Spade calls "administrative violence," distributing safety, freedom of movement, and gender legitimacy only to those who can and will submit to the surveilling gaze of the state.[47] In the military, administrative violence is done by the medico-legal gatekeepers charged with sorting trans servicemembers into the institution's binary sex segregation systems. Regardless of their ability to abide by the new sex classification regulations, trans women are also seen by cisgender servicemembers as invaders and gender pretenders who pose harm to cisgender women. Women are thereby divided from each other through this trans/cis binary and prevented from working together to challenge their mutual marginalization.

STUDYING THE US MILITARY

How do you study a problem like the military? With millions of members dispersed across a vast array of occupational specializations and geographic locations, there is no singular workplace experience or culture to investigate. Rather, the military is an assemblage, inclusive of "varying degrees of fragmentation, incoherence, ambiguity, and other disjointed elements and seemingly incompatible cultural tools."[48] Given this challenge and the relative dearth of research documenting the cultural impact of gender and sexuality policy change within this broad institution, I opted for breadth over depth in my data-gathering approach, spending five years conducting interviews with cadets, servicemembers, and veterans across an array of the military's occupational locations. Because policy becomes legitimized (or delegitimized) through institutional actors, interviews that reveal how these various actors imagine and interpret their experiences help us understand the construction of classificatory systems, symbolic boundaries, and identities.[49]

The churn of policy change throughout data collection complicated the data analysis process. The policy conditions that interviewees were responding to shifted nearly every year, especially as they pertained to trans inclusion. The underlying themes that emerged from respondents' narration of these policy changes, however, remained constant: the participants I interviewed in 2015 were grappling with the same questions and concerns as those in 2020. As a result, in this book I do not take a chronologically comparative approach but examine how divergent logics of inclusion circulated for each policy across this five-year span.

The first wave of interviews with cadets, servicemembers, and vets yielded a very white sample. I responded to this insufficient representation of people of color by recruiting more participants of color through snowball sampling, then, again unsatisfied, moving to targeted sampling. From this, I recruited an additional seven participants of color and interviewed six, five of whom were Black and/or Latine, for a total of twelve interviews with non-white participants, a little less than 20 percent of interviews.[50] My objective was to oversample people of color, but the final sample falls well below even proportional representation (similar to the US population, roughly 40% of all military personnel are non-white). I intended to collect twenty additional interviews during targeted recruitment, which would have made roughly half of the sample people of color. However, the window of time I had to complete these interviews coincided with the COVID-19 pandemic. This limited both my own availability and that of prospective participants; I felt increasingly uncomfortable asking military personnel to carve out time for an interview that could otherwise go to the heightened demands for work, childcare, and self-care the pandemic necessitated. This context matters, but it does not change the fact that these data fail to meet an important criterion of sample diversity. Race did emerge as a relevant factor that shaped participants' experiences of gender and sexual privilege and marginalization; more interviews with people of color would have benefited the project.

My data include fifty-three interviews with future, present, and past generations of servicemembers and eight with key policy stakeholders, for a total of sixty-one interviews. The military personnel in the sample include roughly equal numbers of men (N = 25) and women (N = 32) and a somewhat comparable number of cisgender heterosexuals (N = 34) and LGBTs (N = 23).[51] It includes participants from the Navy (N = 14), Air Force (N = 12), Army (N = 12), Marine Corps (N = 3), and Army ROTC (N = 16). The average age of servicemembers was 33 (with a range from 18 to 63 years), and the average years of service was nine (with a range from one to twenty-eight years). The military personnel sample is largely white (N = 43); the twelve people of color in the sample identified as Black (N = 4), biracial (N = 2), Latine/x/o/a (N = 3), and Asian (N = 3). Three participants declined to answer the survey item on age; two participants declined to answer on race.

Of the eight policy stakeholders I interviewed, four were servicemembers and veterans, so they are also included in the preceding demographic counts. The stakeholder interviews provide context for how the military's policy changes unfolded behind the scenes: the backroom deals, chance encounters, strategies, and staged events that smoothed the way toward policy change, as well as the unexpected blockades and reversals that threatened these changes (successfully so, in the case of trans inclusion). Stakeholders held a variety of institutional positions, from high-ranking Department of Defense (DOD) officials to journalists and documentarians who courted favorable public opinion for gender and sexuality policy change. For this book, I interviewed Eric Fanning, former secretary of the Army and former undersecretary of the Air Force; Alex Wagner, Fanning's former chief of staff and organizer of the Pentagon's first Pride event; Greg Brown from the Office of Military Personnel Policy; Brenda "Sue" Fulton, core organizer for both the DADT repeal and trans inclusion; Blake Dremann, Navy commander and president of SPARTA, a trans servicemembers' advocacy organization; Brynn Tannehill, SPARTA board member, journalist, and trans inclusion activist; Amanda Simpson, former deputy assistant secretary of defense for operational energy and first openly transgender presidential employee; and Fiona Dawson, LGBT activist and director of the film *TransMilitary*.[52] These interviews were especially useful for constructing a history of transgender exclusion/inclusion, since the relevant changes to medical regulations are so recent that little has yet been published on the subject.

TOWARD LIVABILITY

If my orientation toward the military as an institution is decidedly antagonistic, my relationship to its members, especially the LGBT people who serve within it, is much less so. Competing interests between critiquing the institution and honoring the desires of those serving openly for the first time presented a formidable dilemma in writing this book. How could I possibly advocate for inclusion into this institution? Yet how could I disregard or disrespect research participants' desire for that inclusion, to the extent that many made painful and courageous sacrifices to carve out room for themselves and others? Geographer Gavin Brown has argued that although homonormativity "has been used to neocolonial effect on the global political stage," its critics are too dismissive of the affective power of recognition.[53] Visibility and inclusion have opened up positive opportunities for many—myself included. Brown argues that "critical queer scholars and activists need to be more reflexive about their own complicity in reproducing forms of privilege if they are to help foster more just social relations."[54] To that end, I have tried to acknowledge and appreciate the good that policy change has done for some research participants even as I emphasize the harmful trade-offs of the homonormative bargain.

I also take to heart an observation by Aaron Belkin, a leader in the fight for LGBT military inclusion. Belkin writes that anti-militarism activists and scholars have a "disinclination to acknowledge that the stakes that the pro-military LGBT advocates have been fighting for are important."[55] The stories I hold stewardship over include many compelling examples, and more than once I have been moved to sympathetic tears (both sad and happy). I want to advocate for the marginalized servicemembers who shared their struggles and victories, who made themselves vulnerable in this research process, as much as I want to advocate for those experiencing the negative consequences of inclusion.

Deploying queer critique in interview-based and ethnographic research always entails this challenge. It is more straightforward, at least for me, to critique homonormativity within more removed source material: texts, archives, objects of material culture. It feels more fraught to do so when the data take the form of the experiences and opinions of those living with the stakes of the homonormative bargain. Yet this ethical dilemma is what in fact necessitates the increased incorporation of sociology into queer theory and vice versa. It is an invitation to consider and build from Gavin Brown's critique of homonormativity-as-theory.

Sociologist Steven Epstein has highlighted the irony of sociology's annexation from queer theory, in which the humanistic disciplines reign supreme.[56] It was, after all, sociologists who first asserted the claim that sexual identities are products of power and modes of discipline, well before Michel Foucault and others articulated the same. Nonetheless, the empiricist pursuits of sociology position the field as suspect, forever accused of restabilizing and reinscribing the discursive power of sex, gender, and sexual identity by using them as categories of analysis. It's true that sociology can inform laws and policies that harm queer and trans people; the architect of DADT, for example, was sociologist Charles Moskos. While acknowledging the harm done by the disciplining gaze of sociology and social science more generally, I am yet convinced that a queer sociology can also deepen the queer critique of power relations by demonstrating how they operate in and through the real lives of real people. Scrutinizing people rather than texts makes for a much messier site of analysis, but is it not "the mess" that queer theory purports to value as a mode of resistance?[57] Speaking to those who feel its effects offers crucial insight into discourse's creative power. It is much harder, but all the more necessary, to bring sociological insight to bear on queer theory through such an analysis.

One such pairing of queer theory and sociology—Laurel Westbrook's use of Butler's concept of livability to scrutinize the conditions that make trans lives unlivable—serves as a point of inspiration for this book's undertaking.[58] Livability is an ethical barometer for LGBT activism. As Westbrook's *Unlivable Lives* demonstrates, anti-violence activism on behalf of trans people endeavors to make transgender lives more livable yet also reproduces certain conditions of unlivability; in its use of the politics of visibility and vulnerability, such activism unwittingly positions trans lives as inevitably marked by and made legible through violence. Using sociological methods, Westbrook's research shows that these fear-based tactics take a heavy emotional toll on transgender people. They erase livable "possibility," defined by Butler as "the ability to live and breathe and move" without being immobilized by fear.[59] Through queer sociological insight,

Westbrook develops a robust account of what social movements and their tactics can do to make lives more (or less) livable.

Following Westbrook and Butler, I consider livability/unlivability in the context of the US military. Greater inclusion can improve livability for the cis straight women and LGBTs who find meaning, fulfillment, and sustenance through service while also perpetuating unlivability for others, including those who experience violence and death as a result of their participation. And it reinforces the unlivablity of lives outside military inclusion, marking them for disposability, alienation, and domination. The necropolitics of war and militarism—the political power to let live and let die—shape global conditions of livability in ways that must be reckoned with in any analysis of inclusion's benefits.[60] Accordingly, this book is a critique of the military as an institution and of the homonormative bargain as a political phenomenon. It is not a critique of the people who must find a way to survive in those contexts. I believe that a queer feminist politics proliferating new forms of livability *is* possible. Throughout this book, I draw on the insights of queer, feminist, and trans modes of resistance, foregrounding the insights of queer/trans of color critique and transnational feminism to make sense of the complex conditions through which livability and unlivability are produced.

ORGANIZATION OF THE BOOK

A Few Good Gays unfolds in four parts: repealing DADT, ending combat exclusion, removing medical restrictions on transgender service, and a conclusion synthesizing the significance of gender and sexuality policy regime change for evaluating contemporary gender and sexuality ideologies. I have organized the book in this way to allow those readers with specific interests in one policy over the others to most easily satisfy their curiosity, but without introducing undue redundancy across the text. Thus, in chapter 1 I lay the groundwork with a comprehensive history of the military's management of homosexuality, including the development and eventual repeal of DADT. Through previously published research and my own interviews with prominent policy stakeholders, I show how repeal advocates successfully used the repertoires of science, security, and familialism to make open LGB service more palatable. I also consider the political implications of these choices, both informed by and reinforcing the homonormative bargain.

When I embarked on this research, I expected to find significant resistance and hostility toward LGB inclusion. Yet as I show in chapter 2, I found the opposite. The near-universal approval of the DADT repeal and positive opinions about LGB service demonstrate the bargaining power of homonormativity. In this chapter, I analyze the inclusionary logics—appeals to professionalism, tolerance, and diversity—that led to favorable opinions of LGB service and consider the ways interviewees made sense of the repeal's significance by analogizing sexual integration to racial integration. These "like race" analogies, although effective, incorrectly position race and sexuality as parallel rather than mutually constitutive forms of domination, dampening potential challenges to these compound inequalities. Where sexuality and race are treated as separate and equivalent expressions of difference, they are reconfigured as diversity "value-adds," providing additional cover for the role of the US military in sexual, racial, and religious conflicts across the globe and, again, precluding coalitional mobilization within its ranks.

The homonormative bargain makes some LGB lives more livable, but it comes at the very dear cost of making other queer (and queered) lives increasingly unlivable. One of several strings attached to that bargain is the responsibility to contain any queer and feminine contamination that might otherwise sneak in. As a result, LGB servicemembers are expected to keep their sexualities to themselves whenever possible, contributing to two-tiered interactional expectations for straight and LGB servicemembers. In chapter 3 I show how the inclusionary logics of professionalism and tolerance delimit LGB comportment and set the conditions of acceptance. LGB servicemembers are required to contain just about all expressions of sexuality or gender nonconformity at work; those boundaries are enforced through interactional practices, including the use of threats, harassment, alienation, and teasing as mechanisms of queer social control. Gay and bisexual men are governed by femmephobic surveillance of their gender performance. By contrast, lesbian and bisexual women's gender nonconformity can fly further under the radar, but even this is heavily attenuated by race. Ultimately, the enactment of LGB inclusion actually sustains and even strengthens the racialized heterosexual matrix through surveillance and control.

Part 2 turns to how the suppression of queerness enabled by the homonormative bargain has created a different, more negative reception toward women in combat. First, in chapter 4 I consider the evolving role of women in the military, in which they have been held apart from men through various mechanisms designed to preserve its gendered organization. Sociologist Joan Acker's theory of gendered organizations holds that even ostensibly gender-neutral organizations are in fact deeply imbued with gendered norms and practices that ultimately sustain gender inequality. In the military, this is accomplished in part through patriotic paternalism, which uses the parlance of benevolent sexism to define women as vulnerable: not the agents but the objects of patriotic rescue. I then analyze the liberal feminist response to patriotic paternalism, which demands equal access to combat without challenging the ethics of combat itself. In detailing the history of the combat exclusion rule and its eventual repeal, chapter 4 establishes the conditions research participants respond to in chapter 5.

The acceptance, begrudging or otherwise, that was extended to open LGB service did not extend to the prospect of women in combat, with both men and women alike resisting this new site of gender integration. In contrast to the expectation that LGB servicemembers will keep their sexuality strictly "off the clock," few interviewees believed straight men ever could or even should. Not only did they state that women may be physically and/or psychologically unfit for service, they argued that women will be distractions for straight men's unavoidable, primal sexual urges. Patriotic paternalism shapes both the discourse on women in combat and the treatment of women throughout the military. Gendered and sexual harassment are used as weapons that remind women of their subordination under the cover of a victim-blaming logic: *men simply can't help themselves.* Where respondents spoke of inclusion in voicing support for the DADT repeal, here many drew on logics of exclusion, deploying biologically determinist arguments about male and female capabilities and the dangers of privileging "political correctness" over safety or practicality. This distinction between gender and sexual inclusion, partly the result of homosexuality's uncoupling from effeminacy, has given rise to femmephobia as an increasingly relevant axis of subordination. Femmephobia is in fact a driving force behind reactions to all three policies, and its penalties accrue accordingly.

Part 3 of the book turns to the question of transgender inclusion, starting in chapter 6 with a history of trans service and military policy. After the repeal of DADT, much of the LGBT social movement energy (and funding) fell away. Only a determined group of policy entrepreneurs continued to work toward trans inclusion. They scored a major victory in 2016 when the Pentagon announced it would implement new policies to recruit and retain trans troops, but found themselves back in court when the Trump administration reversed trans inclusion with a single tweet. In 2021, the Biden administration swerved back yet again. This chapter compares the dynamics of homonormativity with those of transnormativity to show how discursive differences between them contribute to the patterns I find in policy reception. Additionally, because there are so few accounts of the transgender military experience, I use chapter 6 to help fill that gap, drawing on interviews with policy stakeholders and beneficiaries who experienced the fluctuations of trans military policy.

Chapter 7 analyzes participants' reactions to open transgender service. While their opinions on LGB and women's inclusion were opposed, those regarding transgender inclusion were more varied and ambivalent. Some research participants used comparisons to DADT and LGB inclusion to explain their support for trans inclusion; these participants applied similar logics of professionalism, tolerance, and diversity, arguing that as long as trans servicemembers can do their job just as well as the next (cisgender) one, inclusion is a nonissue. Others compared trans service to women in combat, emphasizing the biological "truths" of sex and gender and suggesting a gender panic is at work in this heavily sex-segregated institution. The trans ban tug-of-war between Barack Obama, Donald Trump, and Joe Biden further complicated the process of transgendering the organization, forcing trans servicemembers into a state of political and symbolic liminality. In this chapter I consider both the constraining and creative possibilities of this liminal position, connecting it to the production of transgender epistemology.

Finally, chapter 8 summarizes how these policy tensions emblematize significant shifts in twenty-first-century gender and sexuality discourse.

The homonormative bargain set into motion the militarization of LGBT identities and the complicity of LGBT politics with misogyny, femmephobia, and empire. Tying together the first three parts of the book, the conclusion presents suggestions for military policy, the expansion of alternatives to service for resource-poor LGBTs and others, and the rearticulation of social movement priorities. In appendix A I detail my methodological decisions and dilemmas, particularly the challenges of studying change as it occurs, conducting in-depth interviews in the military context, and striking a balance between feminist research methodology and queer critique. Appendix B provides a table of demographic information for the sample, and appendix C includes the semistructured interview guide.

PART 1 Repealing Don't Ask, Don't Tell

1 "The Hard Work to Get Me in the Door"

A HISTORY OF THE GAY BAN

The year Shannon joined the Navy, a new military policy called Don't Ask Don't Tell was on everyone's lips.[1] Yet fear of expulsion on the basis of her sexuality was not yet top of mind. "I didn't know that I was gay when I first came into the military," she explained. Ironically, it was entering the military, an institution that forbade it, that brought about that realization: "Being in the military and being exposed to different people and different cultures and talking to people, I'm like, wow, my eyes are open." When these experiences "opened up [her] aperture" to the many possibilities of self-making, Shannon, now a 45-year-old Black cis woman, was elated and terrified. She was a lesbian, and as a result, she was a target. Just as quickly as she discovered her sexuality, she had to conceal it:

> I had to really hide being gay, I had to wear two faces. . . . I would purposely have "boyfriends," because I wanted people on the ship to know I was not gay, because just imagine—if someone didn't like you, they can ruin your career! . . . I [would] go hang with [gay] friends away from the ship, I wouldn't allow people to take pictures of me if we were in a gay club. It was a totally different life. I had to hide. I also couldn't put up pictures in my office. People looked at me like, oh, you're not family oriented or anything like that, because I didn't have pictures up. [But] that's because

> I *couldn't* put pictures up. Until Don't Ask, Don't Tell was repealed. . . . I lived a double life.

Shannon lived this way for almost twenty years—long enough that she was surprised by her reluctance to live openly by the time the repeal came to pass. "I've been socialized into living a double life so long that it's like I was playing double dutch. It's like, I don't know, can I really jump out and be like, 'Hey, I'm gay?'" Still, she said, she "wanted to be that light for other people to feel like they can open up." Her promotion ceremony, in which "your whole command just comes out, they are all around you, watching you get [your new insignia] pinned on," presented a moment to shed her double identity. Like many of her straight colleagues, Shannon asked her spouse, a woman, to do the pinning. When I asked how that moment felt, she said simply: "I felt released." Shannon's story illustrates both the emotional toll of DADT and the catharsis of its repeal for those who served beneath its weight.

The repeal of DADT had been in effect for two decades when Cristina (26, biracial cis lesbian woman) enlisted in the Navy. Like Shannon, she joined with only a nascent sense of her sexuality ("I was not very far along," she explained). Of coming into a lesbian identity during service, she recalled, "It just took me a really long time." Still, when she got there, Cristina felt comfortable being out: "So many people have done the hard work to get me in the door." Her own captain, she said, had been "terrorized during her time in the Navy, just for loving who she loved." But her captain persevered, Cristina explained, so that people like her would not have to suffer the same; that perseverance meant Cristina felt supported and affirmed when she came out: "The biggest obstacle was just myself." In the newly inclusive policy era, Cristina did not feel compelled, as Shannon had, to disguise her sexuality in the Navy.

Taken together, Shannon and Cristina's experiences are emblematic of the predominant narrative I heard as I spoke about the post-DADT military with servicemembers and policy stakeholders: the repeal marked a progress from repression to freedom. Unfettered by institutional constraints on asking and telling, the only thing standing in the way of the good life is one's own fear of living out loud. In this chapter, I trace the gendered historical developments condensed into this narrative—namely, the state management of gender and sexual "perversion" that was central to the making of the modern military and indeed, to the legitimacy of the US state-making process. In some ways, homosexuality is in fact constitutive of the military itself, despite going by other names and definitions throughout its history. Contrary to what we might expect, there was significant fluctuation in the definition and enforcement of different iterations of a "gay ban." The movement from gender and sexual perversion to the crystallization of gay, lesbian, and bisexual identities rendered them threats within this intimate institution. Using the discursive tools of science, security, and familialism, the repeal campaign succeeded in the formal removal of the stigma of gender nonconformity and sexual perversion from LGB identity, but at what cost?

MILITARY SERVICE AND THE MAKING OF THE STRAIGHT STATE

Historian Margot Canaday argues that US state making differed from its European predecessors in its reliance on the regulation of homosexuality to define citizenship and national belonging.[2] Certainly such regulation is part of state making elsewhere; as sociologist Jyoti Puri's analysis of antisodomy law in India demonstrates, the governance of sexuality is a prime tactic used to reinforce and relegitimate states, especially when they are under threat.[3] Canaday's point is instead that the coinciding production of the United States as a global power and a sexological science of gendered sexual perversion led to a reciprocal and reinforcing relationship between US statehood and the homo/hetero binary. In the United States, the category of the homosexual was developed through state regulation of gender and sexuality, and the state itself was developed and legitimated through its surveillance, punishment, and expulsion of gender and sexual deviance. Homosexuality as we would come to understand it in the latter half of the twentieth century was made, unmade, and remade through a tangle of legal and administrative processes Canaday summarizes as the "bureaucratization of homosexuality." The military was a central site of this bureaucratizing project, along with immigration and social welfare offices and policies. Well before World War II, the commonly cited starting point for the systematic purging of homosexuality, military leadership was actively regulating its practice. At that time, because homosexuality was first understood as a matter of gender indeterminacy rather than sexual object choice, regulation took the form of processes designed to ferret out gender nonconformity, especially in men.

Medical clearance exams in the 1910s and 1920s included scrutiny of recruits for embodied gender difference. Doctors searched for signs of potential perversion, including bodily markers of deviance from masculine ideals, using narrow waists, wide hips, limited muscularity, and other "feminine" traits as criteria for service exclusion. The military also used intelligence tests to help identify such perverts but quickly concluded the homosexual was an intelligent psychopath, able to elude such barriers. Anxious about this psychological evasion, the military codified physical examinations as the standard screening protocol by March 1918. This amplified the growing preoccupation with finding physical "tells" of homosexuality, an effort imbricated with eugenicist logics and an interest in upholding white supremacy and compulsory able-bodiedness.[4] The somatic inferiority of white homosexuals was thus theorized as a form of racial regression, or a dangerous devolution toward the more "primitive" races, and thus in need of containment.[5] Embodied gender ambiguity was also positioned as a quasi-disability.[6] Gender and sexuality studies scholar Jacqui Alexander argues that citizenship, a status for which the military is a prime vehicle, is premised on the heterosexual, productive body; I add that it is also a cisgender body, held in contrast to the embodied deviance of transgender.[7] To face military rejection on the grounds of gendered deviance was to be excluded from the body politic.

Curiously, the actual enforcement of these regulations was highly uneven. Then as today, the offices performing clearance exams were overwhelmed, understaffed, and sometimes uninformed about the protocols. Moreover, the military was routinely in need of more bodies. Its regulatory policies focused on bringing people *in* rather than keeping them out, a fact that distinguishes the establishment of sexual citizenship through the military from its function in immigration and welfare policy.[8] The limited and selective enforcement of gendered medical criteria would become a hallmark of the military's approach to sexual regulation over the coming century, relaxing in times of crisis, when the existence of the regulations was more important than their enforcement.[9] Through the *appearance* of prohibition, more lax recruitment practices could build the ranks without threatening the moral character of the armed services.

Masculinity was central to that morality and, not incidentally, to morale. Heterosexuality was itself an emergent concept and a tenuous accomplishment; the gender ideology of the time presumed the distance between normal men and women was so vast as to require a good ideal of coaxing to bring them together into the successful formation of a nuclear family.[10] Some experts wrung their hands with worry: what if the homosociality and masculine exuberance of the military thwarted the normal course of heterosexuality? That is, they wondered whether "being so robustly male, there is no place in a soldier's heart or sexual impulse for anything not vehemently manly," like women and family.[11] In response, the armed forces relied on regulation of gender nonconformity and sodomy to defend against accusations that its gendered organization might foster sexual perversion.

Sodomy was prohibited in the military as early as the 1917 Articles of War, but the use of sodomy statutes to police homosexuality only became routine—if still selective—in the 1930s. The definition of homosexuality was transitioning from gender confusion to sexual proclivity, but sodomy prohibitions were enforced in gendered ways. Masculine men receiving pleasure from effeminized "punks" who could be "used as a girl" were considered redeemable, while the feminized men who were being used were not.[12] A certain amount of sex between men was acceptable, even to be expected, within the confines of the military, so long as it did not threaten the institution's masculine character.[13] In the 1940s alone, definitions of homosexual behavior shifted rapidly, and the Army revised its policies on homosexuality forty-one times. Finally, in 1950, the Uniform Code of Military Justice (UCMJ) established a durable anti-sodomy policy that applied across all of the armed forces. The UCMJ's definition included "unnatural," nonreproductive forms of sex between men and women, but in practice, enforcement targeted men engaged in erotic acts with each other.[14] The policy remained inconsistently applied, to the degree that commanders could "reclaim" men discharged for sodomy if there was a compelling need for their service.[15]

Early on, the military retained a relative indifference to (and ignorance of) women's homosexuality. That changed drastically in the early Cold

War era. Suddenly, women went from being a small fraction of the armed forces' homosexual discharges during World War II to becoming the target of an intensive lesbian purge. In the postwar period, women began to be discharged as homosexuals at a rate three times their proportional military representation.[16] With the war winding down, women's military service was no longer considered a temporary, heroic service to the nation, but rather another threat to the masculine institution and the American nuclear family. When some women opted not to return to their rightful places in the domestic sphere, Canaday writes, "they were seen as choosing the military (as opposed to marriage) . . . automatically suspect, considered overly ambitious and unlikely to be satisfied by the things that 'normal' women wanted."[17] Not only did their recalcitrance upset expectations about the gendered division of labor outside the military, it warned they might intend to be permanent intruders into this, the boys club par excellence. Anti-lesbian regulation ramped up, and hypersurveillance for signs of potential "lesbian tendencies" kept women's institutional membership provisional, ensuring "the subordination of women as a class."[18] For many decades to come, lesbian baiting, or threatening to report a woman as lesbian, would enable sexual violence against women in the service.[19]

The lesbian purge's control tactics were incredibly invasive and largely psychological. Compared with the medical regulations and sodomy statutes that policed men's homosexual potential, it was *emotional* intimacies between women that were the site of investigation. Investigators searched servicewomen's correspondences, followed them on outings, and pitted friends against each other in interrogations. Military records demonstrate a profound puzzlement about what lesbian *sex* might entail; in more than one instance, women engaging in oral sex evaded expulsion thanks to the bafflement of those who caught them.[20] The visible gender transgression of butch and masculine women did not go unnoticed, yet the military's obsession with locating perversion on the body was not the same for women as it had been for men. This was in part an artifact of timing: by the time the lavender scare set its sights on women, the sexological literature had moved homosexuality much further toward sexual object choice than embodied gender inversion.[21] Additionally, by simple virtue of their participation, women in the military were already regarded as gender transgressors; the institution aimed to manage that through uniforms and grooming standards that emphasized femininity and visually marked women as not-quite soldiers, sailors, and so forth. Surveilling lesbianism, then, went beyond the body. Containing their contaminating influence required policing women's emotional relationships and subjecting them to consistent, even obsessive, harassment and humiliation. Any woman who dared aim too high in her ambitions was at risk.

While the techniques of enforcement differed, by midcentury the military was moving toward a gender-neutral approach to anti-homosexuality enforcement. This reflected the crystallization of the homo/hetero binary as we now know it. In 1962, policy changes broadened the net of homosexuality-related discharges for men and women alike. The new regulations authorized the dismissal of any servicemember who "engages in, desires to engage in, or intends to engage in homosexual acts."[22] No longer a behavioral misstep, same-sex sexual desire was cemented in this language as a defining moral characteristic unbefitting military service.[23] Once again retaining their options, however, commanding officers held wide discretion, with some continuing to differentiate between amoral, "true homosexuals" and straight servicemembers enticed into same-sex intimacies by circumstance (men) or seduction (women). But that latitude was coming to an end.

In 1981, a DOD directive clarified the dismissal procedure and restricted commanders' discretion in determining what constituted an unacceptable aberration in conduct. The wording now *mandated* the discharge of any servicemember who "engaged in, has attempted to engage in, or has solicited another to engage in a homosexual act."[24] The politics of gay visibility had erased the distance between "true homosexuals" and "heterosexuals led astray." To borrow from lesbian literary great Gertrude Stein, the military had declared a homosexual is a homosexual is a homosexual.[25] Splitting hairs over how much or what kind of queer sex made one quintessentially homosexual was becoming a thing of the past as the nascent Religious Right fought to withhold and remove gay rights. Their backlash politics—repressive, right-wing, and reactionary, provoked by (and aimed at preventing solidarity among) women, people of color, and homosexuals demanding equality—helped win Ronald Reagan the presidency. His administration's support for the zero-tolerance gay ban was a foregone conclusion.[26] The DOD directive was challenged in a half dozen high-profile court cases but remained largely intact for a decade. Court rulings, military policy, and political power brokers aligned around the gay ban. By the 1990s, however, politicians on the left, including soon-to-be president Bill Clinton, recognized "gays in the military" was becoming a wedge issue—one they could and would capitalize on.

DON'T ASK, DON'T TELL . . . DON'T DISRUPT THE STATUS QUO

Promising an end to the gay ban was a calculated risk for Clinton's presidential campaign. The gamble paid off, and he was elected in November 1992. Just days after his inauguration, Clinton told the press he intended to challenge the disqualification of gay, lesbian, and bisexual servicemembers "solely on the basis of their status" as LGBs.[27] Declaring all "American citizens who want to serve their country should be able to do so unless their conduct disqualifies them from doing so," Clinton drew a distinction between status and acts. The rhetorical move was a delicate maneuvering of the era's culture wars. The administration rather elegantly sidestepped the adjudication of the "problem" of homosexuality in the military; under the illusion of status-based inclusivity, the gay ban's prohibitions on homosexual *behavior* would remain intact.

Clinton's initial plan would have allowed for open yet sexually abstinent service for LGBs. Ultimately, this clever sleight of hand was still a bridge too far for Congress, the Joint Chiefs of Staff, and top military brass. They saw even this perfunctory gesture of inclusion as a threat to the military's authority. Swift and unequivocal resistance from the DOD made it impossible for Clinton to carry out his full commitment.[28] Secretary of Defense Les Aspin was charged with drawing up a new policy that would allow for open service, but the DOD rejected the initial proposal outright. After a long and protracted battle, the compromise policy that emerged was but a timid step beyond absolute exclusion. Don't Ask, Don't Tell, Don't Pursue (10 U.S.C. § 654), shorthanded as Don't Ask, Don't Tell or DADT, purported to end sexuality-based discharges by preventing supervisors from asking subordinates about their sexuality (Don't Ask, as well as Don't Pursue) and ensuring the continued silence of forcefully closeted servicemembers (Don't Tell). Sue Fulton, an Army veteran and pivotal figure in the later efforts to repeal DADT and the trans ban, described the flimsy hope that offered: "When Don't Ask, Don't Tell happened, we thought, 'well, it's not everything we wanted, but if they just leave people alone, that would be something.' Of course, we now know it was never as advertised, it was just another version of the gay ban." Eric Fanning, who served on the House Armed Services Committee at the time, recalled of the period:

> It was enormously frustrating. I would've liked to wave a wand in 1993. If you think the debate was difficult at the start of the Obama administration, [the Clinton administration] was a very different time in history. There weren't openly gay people. I felt like I was the only one in the entire Pentagon. You know, people take license to speak more directly when they don't think the subject of whom they're speaking is in the room.... It was not an enjoyable experience to listen to [the chiefs] talk about gays in the military.

DADT was a Trojan horse, smuggling in "more arbitrary, wide-reaching, and unpredictable" antigay enforcement packaged as a progressive update to DOD policy.[29] DADT allowed for discharge if a "reasonable person" could ascertain or assume a servicemember's *propensity* for homosexuality, even in the absence of a disclosure or an act. This incredibly subjective criterion meant that anything, from sitting too close to a fellow servicemember to not adhering strictly enough to gender norms, might trigger investigation and discharge. Both straight and gay servicemembers now had to carefully monitor their behavior (including nonsexual behavior). The fear of queer contagion from the early twentieth century was revived, bridging the eugenicist ideals of past policy with the stigma attending the AIDS crisis. The military stoked fears of the "diseased and depraved homosexual" who would corrupt the morals, morale, and very health and vitality of the troops.[30] Once again, it would go to great lengths to ferret out the dangerous scourge and protect the virility of the service and the country.

Some thirteen thousand servicemembers were separated from service under DADT.[31] We can expect this figure would have been larger save for recruitment and retention needs; as in earlier periods, the number of homosexuality-related discharges waxed and waned depending on whether the military could spare troops in the moment. The policy was also leveraged to control and subordinate women, who were statistically more likely to be discharged under DADT than men, reminiscent of the Cold War–era lesbian purges.[32] At the time, only 13 percent of the Army's membership was women, yet they made up 41 percent of its DADT discharges.[33] And Black women were especially at risk, discharged at a rate three times their rate of service.[34] It's little wonder, then, that women like Shannon, whose story opened this chapter, engaged in the active performance of straightness. Her continued service depended on staying off the military's gaydar.

FROM MORALITY TO MORALE

Early opponents of DADT faced an unfavorable political and cultural climate. In 1994, Republicans won the congressional majority, letting them handily defeat legislative attempts to repeal or modify the dictates of DADT. Around the same time, Congress successfully enacted a homophobia-motivated bill requiring the expulsion of soldiers diagnosed with HIV (repealed the following year). No longer simply a wedge issue, gays in the military became, for politicians, a "political plutonium" to be avoided at all costs.[35] After the initial repeal attempts were scuttled in the Senate, the policy fight went dormant.

Outside the halls of Congress, however, the struggle continued. The civilian groundswell of support for gay rights was increasingly reflected in court decisions rather than legislative jockeying. In 2004, three judicial rulings—*Log Cabin Republicans v. United States*, *Cook v. Rumsfeld*, and *Witt v. Dep't of the Air Force*—undermined, without displacing, DADT.[36] (Notably, the involvement of the Log Cabin Republicans, a coalition of LGB conservatives, was a herald of the impending homonormative bargain, through which the political strategy of gay rights foreclosed the gay liberation movement's expansive possibilites.) *Witt v. Dep't of the Air Force*, in particular, provided new leverage for challenging DADT dismissals by establishing what was called the "Witt standard." Named for appellant Sgt. Margaret Witt, the Witt standard established the legal right for an accused servicemember to compel the military to prove they posed a specific threat to order and morale, above and beyond any inherent threat posed by LGB presence. In other words, the morale claim had to be backed by evidence of misconduct.

The claim that open service threatened the moral order of the military was losing credibility by the close of the century.[37] DADT's defenders were obliged to lean into more objective and value-neutral rationales to justify its maintenance. In a shrewd spin, they now argued the policy was not discriminatory and in fact, that the opposite was true—it was a tool to *prevent* discrimination.[38] Open service, they claimed, would mean gay/straight antagonism, with deleterious effects on unit cohesion and, in turn, national security. Ironically, they used Clinton's report, commissioned to challenge the gay ban, to urge its continuation, cherry-picking evidence of homophobic attitudes to suggest open service would destroy camaraderie and inhibit recruitment and retention.[39] The problem, they argued, was the regrettable but inevitable resistance of straight servicemembers—and that meant keeping DADT in place.

In response, repeal advocates made their own savvy pivot.[40] Like their opponents, repeal enthusiasts turned to social science. If DADT's defenders wanted to move to cohesion, morale, and national security as their new stronghold, then its detractors would bring the fight to them.[41] They took a two-prong strategy, first using social science, including a battery of new studies proving the 1993 report's findings were out of date,[42] to counter claims about military readiness and national security vis-a-vis open service.[43] Second, they engaged a "hearts and minds" approach to demonstrate the human costs of DADT by capitalizing on the institution's commitment to supporting military families. Both approaches were made possible, and ultimately successful, by the political transition from gay liberation to rights detailed in the introduction of this book.

Science and Security

Military readiness refers to the forces' essential capacity to ensure US security.[44] In the case for its continued relevance, DADT was characterized as vital to readiness: a policy meant to prevent threats to the crucial criteria of cohesion, morale, recruitment, and retention. A coterie of policy entrepreneurs working for repeal—"skilled hunters that [sought] openings" and "savvy outcome brokers[s]" who exploited those opportunities—included groups like OutServe, the Palm Center, and the Servicemembers Legal Defense Network (SLDN).[45] They, too, took up the language of readiness. Aaron Belkin, director of the Palm Center, detailed their approach in the book *How We Won*:

> In order to win repeal, I believed that we had to prevail on the national security argument. And instead of coming up with a new frame, we should use the one that conservatives had invented. But, we should flip it on its head. My message was this: It wasn't gay soldiers that harmed the military. It was discrimination.[46]

The premise of this revised persuasion campaign was that inclusion would significantly improve, rather than endanger, readiness. As Belkin hypothesized, the newly emergent research overwhelmingly disproved the idea that open service dampened military readiness. In fact, it suggested the opposite: the lying and covering required of LGB servicemembers interfered with the recruitment and retention of excellent servicemembers and encouraged harmful and divisive hypervigilance and secrecy within the ranks.[47] Harkening back to Shannon's story, the data show that DADT hardly inspired fraternal bonds between gay and straight servicemembers.[48] Therefore the policy's continuation not only hindered recruitment and retention, it diminished unit cohesion. Policy entrepreneurs like Belkin took every opportunity to discuss and disperse these findings through academic, professional, and media outlets. As the repeal inched toward political feasibility, the Senate Armed Services Committee commissioned an updated study from RAND. This time, the findings showed that military readiness would not be negatively affected by a DADT repeal.

Revealing that readiness—or at least its constitutive elements—was durable without DADT allowed repeal advocates to turn to the core motivation for readiness: security. Did the policy damage the country's safety and standing in the world? As the newly formed homeland security apparatus ballooned and leaders beat the drum for the amorphous war on terror, the nation's military and intelligence outfits sought to identify the security failures that had left them on the back foot on 9/11. When Lt. Dan Choi, a West Point graduate, decorated officer, and Arabic linguist for the Army, appeared on the *Rachel Maddow Show* to protest DADT, he was discharged. Choi became an outspoken activist, drawing attention to the fifty-nine Arabic language specialists who, like himself, had been separated from military service under the auspices of DADT. Gay rights organizations seized on this high-profile discharge and the intimation that dismissing these uniquely skilled servicemembers weakened the United States and left it vulnerable to further attacks. The Human Rights Campaign sponsored a speaking tour, The Legacy of Service, that amplified the message:

> [Former Army linguist Alexander] Nicholson implied that the DADT policy was directly responsible for the September 11 attacks. He explained that two key phrases—"tomorrow is zero hour" and "the match begins tomorrow"—were intercepted by the Pentagon on September 10 but not translated until September 12. He theorized that, if not for the ban, one of the recently fired but highly qualified gay linguists would have been on staff to receive the collected intelligence and could have prevented the terrorist attacks. . . . From this perspective, to call for the repeal of DADT was not to advocate on behalf of a narrow special interest group; rather, it was to support an essential tactical move in the War on Terror.[49]

Repeal advocates also pointed out another security risk: the potential for DADT-related blackmail. If servicemembers cannot serve openly, they argued, they could be extorted by the enemy. Open service, by contrast, would remove this possibility, uniting (and possibly expanding) the armed forces against their enemies. In the era of what Inderpal Grewal calls the "security state," this framing was brilliant—it securitized the issue, making open service all but politically unassailable.[50]

Successfully reframing DADT as a security risk, of course, was a Faustian bargain. Framing open service as a matter of national security necessitated full complicity with the violence of American empire. Grewal argues that securitization is a response to American anxiety, to its perceived losses in global dominance, racial sovereignty, and economic weakness. Securitization seeks to protect US status as an "exceptional nation," but insists its security demands the insecurity of others. As gender and sexuality studies scholar Chandon Reddy's work shows, securitization promises freedom *from* violence; in actuality, it produces freedom *with* violence.[51] Under the auspices of the security state, the military is reified as the site of rational, legitimate violence wielded against the irrational, uncivilized terror of a racialized and queered Other.[52]

Similarly, a securitization-based DADT repeal promised freedom from violence. In its enactment, LGB servicemembers were promised to be freed from the threat of homophobic violence at the same time the liberal nation-state would be freed from the forces of Islamic extremism; it even suggested the oppressed Muslim homosexual can be freed from sexual repression under terrorist regimes.[53] Yet the reality—freedom *with* violence—cannot make good on these promises. First, the harassment of gender-nonconforming LGB servicemembers has persisted, if not been exacerbated, as I show in chapter 3. Second, even after decades, the war on terror remains an albatross around the necks of liberal democracies; its end seems nowhere in sight. Third, queer life in the Middle East is actually made *more* vulnerable by US interventionism; an entire generation has now never known life outside of *al-wad*, the "situation" of everyday violence, disruption, lack of basic services, and constant fear.[54] The repeal's promise of security certainly does not extend to them, whose lives are expendable—nothing but collateral damage in the global fight against terror.[55]

The repeal and its reliance on securitization as a primary rationale is one part of the package that gender and sexuality scholar Jasbir Puar calls "homonationalism," the seduction into the fantasy of sexual exceptionalism.[56] Homonationalism builds on the idea of the United States as the exceptional nation-state: the iconic liberal democracy at the center of global politics, the "shining city upon a hill," as Ronald Reagan called it in his presidential farewell address.[57] Likewise, *sexual* exceptionalism grants the United States moral authority on questions of sexual regulation.[58] Even though that exceptional statehood was built on the containment of homosexuality's moral repugnancy, the politics of homonormativity recuperated homosexuality from the perverse.[59] Homonormativity thus produced homonationalism by "transform[ing] previously pathologized homosexuals" into "respectable homopatriotic citizens."[60] The resulting nationalistic zeal enmeshes patriotism and Pride, the premiere brand of LGBT identity.

This sexual exceptionalism can only be successful insofar as a nation can "gloss over its own policing of the boundaries of acceptance gender, racial, and class formations."[61] For the United States, LGB service creates a smokescreen, diverting attention from its failings to spotlight homophobia, gendered violence, and sexual "perversity" elsewhere.[62] Homonationalism allows the United States to position itself as gay friendly on the global stage and to shore up its liberal democratic bona fides. Homonationalism is not unique to the United States; it is not an attribute that a country either has or doesn't have. It is "the field within which demarcations of nation-states as 'progressive,' 'gay-friendly" 'tolerant,' and 'homophobic' have salience in the first place." Homonationalism is a "hermeneutic that asks how and why 'how well do you treat your homosexuals' . . . emerges as an arbiter of the capacity for national sovereignty, for governance and self-determination."[63] Through such rhetorics, gay rights are Occidentalized and homophobia is Orientalized.[64] The Middle East is continually framed by liberal Western democracies as the supreme site of homophobic violence, one more reason it must be targeted for continued military occupation and intervention. By contrast, pinkwashing helps the United States and other countries position themselves as particularly modern and democratic, despite their inattention toward domestic homophobia and their responsibility for creating the political conditions that violently prohibit homosexuality elsewhere.[65]

Family Ties

The pragmatic approach of marshaling social science and security to the DADT repeal covered a lot of ground, but the second prong, the "hearts and minds" campaign, was no less important to the movement's tactical repertoire. Generic appeals to rights and fairness were ineffective, given that the military has retained greater latitude to impinge on its members' freedoms, privacy, and right to work than have civilian employers. It is a wholly unique workplace, with higher stakes and tighter regulation on its members' civil rights, as Clinton proclaimed in his first presidential press conference:

> Military life is fundamentally different from civilian society. It necessarily has a different and stricter code of conduct, even a different code of justice. Nonetheless, individuals who are prepared to accept all necessary restrictions on their behavior, many of which would be intolerable in civilian society, should be able to serve their country honorably and well.[66]

In an institution premised on national rather than individual sovereignty, appeals to rights based in civilian logics can go only so far. Instead, policy entrepreneurs wisely used the distinct conceit of the "military family" to promote change. Many gendered organizations are reliant on the invisible and uncompensated labor of partners, often wives, whose work facilitates the long hours, focus, and commitment they require. In the military in particular, spouses are expected to shoulder the burdens that allow for everything from servicemembers' overnight work rotations to moments-notice deployment. In our conversation, Eric Fanning summarized:

> In many ways, the military is still built on a 1950s culture and family construct. . . . The military as it exists wouldn't work if you didn't have a lot of trailing spouses who are opening houses, closing houses, getting kids in and out of new schools, what have you. It's very hard not to have that team and do what someone is asked to do in uniform.

The uniquely burdensome demands of such arrangements spawned their own cultural archetype: the military wife. She is celebrated through Military Spouse Appreciation Day; spousal support services; military balls; pinning ceremonies; and rituals like the "hail and farewell," during which families celebrate (and are celebrated for) spouses' departures to and returns from deployment. Military spouses work together to maintain and support both their own individual families and the symbolic family of the military community, from the unit level to the global sprawl of the US armed forces. On military bases, the commander's wife is treated like the "First Lady of the base," in Eric Fanning's words, the beneficent maternal figure presiding over the spousal collective.

In our interview, Sue Fulton pinpointed a specific meeting as the watershed moment in the repeal process. The DOD's Comprehensive Review Working Group (CRWG) on DADT sat down with the partners of active duty LGB servicemembers. She explained:

> When they hear somebody saying, "I can't pick up my partner from the hospital after his knee surgery, I can't pick the kids up after daycare, I can't go shopping at the commissary. . . . When he comes back from Afghanistan, when she comes back from Afghanistan, when she comes back from Iraq, I can't be at the welcome ceremony." And they were staggered by it. One senior officer, I don't know whether it was a colonel or brigadier or general, said, "My wife wouldn't have allowed me to stay in the military if I had to put up with that." They really, finally, *finally* got it.

In other words, the appeals to the military family (and how DADT hindered military spouses' ability to support servicemembers) were far more compelling than other pleas for equity or fairness. The Army's motto, "Mission First, People Second," is illustrative: if repeal advocates could show that readiness would not be compromised by open service (mission first) *and* that the repeal was in the best interests of military families (people second), then open LGB service could be presented as essential to the continued health and success of the armed services. The face of the fight would not be individuals seeking rights, but families sacrificing for the nation.

The military family also refers to the less literal "band of brothers," led by the father figure of their commanding officer (whose wife, the First Lady of the base, tends the home fires). That "family" is united by the uniform, a venerated symbol of kinship. In our interview, Eric Fanning explained that "the Marine Corps was the most resistant to the change" of DADT repeal, but once it passed, the Marines' commandant James Amos and senior enlisted released a surprising video statement.[67] He remembered them saying something "along the lines of 'anyone wearing the uniform of a Marine is a Marine, period.' Hard stop."

> The minute that the chiefs look at someone in their uniform, they're like, "I'm responsible for that person. Everyone backs away. That's a Marine/soldier/sailor/airman. I got it." Once that uniform's on, it just changes their mentality. . . . It is binary for them. "That is my Marine." Yesterday, "I don't want a gay being a Marine." Today, "he's a Marine, he's my Marine. I gotta take care of him. . . . My Marine's got a job to do, and my Marine needs to be treated fairly." . . . Once you got them in, and said to the senior uniformed leadership, "They're yours now," they're like, "Yeah, they're mine. I'm responsible for the wellbeing of the people who put on the uniform in my service."

Repeal advocates appealed to the institution's inherent duty-bound paternalism to coax leadership into accepting change. They also sought to mobilize the sense of sibling solidarity in the bonds among servicemembers. For example, when I later interviewed Joanna, a 41-year-old white cis straight woman, she told me:

> [In the Air Force], we definitely have a real family feeling. It's not just the people that you see from 7:30 to 4:30 every day. . . . When you start deploying . . . you learn about them and what makes them tick and their families

> and their kids and all that. It's a real family feeling. The most amazing thing about being part of the Air Force that I've ever seen is, when somebody is in need, you don't have to ask, "Hey, does anybody want to help these folks out? They're having an issue." People just jump up. . . . Whether it's big or small, you're just down on your luck and everything keeps going wrong, or whatever it is, folks come together. You get more help than you ever thought you could need or want. When you're a young airman and you first come in the Air Force, you get your supervisor . . . the person that is kind of like your big brother or big sister. In a *lot* of ways, it's like a family, insomuch as you might have a big brother who loves you, who's going to take care of you, might kick you in the ass when you need it, but he's doing it because he cares.

Capitalizing on these family values, repeal advocates took a tack that marriage equality activists and other movements have found fruitful, and it was distinctly successful in the military context, where familialism is so central to the institution's self-image.[68]

By using family as the emotional entry point, repeal advocates further embedded familialism and all it entails into gay rights politics. Despite the gender-neutral language of "military spouse" that has become the more common parlance, the division of labor expected of such households is still deeply gendered. Familial logics, especially to the extent that they align with or reinforce the patriarchal, white, and middle-class nuclear family ideal, help coalesce homonormativity. The ideological system of homonormativity is "anchored in domesticity."[69] The homonormative bargain begs incorporation into the conservatizing institutions of marriage and parenthood, while narrowing the menu of possibilities for challenging antipathy to queerness in the military and beyond (see chapter 3 for servicemembers' lived experiences of this bargain's negative repercussions). Moreover, the gay rights movement's co-optation of familial logics extends the legitimization of US imperial ambitions. As Dean Spade and Craig Wilse write, "Imperialism and militarism are always, among other things, sexual and gender projects that use sexual, gender, and family norms as technologies of intervention and violence."[70]

ANATOMY OF A REPEAL

Due to the diligent efforts of policy entrepreneurs, The Military Readiness Enhancement Act was put before Congress in 2005, 2007, and 2009. If passed, it would have replaced DADT and amended Title 10 of the United States Code to include a nondiscrimination policy for sexual orientation.[71] Each time, the act stalled in committee. In 2009, the Palm Center published a report laying out the political, legal, and regulatory path to ending DADT by executive order.[72] While keeping pressure on Congress, this move pressed then president Barack Obama to take executive action. He demurred, though he threw public support behind a legislative repeal of the policy.

Greg Brown, who worked in the Office of Military Personnel Policy at the time, described for me the flurry of panic in the secretary of defense's office when Obama first broached the topic during his presidential campaign:

> The policy had been on autopilot forever, there was really nothing to do with it. The first time [Obama] mentioned it, we all looked at each other and said, "Holy shit, if he is elected, we are ill-prepared to—we do not understand what went into this policy! We don't understand the social science behind it, the military readiness aspect of it, the legal parts of it—." . . . We were so ill-prepared that we just panicked. When it became clear that he was going to win the election—there's normally an understanding in the Pentagon that you do not start working new administration's projects until the inauguration, but on this one we just started building a knowledge library and getting the numbers and calling people and reading congressional testimony and just trying to figure out what went into this thing and how we would go about deconstructing it if it came to that. I like to [describe that time by saying that] I had a full head of hair prior to that, and I don't have much of it left!

Brown, who would go on to support the repeal as well as transgender inclusion, admitted his initial instinct was resistance. He assumed the policy was in place for good reason. His turnaround included a lot of unlearning:

> We were not convinced that the current policy, the Don't Ask, Don't Tell policy, wasn't the best policy if you look at it in terms of military readiness, because geez, there was a law! [We assumed] people had done research, made the good order and discipline argument [in an objective way]. . . . We just all assumed there was something to this policy, so our goal was not to overturn it. Our goal was to understand it and then provide sound military advice as to what is the best way going forward, taking into account *only*

> military readiness. Again, it seems so silly now . . . but we didn't know. [A new RAND report] was commissioned by the Secretary of Defense. [I read] the 1993 study, which had also been commissioned and then conveniently ignored—eventually, I used to walk around with it. It was the Rosetta Stone, where we were going to end up going. By this time, and [with] the new RAND study, we quickly got over [resistance]. . . . It did not take long before you realized the argument [for keeping DADT] was built on lies, built on prejudice, built on old data—built by well-meaning, but ill-guided people.

So fortified, the push for the repeal led Rep. Patrick Murphy to introduce an amendment to the National Defense Authorization Act with Obama's support. The amendment, which would have ended DADT and added a sexuality nondiscrimination policy to the UCMJ, passed the House in May 2010 but was filibustered in the Senate by Sen. John McCain.

By November of that year, the DOD's working group had released its implementation plan for a repeal. After more congressional hearings, including supportive testimony from Chairman of Joint Chiefs of Staff Admiral Michael Mullen, the amended Defense Authorization Act was reintroduced and again filibustered. Undeterred, Senators Joe Lieberman and Susan Collins introduced one more last-minute, standalone bill in December. Called the Don't Ask, Don't Tell Repeal Act, this measure passed both the House and Senate. It was signed into law by President Obama on December 22, 2010, and stipulated full implementation as of September 20, 2011.

The DADT repeal ended military disqualification and dismissal on the basis of sexual orientation. Even so, it was not nearly as expansive as it could have been or as many hoped it might be. Unlike its predecessor, the Military Readiness Enhancement Act, the repeal did not prohibit discrimination and harassment on the basis of sexual orientation (that would come in 2015, when the military added sexual orientation to its nondiscrimination policy). Nor did it decriminalize sodomy, leaving that for UCMJ changes in 2013. Same-sex spousal benefits also lagged for years. When I asked Greg Brown about the omissions, he said they had been strategic:

> We tabled a few things because we knew they would be contentious: . . . benefits for partners, collection of military records, nondiscrimination, removing sodomy from the UCMJ. . . . There were some issues that we just set

> aside because our phrase was, "Let's just get to second base, take a breath, and then we'll bunt the guy over to third and they will hit a sacrifice fly and get it all." In the end, we got it all. Now [the end of] DOMA [Defense of Marriage Act, 1996] helped, we could not have got it all without [that repeal]. The [partner] benefits, we were very limited by what we could do by DOMA language. But we accepted incrementalism as the daily strategy.

Eric Fanning recalled the day Obama signed the Repeal Act into law: "They had such a big signing [event] they had to do it in the Department of the Interior room so they could have more people in. That night, everyone was celebrating, excited and emotional." People were curious about the Pentagon's reaction, "as if they were expecting there to be either an open revolt or a champagne celebration." Instead, the reception was a preview of what I would later hear from cadets, servicemembers, and veterans: "Nothing happened in the Pentagon," Fanning remembered. "They were focused on wars, budgets, like it is every day. Because this had gone on so long, when it was finally certified, people were like, 'Didn't we do this already?'" An entire century of exclusion, activism, court fights, and legislative back-and-forth meant that, when DADT ended, it was not with a bang but with a shrug.

When the repeal passed, predictions about its reception were mixed. Some, like Fanning, argued that the organizational culture of the military had already moved toward open service and anticipated very little if any conflict.[73] Hopeful forecasters thought the repeal would pave the way for the end of gender-based combat exclusions and trans service (indeed, these came in 2013 and 2016, respectively).[74] Others were skeptical the repeal would really improve working conditions for LGBs, given the durability of the homophobic and femmephobic rituals and practices of the military.[75] Critics anticipated that LGB servicemembers would continue to deal with isolation and closeting, even possible swells of homophobic violence, in the wake of the repeal.[76] Mental health professionals prepared for a flood of LGB patients experiencing stress and suicide risk and warned of a potentially increased risk of self-harm.[77] The current research shows that, indeed, LGB servicemembers and veterans fear disclosure and on average accrue negative mental and physical health outcomes beyond those experienced by their straight peers.[78] Still, from the vantage point of ten years post-DADT, the repeal appears to have been neither crisis nor revolution, for better or worse.[79]

The language of the repeal relied on rights to privacy, respect, and dignity as its primary rationales. That first point has been particularly common—and successful—in securing LGBT legal protections outside the service. For example, in the landmark case *Lawrence v. Texas*, the Supreme Court found criminalization of sodomy unconstitutional on the grounds that it violates the right to privacy between consenting adults. Though effective, the privacy rights strategy is also deeply homonormative. Privacy is figured as an individual possession, not a collective resource, and conditions like poverty, homelessness, incarceration, and abusive relationships structure who can and who cannot afford it. Moreover, defining sexuality through privacy and dignity facilitates homonormativity by splitting private from public behavior. Conceptualizing sexuality as what one does "in the privacy of the bedroom" implies the possibility of a decidedly unqueer presentation of self in the public sphere. Put differently, a person deserving of privacy is one who is able to act with subtlety and discretion in public, complying with heteronormative social norms in exchange for protected privacy "at home." These are not mere semantics; the homonormative coding of the repeal plays out in how servicemembers incorporate—and continue to exclude—LGBT people in the open service context.

CONCLUSION

Advocates who worked tirelessly to dismantle the ban saw the repeal as a win not just for servicemembers, but for all LGBT Americans. In a dialogue between Aaron Belkin and legal scholar Dean Spade, an outspoken queer critic of the push for inclusion, Belkin made this explicit:

> Discrimination against LGBT service members is dangerous. Critics sometimes think that the inclusion campaigns were pursued for the sake of the troops, and to a certain extent, that is correct, in that military discrimination destroyed many lives and led to murder, rape, suicide, and more. What prompted me to work on this issue for the past twenty years, however, is not just the welfare of the troops but also Eve Kosofsky Sedgwick's (1990) point that appropriating someone's right to name their own identity is a "consequential seizure," and Janet Halley's (1999) point that if the legal mechanism embedded in DADT had spread to other statutes, that would

> have been a step along a slippery slope to a totalitarian outcome. . . . There's a lot more to be said about that, but the main point is that military discrimination against LGBT people is dangerous, not just because of the impact on the troops. So, not standing up to it was not an option, at least from my point of view.[80]

Belkin's is a crucial point that cannot be lost in my analysis of homonormativity and homonationalism. Advocates have dedicated their lives and careers to inclusion because they have a front-row seat to the literal and representational consequences of exclusion. In my discussions with servicemembers, I heard what Belkin saw: the direct and indirect stakes of open service. The toll exacted upon those who had to survive—and those who were unable to survive—the ban is staggering. It would be impossible for me to absorb such stories and walk away wishing that open service didn't exist. I also saw the indirect stakes Belkin mentions as I listened to straight and cis servicemembers reevaluate their homo- and transphobic belief systems through open service.

In the same piece, Belkin laments that queer critics have paid inadequate attention to these stakes. Indeed, when debates happen at an academic remove, it is hard to grasp the ways the repeal provides on the ground. At the same time, I think of Eli Massey and Jasmin Nair's critique of "inclusion in the atrocious": "It has long been the case that the most vulnerable populations—queer, trans, and the poorest among us—are disproportionally the ones who end up becoming cannon fodder, while the children of the wealthy get to stay at home."[81] It is perverse, Massey and Nair continue, to tie access to basic resources (wealth, health, education, citizenship) to the conditions of military service. Pointedly, they ask, "What can possibly be good about a society where [LGBT] people must sign up for the possibility of losing life and limb in order to be guaranteed such basic entitlements?"

Critics like Massey and Nair *also* have front-row seats to the ban's consequences; they are simply facing a different part of the stage. The pragmatist/idealist and incremental/transformational binaries that frame these debates can obscure the shared concern at their core: the constellation of harms that are both alleviated and exacerbated by inclusion. Is it possible to stand between the benefits and the dangers of military incorporation, refusing to choose sides? Taking inspiration from Reina Gossett,

Eric Stanley, and Joanna Burton's analysis of the politics of trans visibility, I endeavor in this book to continually seek out the "trap door" between these two stages, a passageway out of these binaries.[82] Keeping in mind this both/and perspective, itself a characteristic of queer critique, I turn now to how people inside the military institution received and interpreted DADT's repeal, demonstrating the simultaneity of harm reduction and harm aggravation in open service implementation.

2 "What They Do in Their Private Life, I Couldn't Care Less"

STRIKING THE HOMONORMATIVE BARGAIN

General Merril McPeak was the Air Force chief of staff at the start of DADT. On the eve of its repeal, he published an op-ed in the *New York Times*, offering one last, impassioned plea for its maintenance.[1] Morality appeals having long since lost sway with the public, General McPeak turned to the rationale of national security. A sexuality-based ban, he argued, was not an act of discrimination but a carefully considered and necessary restriction on service like so many others. "The services exclude, without challenge, many categories of prospective entrants," McPeak wrote. "People cannot serve in uniform if they are too old or too young, too fat or too thin, too tall or too short, disabled.... [S]o why should exclusion of gay people rise to the status of a civil rights issue?" Of course, he assured readers, he believed that "all *people* are created equal." He simply didn't "believe that such equality extended to all *ideas* or all *cultures*"—including the idea of open service or the "culture" of homosexuality. "We know, or ought to know," he continued, "that warriors are inspired by male bonding, by comradeship.... [T]o undermine [this] cohesion is to endanger everyone." "Some will see these ingredients of the military lifestyle as a sort of absurd, tough-guy game played by overgrown boys," he allowed, yet argued they were essential to the lynchpin of the military's continued success: its readiness. "I do not see how permitting open homosexuality in these communities enhances their prospects of success in battle," he concluded. "Indeed, I believe repealing 'Don't Ask, Don't Tell' will weaken the warrior culture at a time when we have a fight on our hands"—the fight against the forces of "radical Islam" threatening the foundations of American freedom and democracy.

McPeak's comments are the sort that kept DADT in place for decades. The servicemembers I interviewed, however, found them out of step with the modern military. The tactical repertoires of the repeal's champions (see chapter 1) had successfully reversed McPeak's assertions about DADT and the war on terror, turning the repeal itself into a convincing strategy of securitization.[2] Still, I expected I would encounter in my interviews some resistance to the repeal among the rank and file. At the very least, I thought the repeal would be treated as a transformative moment in military history. To be sure, for many LGB servicemembers, it was. Nonetheless, both straight and LGB servicemembers described the repeal as Eric Fanning did in the previous chapter: neither an open revolt nor a champagne celebration, but a pen stroke that brought the letter of the law into alignment with the spirit of contemporary service.

Today's armed forces are branded as professionalized, tolerant, and diverse, leaving little room for overt expressions of homophobia. Like other organizations—the corporation, the university, and so forth—the military has experienced what gender and sexuality studies scholar Sara Ahmed calls the "institutionalization of diversity."[3] In this configuration, diversity is a high-demand currency that credentials institutions as enlightened, benevolent, and thoroughly (neo)liberal. It is a "value-add," in corporate speak, that improves marketability.

Diversity today is both a tool and a criterion of recruitment into institutions. For example, Navy recruiter Shannon, whom we met in chapter 1, described a recent initiative to identify "any biases in our training programs for recruiting . . . that can possibly hinder us from ensuring that this all-volunteer force" is manned with the best possible talent. Her words were telling:

> We're looking at marketing and advertising. How do we reach the families? How do we get over the historical negative perceptions of the military that

> people believe that, hey, you can only come in to be third-rate? . . . How do we get to these diverse populations? That's what we're exploring now.

Opinions like McPeak's directly contradict the official line of today's military: rights, respect, and recruitment *should* be "extended to all ideas [and] all cultures," not just those of white, straight, cisgender candidates. The incorporation of sexuality and gender expression into the frameworks of tolerance and diversity was no foregone conclusion, however; it was facilitated by the strategic decisions made in the pivot from gay liberation to gay rights.

In 1980, lesbian feminist Adrienne Rich coined the concept "compulsory heterosexuality," referring to the social forces that compel people, especially women, into its waiting, stifling embrace.[4] A few years later, fellow lesbian feminist Monique Wittig articulated the "heterosexual contract" to refer to the social conventions and language of how we cooperatively live, function, work, and marry that "show on the dotted line" that what we refer to as the social contract actually "consists of living in heterosexuality." Heterosexuality, Wittig reasoned, is "an ideological form which cannot be grasped in reality, except through its effects, whose existence lies in the minds of people, but in a way that affects their whole life, the way they act, the way they move, the way they think."[5] DADT was a compromise, an attenuation rather than a repudiation of the heterosexual contract at a time when its taken for granted-ness was under threat. The "ingredients of the military lifestyle" referenced by General McPeak, namely homo- and femmephobic exclusion, maintained their nonnegotiable status long after other institutions had begun to concede these points. The continued discrimination was deemed necessary to continued US security and sovereignty.

However, by the late 2000s, the politics of visibility and normalization that came to characterize the gay rights movement successfully broke the exclusivity clause of the heterosexual contract by negotiating the homonormative bargain. Under its terms, some LGBs are granted "the 'measures of benevolence' afforded by liberal discourses of multicultural tolerance and diversity," including the ability to serve openly in the military.[6] Repeal advocates could successfully debunk the myth of DADT's necessity through empirical research and turn the military's familial culture to its advantage, as detailed in the previous chapter, so long as they abided by the terms of the homonormative bargain and its assimilative aspirations.

That bargain made life more livable for many, but as I will show, only by conceding to increased unlivability for so many others. The terms and conditions of gaining "respectably queer" status include the active suppression of the "unpredictable, unprofessional, messy, or defiant" differences that constitute queer culture.[7] The respectable queer is, as a result, a queer subject in name only, the substantive queerness having been displaced onto others who suffer further marginalization under the homonormative bargain. Whether it does or does not manifest as an LGBT or queer *identity*, continued sexual or gendered perversion is a queer *relation*. Further, under the homonationalist imprimatur, the perversion that once characterized the American homosexual subject is sited in racialized Muslim foreigners, defined as perverse by their proximity to terrorist potentiality. Their queerness marks them for death or debility, acceptable collateral damage in the war on terror.

Being vacated of one's queerness is a mournful, painful experience that subjects the repatriated LGB citizen to social control processes that closely discipline and punish any breach of this homonormative social contract. In the pages that follow, I show how individuals' own narrations and recollections about the repeal's reception are constituted and expressed through homonormativity. This analysis of the participants' logics of LGB inclusion reveals the specific contours of that bargain as they play out in the military context.

THE BIG (NON) EVENT

I anticipated that the repeal's rollout, the culmination of decades of impassioned debate and policy shifts, would be remembered by current, former, and future military personnel as a watershed moment. Instead, the vast majority framed the long-awaited transition as a nonevent, a blink-and-you'll-miss-it moment. Alyssa (34, cis straight woman, race not given), who served in the Air Force through the repeal and its aftermath, described:[8]

> I [thought] the reality of the situation is it's going to be a nonevent. . . . You go to work on Monday morning, on Monday afternoon it's repealed, and on Tuesday, you do exactly the same thing you did Monday morning. I said, "Nothing's going to happen." Everybody thought I was crazy. Then when it got repealed, nothing whatsoever changed. Nobody resigned. . . . The reports that I saw were that not a single person resigned for that reason. We were all of the general mindset, "Why is this even a thing that has to be repealed?" It was a non-thing to us, other than, "Oh my God, finally the military got it right."

Alyssa welcomed the repeal and said that even those who resisted it were surprisingly subdued at its inauguration. She continued, "The higher up [the ranks] you went, the more [the repeal] became 'a thing', but they also knew the writing was on the wall." Unlike General McPeak and other retired personnel, "people that did have a problem with it of the higher ranks tended to respond with . . . 'Whether or not you agree with it, this is the law, get used to it.'"

When I asked Maryann (31, white cis straight woman, Navy) if she recalled the "water cooler conversation" during that period, she responded, "I didn't hear a whole lot of people too worried about it. A lot of what I heard was 'I don't care what you do on your weekends.' That was kind of a consensus that kept going.'" Ben, a 35-year-old white cis gay Air Force veteran, concurred, describing the "incredibly minor" impact of repeal: "People have probably joined that wouldn't have before. A couple of people have probably gotten out or have not joined because of it. Okay, we don't want you anyway." Just a few decades earlier, homosexuality was an all-encompassing, pathologizing status. Now Maryann, Ben, and their colleagues understood it as something "minor" you "do on your weekends," a leisure pursuit akin to camping or golfing.

Brian, a 40-year-old white cis straight man in the Navy, contrasted the anxious tone of media reports with the reality as he experienced it: "I remember conversations [on the news] where it was like, 'This is going to be terrible, there's going to be violence, there's going to be fights in the barracks, there's going to be all these dramatic negative consequences.'" Yet Brian and his coworkers "sat there, pre-repeal, saying, 'There's not going to be any of that. There's going to be a collective yawn and people are going to go on with their lives.' . . . From our perspective, that's basically what happened." Similarly, Hank (30, Black transgender straight man, Air Force veteran) reported: "A lot of higher ranking people didn't think it was a good idea, they thought that mass chaos was going to ensue." Instead, "I heard of a few people coming out . . . one or two people . . . but for the most part . . . it was just like, 'Okay, that happened. We're glad it happened, but we're still just kind of living life every day.'"

The narrative of the repeal as a nonevent threaded through discussions of its longer-range impact. Crystal (37, white straight cis woman, Air Force) said that, in the years since, "I haven't noticed a huge change myself. . . . In leading up to the change, everyone was really nervous, it seemed like. . . . Then after the change happened, [people] were like, 'Okay, this happened. Either we can talk about it, or we can get back to work.'" Like Hank, Crystal recalled rampant fears about the moment of repeal: "Everyone stop what you're doing and stare at the person who's gay sitting next to you and make them uncomfortable." But, she said, "I don't feel like that was what happened. That's [just] what the military was afraid was going to happen." Admittedly, she added, there was a period of adjustment as LGB servicemembers came out after so many years of suppression:

> In the beginning, I don't want to say it was a big deal, but there were the people who you were kind of wondering if they were gay or not. Then they would just kind of start talking about their significant other in a manner where you realized, "Oh yeah, they were gay." . . . I did have to kind of control my facial expressions or my reactions so I didn't make them feel bad for telling me or announcing it or admitting anything. Just trying to make it a normal part of the day. Like you said, before that, we were supposed to not talk about it. All of a sudden, everyone had to make this mental change where, "Okay, it's okay to talk about. Don't have any reactions."

Crystal's self-monitoring of facial expressions and reactions illustrates the interactional work incumbent upon straight allies under the homonormative bargain. What makes LGB service palatable is its unremarkability. Producing that unremarked upon-ness is an ongoing accomplishment that can require the suppression of an affective response, positive or negative. Not only did servicemembers understand it was unacceptable to chastise or exclude a peer who came out, they absorbed the idea that they shouldn't congratulate or celebrate them. A polite poker face was the only "right" reaction.

Out of all research participants, only Kyle, a 51-year-old white cis straight Navy veteran, described the transition as disruptive or sudden. He offered a metaphor: "You cannot just drop a baby on someone's doorstep and think they're going to be ready to take care of it. They should have eased into it." To him, it was like, "All of a sudden you've got this big change of policy. That's what puts people, what gets them in an uproar." By contrast, "People adapt well to incremental change. As long as it's a little bit by little bit by little bit, it's a lot easier and it's a lot safer, too." By contrast, Ritchie (50, white cis straight man, Navy veteran) told me that "long before Don't Ask, Don't Tell went away," he was working with known LGB servicemembers. "While they didn't talk about it, it was known and it was no big deal." He went on, "Everybody was cool with them and there was no one I knew who was gay who ever had a problem. . . . Everybody just understood and nobody ever made a big deal of it." After probing, Ritchie allowed, "Sure, there might've been a little bit of jokes, 'Hey, you know, Such-and-Such over there, he's this, that, or the other, ha, ha, ha. Big deal.' [But] everybody treated each other well and it was never a big deal."

Brian had similar memories:

> There were a lot of people that either had already come out or were just an open secret. They were just, "I'm going to live my life. You do what you will with it," type of attitude. Nobody was doing anything about it because as the culture changed, people didn't really care that much. I can think of two people that I knew, both at the Pentagon, who came out, quietly and just as a matter of, like, "This is my life. This is who I am."

He detailed the "open secret" of two coworkers' sexualities during DADT:

> In my first squadron, we had two women in the squadron that were gay women, . . . one of them pretty much openly. By "openly," I mean she was a warrant officer in our squadron and she would come to the Christmas party with her girlfriend. It was just, "This is my friend Susan," but it was quite clear to everybody they were in a relationship with each other. The other one was our command master chief who was more. . . . This sounds horrible, but she fit many of the stereotypical characteristics of being a gay woman. . . . She never brought her girlfriend to any squadron events, but you would see her out in town.

Brian's coworkers served from inside a "glass closet": social cues and gender presentation outed them, even in the absence of a formal disclosure.[9] Christopher (cis straight man, Army veteran, race and age not given) said that lesbian soldiers were a "well-known but well-kept secret" since he first joined back in the 1970s. This liminal space between detection and disclosure expanded under DADT. While on deployment, Christopher said, LGB servicemembers tended to be more open about their sexuality: "Not like coming out of the closet and announcing you're gay, but it was obvious that they had their past, had their 'little thing' going on or whatever." Sociologist Shawn Trivette argues that the silences forced by DADT paradoxically produced a "queer space" within the military.[10] Ritchie, Brian, and Christopher were acclimatized to open service by virtue of their straight observations of that queer space: a space made obsolete by the repeal, at least on paper.

LGB Experiences of DADT and the Repeal

During its tenure, the strange compromise of DADT installed glass closets across the entire military. The "don't ask" of it, as well as the lesser known "don't pursue," meant that in relatively gay-friendly units, LGB sexuality was seen and tolerated, but only obliquely acknowledged. Coworkers sometimes engaged in teasing, which skirted the official prohibition on asking and telling by providing just enough plausible deniability for both parties. Even so, these jokes could put LGB servicemembers at risk. When they entered the public domain of a unit's cultural commons, LGB servicemembers could easily lose control of the circulation of potentially damning information and innuendo. Courtney, 44-year-old Black cis lesbian woman and Navy veteran, explained:

> On my first ship, everybody knew about [me]. Or some people suspected, but I had boyfriends too [as cover]. . . . Any new female who would come aboard, . . . I would be one of the first people they see because they have to come to me when they check-in on the ship. I was the one that would be showing them around and stuff like that. But then [other sailors] would be all, "Oh, your girlfriend was looking for you," or stuff like that. . . . Which wouldn't be true, but I was a scared kid.

For people like Courtney, the repeal was far from a nonevent; it meant freedom from the terror that one day, one joke would go too far or fall upon the wrong ears.

LGB cadets, soon-to-be officers in the post-repeal military, recalled with great specificity how the repeal influenced their decisions to join ROTC. For example, Thomas (21, white cis gay man) told me he had been attracted to a military career when he was in high school but had dismissed it as a viable option because of its sexuality-based restrictions. When the repeal was announced in his junior year, he was ecstatic. Years later, he vividly remembered the exact moment he learned that his options had suddenly expanded:

> I had to realize ROTC probably isn't an option for me because I obviously am not going to be comfortable hiding who I am and also being a soldier or an airman or whatever at the same time. That's when I dropped the whole ROTC idea. . . . Then Don't Ask, Don't Tell got repealed—I remember watching it, actually, before hockey practice. I was at home, sitting on my couch and getting ready to go to hockey practice. I was watching CNN, Wolf Blitzer or something like that. I saw it flashing across the screen, and I was like, "Oh my God." . . . It was an awesome moment for me, because now I can serve in the Army. It felt good to know that the country was moving in a new direction, repealing something that was so regressive and homophobic and all these other things. That was a good feeling. That's when I started thinking again, "Maybe I want to do this. Maybe I do want to join the Army because now I can. Yeah!" Senior year, I decided to apply for the scholarship.

Another cadet, Cassie (22, white cis lesbian woman), was unsure whether she would have joined without the repeal. DADT was still in place when she was weighing her options; when I asked whether it factored into her decision-making, she answered, "Ultimately no, because I was really lucky that it was repealed before I got in." She continued, "It's hard to say if I would have or would not have joined if it was still on. . . . It sucks for those people who went their whole lives not getting to be out." Even some cadets who joined ROTC after the repeal felt its impact. Despite the availability of open service, Julie (20, white cis bisexual woman) was unsure whether the culture would really change. Her own ROTC program was supportive of her open sexuality, yet Julie worried about meeting other cadets during summer training. When she got there, though, she "realized that [most cadets] were like, 'Okay, yeah, and who cares?'" She called this blasé attitude about homosexuality a "casual effect from the repeal" that made her less anxious about life as an officer after graduation.

Some enlisted servicemembers who joined after the repeal shared similar stories. Justine, a 33-year-old white cis lesbian in the Air Force, "thought about joining right after high school" but chose not to because of the ban. "That repeal was very important to me in terms of just making that career decision." Her wife, who *did* join prior to the repeal, told Justine "these stories about people who are, you know, good airmen or good soldiers or good sailors who were kicked out of the military just for being gay." These stories were "the reason [she] didn't join." She recalled thinking, "I know there's gay people who did [join under DADT], and I admire that, but I can't imagine having to hide that part of my life."

In the DADT era, Melanie (28, white cis lesbian woman, Army) was terrified of being "found out" as a lesbian during recruitment and orientation. "It made me really nervous," she recalled, especially because "a couple years before I joined, I actually got a Pride tattoo." Military medical processing specifically documents and asks enlistees about any tattoos or other identifying marks; Melanie remembered that to evade detection, "I basically made up a story. I told him that me and my best friend wanted to get our first tattoo together, and we couldn't decide on something. We're both girls, so we got two female symbols, and we didn't have a favorite color so we picked rainbow." Her doctor seemed to accept this explanation—at least, he didn't ask further questions or raise any flags with the higher ups.

Melanie remained scared after enlistment. Two of her friends had already been discharged under DADT, so she worked hard to keep her sexuality completely under wraps: "I would say, probably for the first year, it was pretty tough, because up until the last year that they had [DADT] in effect, nobody talked about it and I felt uncomfortable because I couldn't be myself." Exhausted by the secrecy, Melanie began to come out to close friends as the repeal implementation drew closer: "I slowly started telling a few people, started being myself, and those people were actually pretty accepting of it. There were only a few people that were against it, but not to the point where they would try to get me kicked out or anything." Her selective disclosures remained risky until the repeal was implemented. "It was pretty scary because you don't know how people are going to react to something. . . . You don't know if they'll go and tell someone on you." She continued, 'If you feel like you can trust [people], that's when I would be open with people about it. [But] it was scary either way."

ABOUT TIME

To the vast majority of my research participants, then, the repeal was uneventful. In fact, these interviewees largely supported the DADT repeal. They often characterized the policy as an anachronistic relic that made no sense for the modern military. For example, Air Force veteran Marie (29, white cis straight woman) exclaimed, "It was about time! I was very excited. It was a just step towards [joining] our society in moving in the right direction." The comments I heard directly contradicted the logics used to uphold DADT, including the idea that repeal would irreparably harm unit cohesion. If anything, they argued that it was deception about one's sexuality that impeded cohesion.

April, a 40-year-old white cis straight woman in the Air Force, explained, "If you are fundamentally lying about who you are, you cannot uphold the core values" of the military. In such a situation, she argued, "You are living a lie every day. . . . How can you be a representative of the military in that way? I thought that was a really strong argument" for repeal. Holly (white cis straight woman, Army veteran, age not given) concurred, saying of the repeal, "I think it's great, people shouldn't have to hide anything." Participants framed the closet as an impediment to authenticity and used the popular psychotherapeutic framing of sexual disclosure as essential to happiness. Nate (19, white cis straight man, Army ROTC) enthused, "I'm thrilled. This is something I've noticed a lot. . . . If you have something on your mind, if you have something stressing you, if you have something you're trying to hide from your friends, you just can't perform at the same level. It's so hard to wake up and work out if you've got too much stress going on." Such statements emphasized the policy's potential to hinder effective job performance. Zach (20, white cis straight man, Army ROTC) initially commented, "There shouldn't be any discrimination based on your sexual preferences; I don't think that should hinder your performance at all as a solider or an officer." When I asked, "Do you think it's going to have an impact either in the short term or the long term in terms of the culture of the military at all?," he replied, "I think that culture is already. . . . It's about soldier care and treating people the same and treating people with respect, honestly." Nate and Zach's emphasis on performance as a repeal rationale reflects the neoliberal assurances of the homonormative bargain: rather than queerness's disruption to productivity, homonormativity reinforces it. The repeal is not just about alleviating the psychic stress of the closet for LGB individuals, it's also about how that alleviation enables an ever stronger, better, faster military.

"I DON'T NEED TO KNOW IT"

Only three people in the entire interview sample gave explicitly negative opinions on the repeal of DADT. For all three, the problem was not the existence of lesbian, gay, and bisexual peers per se; it was *acknowledgment* of their sexuality that informed their antagonism. Like many, Christopher, who acknowledged LGB service had been a "well-known but well-kept secret" as far back as the 1970s, believed that sexuality should be irrelevant to the job. "We are all the same," he argued. "I don't care who you are sleeping with at night, I don't care what your body looks like. I know that when you show up at 4:30 in the morning, whether it's to go kill people or it's to go change a flat tire, we all look the same, we all have our standards that we all follow." But for him, this was an argument *against* open service and the DADT repeal. "This is where I stand *against* gays in the military. If you're gay, I don't need to know it—if you're not gay, I don't need to know that either." Christopher went on, "I don't care who you're sleeping with when you go home. I don't care who you're in love with. [But] when you report to work, you're a soldier, that's it, period. I don't know how else to say it." Here, Christopher evoked the military's "mission first" ethos ("you're a soldier, that's it, period") and its commitment to uniformity ("we are all the same . . . we all look the same"), beliefs that animated the responses of those both for and against the DADT repeal. In fact, the idea that sexuality has no place at work has cropped up in my previous work on gay and lesbian teachers and elsewhere.[11] Under the conditions of the homonormative bargain, this idea is increasingly leveraged in favor of rather than against inclusion, but it still affirms the idea that truly *queer* sexualities and genders need to be contained.

Christopher believed that DADT hadn't been a problem in "rank and file situations." "If anything," he continued, "it was put there to protect an individual, so that if I suspected someone to be gay—which I [did] over the years. . . . I couldn't do anything about it and I couldn't hurt that individual just because they were gay. That's all Don't Ask, Don't Tell did." In other words, DADT protected those in his command against the discrimination or termination they might have faced in earlier eras. This was, you'll recall, key to the discourse that had produced the DADT compromise: DADT enabled LGBs to serve without fear by taking their sexuality off the table. In their analysis of DADT rhetoric, Craig Rich, Julie Schutten, and Richard Rogers document the farce of that stated intention to make service "sexual orientation-neutral."[12] Most obviously, heterosexual identity disclosures went unchecked under the policy. Furthermore, the false insistence on the sexually neutral character of the institution laid bare the homophobic dread attached to the potential queerness of the intimate, same-sex proximities in barracks and battle.[13] A member could *be* gay so long as they never acknowledged, embodied, demonstrated, or got in any way too comfortable with their always-unspoken status.

Cal (40, Black cis straight man, Marines veteran) gleefully proclaimed, "I loved the Don't Ask, Don't Tell policy!" He, too, saw value in the policy and how it allowed LGB people to serve, hidden in plain sight. The glass closets engendered by the ban meant that "we all knew coming in who we assumed was gay, but we didn't have a problem with it." Cal believed that "no one I ever worked with had a problem with anybody who everybody thought was gay. . . . Sometimes you might go out, you might see something, but it was no big issue." Unfortunately, he continued, "This thing now of open, come out gay, everybody's out. . . . I guess it's that I'm not adjusting to it right now." He offered a cursory list of ways he thought open disclosure impeded military readiness and efficiency:

> People are [now] wondering, "Okay, now, I got to live in a room with a person who likes me, could possibly like me. Why can't I live in a room with the opposite sex?" Some of the younger guys are like, if it was a guy or female, if it's two females and one [of them] was gay, then the other female would be like, "She likes me, and she gets what she wants, why can't I live in a room

> with a guy and get what I want?" And vice versa. Now that it's open—some of the places are open showers, [and it's like,] "Why do I have to go in here? I'm uncomfortable knowing that that person will be looking at me." Before, you never thought about it. . . . It never came to your head when you went in the shower or did these kind of things, but now that it's out in the open, you start thinking about all the what ifs.

Just as the critical readings of the military's management of homosexuality had asserted, Cal's assessment was that DADT diffused the potential sexual tension of living, working, and going to war in close quarters. Sex-segregated showers and bunks were made symbolically safe by sidestepping their erotic potential. DADT's author, Charles Moskos, compared it to policies and procedures put in place to protect women in the military: "If feelings of privacy for women are respected regarding privacy from men, then we must respect those of straights with regard to gays."[14] This privacy was achieved through silence, using the thin veneer of mutually assumed heterosexuality to alleviate anxieties about gay predation. As Cal said, DADT allowed you to avoid thinking about "it"—that is, that a man showering or sleeping in the bed next to you might be gay and/or find you sexually attractive.

Lily, a white cis straight woman in the Army, gave a personal example on this point. She had lived with a roommate who was rumored to be a lesbian, but DADT and her roommate's discretion had alleviated her concerns that the living situation might be uncomfortable for her:

> [People would say] "Oh, well, she's a lesbian." [I felt like,] "Okay, you're saying she was, but I've never heard that person say she's a lesbian or hit on me, or anything to that effect, so I'm not just going off of what you're saying." [It's] uncomfortable where now, people can just say, right to your face, "Yes, I like women." I guess that's what—before it wasn't hidden, anything like that, it's just it was unknown and it was not talked about, where now you can talk about it all you want. And I'm okay with that, like I said, until it affects me personally. Then I will probably get a little uncomfortable. That has not happened, nothing even close to that has happened, I just—I don't know, we'll have to wait and see.

Once again, repeal antagonists distinguished between living and serving alongside LGBs and living and serving with *openly* LGB peers. Lily said that disclosure "right to your face" was the real source of tension.

Tendering an example, she noted that "some places in the military still have open showers." "To be in a group shower" post-repeal, she said. "No, that makes me a little uncomfortable, I would probably try to avoid that scenario."

This trio of anti-repeal narratives suggests that the objectionable bit of repeal was its disruption to heteronormativity. So long as everyone could be presumed heterosexual, or at least given cover, these respondents believed there was no sexual tension in communal living. By contrast, the repeal made the intimacy of living in sex-segregated spaces all too visible, its erotics and discomforts all too real. I find it striking that all three of these interviewees professed nonchalance about serving with LGBs under DADT. Of course, the possibility of desirability bias is endemic to interview research of this sort; research participants sometimes downplay opinions they believe are at odds with the researcher's. Thus, it is likely that some research participants were savvy enough to avoid espousing explicit homophobia in the context of this study. Nevertheless, as I show in later chapters, participants rarely held back when it came to their disapproval regarding women in combat and trans inclusion. It would be hard for desirability bias to fully account for the fact that none of the people I interviewed outright objected to homosexuality, only its overt embrace. And on this point, respondents converged: DADT defenders and repeal supporters shared the expectation that LGB servicemembers would draw a hard line between service and sexuality. The key difference was whether they believed disclosure alone violated that genteel boundary.

LOGICS OF INCLUSION

Participants of all stripes expressed two primary rationales—what I call *logics of inclusion*—for their support of open LGB service. In the first, participants appealed to the principles of professionalism, arguing that sexual orientation has no bearing on one's ability to satisfy professional norms and succeed according to objective standards of workplace performance. In the second, they drew on the rhetorics of tolerance and multiculturalism to situate LGB sexuality as a valuable form of diversity, increasingly understood as a proxy for an institution's vibrancy and potential for future success.[15] Participants (favorably) compared the repeal of DADT to the military's record on racial integration and religious accommodations. These comparisons do rather a lot of discursive work and reveal the embeddedness of homonormative and homonationalist conceptions of modern military service. Interestingly, though, they should be as applicable to combat gender integration and trans inclusion, yet they were only prevalent in interviewees' narratives around open LGB service, a point to which I return later in the book.

Appeals to Professionalism

ROTC cadets, themselves in the midst of the military's intensive professionalizing process, were quick to identify professionalism as the hinge that opened the closet door, as it were. Cara (22, white cis straight women, Army ROTC), who supported the repeal of DADT, reasoned:

> I just don't see how your sexual orientation should affect you in any way in that kind of an environment, your professional environment. It shouldn't matter. . . . None of that should be brought into your work, in that environment. It doesn't change you as a leader, I don't think, or even as a soldier and the types of tasks you have to do. I think what you do at home and who you love has nothing to do with your professionalism. . . . Gay people are just as competent as professionals as straight people. That's been proven in history.

Twenty-year-old Sean, a cis straight man in ROTC, said much the same: "I think [your standing] should be merit-based. As long as someone interacts with me and they're cool with me, and I'm cool with them, and they're doing their job right, then it shouldn't be my business what they do with their personal life." Sexuality's irrelevance to work performance or competency made closed service illogical to these straight participants, who seemed to have internalized the public-private distinctions incorporated into the logic of the homonormative bargain.

What makes this bargain so insidious, however, is how thoroughly it has been internalized by LGBs seeking inclusion. For example, gay and lesbian cadets Thomas, Michael, and Julie all cited the public/private divide to insist on the immateriality of their sexuality to their service. In fact, because of the institution's professionalism, they argued the military was *especially* compatible with open LGB employment. For Thomas, it was all about the "mission first" principle:

> You're taught the Army is a professional organization, we do our job no matter who we are. We do it as best as we can, every soldier is a soldier first. I think that sort of mentality tends to eliminate some of the differences between people by sexuality. I've always felt [that], as long as I'm doing my job and I'm doing it well, then I'm a good soldier, that sort of thing. . . . Be a soldier, be an airman, or be a sailor or Marine or whatever, then nobody has any right to question what you do in your personal life, because as long as you keep above [the] standard that you need to live up to in order to be in the military, then you should be allowed to be in the military and your personal life is your own life.

His service, Thomas thought, superseded others' rights to question his sexuality, let alone their ability to harass LGB servicemembers on account of their sexuality. Much as service entitles participants to education, healthcare, citizenship, and a living wage, it now entitles LGB servicemembers who can successfully fit in to live a life free from stigma—at least while on the clock. This is the homonormative bargain in action, a "get out of jail free" card for those LGBs who can and will uphold their end of it.

Sociologist Steven Seidman argues that as LGB normalization unfolds, the notion of sexuality as a personhood-defining characteristic is losing relevance.[16] The compulsory heterosexuality that once mandated life in the closet is waning, at least for some. The closet organized the social experience of homosexuality as either "in" or "out"; under such conditions, sexual identity was one of, if not *the* defining element of the self. Since then, homonormativity has lowered the stakes of coming out and enabled other aspects of identity to take primacy (again, only for some). The military's ethos that "every soldier is a soldier first" further minimizes sexual identity as a marker of distinction under open service. Life "beyond the closet," as Seidman calls it, frees LGBs from being defined by sexual stigma, provided they remain willing to abide by the terms of professionalism, respectability, and the private-public split. For instance:

> Michael (22, white cisgender gay man, Army ROTC): I never want [my sexuality] to be something that's focused on. I never want to outright just be

like, "I'm gay." If you ask me, I'll tell you, but otherwise, it's a professional environment. We have a task at hand.

Julie (20, white cis bisexual woman, Army ROTC): I am more private, but for multiple reasons, not only because I'm gay, or a girl instead of a guy, but also for the fact that it's a professional environment, and do I *really* need to talk about this? Because technically, I'm [at] my job. You know what I mean?

Meanwhile, for most straight participants, the homonormative bargain obviated the need for policies like DADT because they understood the workplace as one in which asking or telling was irrelevant. As Nancy (59, white cis straight woman, Army veteran) declared:

> Personally, to me, it doesn't matter, as long as the person does their job. What they do in their private life, I couldn't care less. I think you would probably find that with a lot of people. I think if you're going to accept something like that and have it part of the organization, then just make it part of the organization. Don't be like, "Don't ask, don't tell." Why make it "we won't ask you and you won't tell us and we'll just pretend it doesn't exist"? . . . [Being gay is] pretty acceptable in today's society, just accept it and move on. That's my philosophy.

The threat of queerness is so well-contained under the homonormative bargain that it is unnecessary for straight people to pretend that LGB servicemembers don't exist. And so, for many, masking sexual distinctions with professionalism and exemplary service is the baseline requirement of open service.

Even Christopher, who took issue with the DADT repeal, argued that the problems of open service were wholly beside the point when servicemembers found themselves under attack:

> If that person just lifted that four-hundred-pound box for you and put it on the back of the truck, you don't care if they're gay or not. They just did their job. If that person jumps out of the truck, rolls down, lands beside you, and they're ready to fly down and kill somebody, you don't care what they are. You really don't.

Christopher told me he had worked with servicemembers he knew to be gay or lesbian well before the repeal. While that knowledge was unbidden and, to some extent, unwanted, at the end of the day, "It didn't matter. [If] you survived your convoy when you saw the convoy in front of you, behind you—half of your convoy got hit, it's like 'Shit. We're alive.'" Celeste (25, Latina cis lesbian woman, Navy) affirmed the salience of this perspective on the front lines:

> If you ever actually ask somebody who has served their time in the military in a role close to combat—or anywhere overseas where combat was right at your door—they will always say to you, "I never cared who was the hand picking me up from an explosion or out of a helicopter accident."

Lifting four-hundred-pound boxes, escaping a truck but ready to kill, or whisking a would-be casualty away from an explosion is a high threshold for inclusion, but acceptance forged in fire is fundamental to military culture. Proving yourself a warrior is the quickest route to universal approval.

Sabrina (38, white cis straight woman, Air Force) confirmed this perspective, driving home the point that the referent category for this logic is always assumed straight (using "we" and "everyone" in the following):

> [LGBs] are looked at as an equal as long as they're doing their job correctly. You can carry a gun and stand on this line with me, and you're trained, and you're professional, I don't care what sexual orientation you are. . . . As long as you can shoot your target, and you show up to work, and you look professional, and you are professional, we don't care who you lay next to at night. That's where everyone's at right now.

Travis (20, white cis straight man, Army ROTC) took the "mission first" philosophy even deeper. Beyond job performance, Travis believed even one's inner life should be organized around the "mission first" motto: "To me, it comes down to professionalism. You can be whatever you want and love whoever you want, but if you're on duty—gay or straight, you shouldn't be thinking about that when you're doing your thing." Not only should servicemembers behave professionally and keep their private lives private, it seemed Travis wanted peers to go a step further, to police their very thoughts to excise any stray hint of sexuality while on duty.

These examples all demonstrate that acceptance is conditional, in this case on meeting the strictures of professionalism. Certainly it is reasonable to expect colleagues to do their jobs well and exercise good judgment in terms of sexual conversation while on the job. The striking part is that these comments imply that an LGB servicemember's lapse in asexual presentation of self might disqualify them from acceptance. This is hard to imagine should a straight male servicemember mention his wife or having gone on a date over the weekend. So why would an LGB servicemember's failure to successfully perform professionalism make their sexuality suddenly relevant? The answer, I argue, is homonormativity and its attendant bargain: inclusion and acceptance for some in exchange for normalcy and discretion. LGB servicemembers are acceptable, but only insofar as they keep LGB *sexuality* out of heterosexuals' awareness—they have granted acceptance, and could always take it away.

Sabrina's reference to "look[ing] professional" particularly piqued my interest. In the literature on sexual discrimination in employment, the importance of "looking good and sounding right" is a resounding theme.[17] If LGBs can achieve, or at least approximate, the same professional "look" as their heterosexual counterparts, they do not queer the institution. Research, including my own, has detailed how professionalism, a seemingly neutral standard, is in fact constituted through whiteness, cisness, heterosexuality, and classed norms of comportment.[18] By contrast, flamboyance, exuberance, and spectacle are queer aesthetics that were forged in difference: Blackness, transness, the dark backrooms of working-class gay bars.[19] Queerness stands in opposition to the more subdued and colorless norms of professional comportment. Queerness fundamentally *resists* privacy, discretion, and normalcy; it cannot be incorporated into the military. To be included, LGBs must dim or even snuff out their queerness, as the next chapter illustrates in detail.

Tolerance and Diversity Discourse

In addition to professionalism as a logic of inclusion, participants narrated their approval of open service through the logics of tolerance and diversity. The concept of tolerance has done a significant amount of heavy lifting as a civil rights strategy, gay rights included. In the 1970s and 1980s, the newly formed Religious Right cut its teeth on campaigns like the Briggs Amendment, a California ballot proposition that would have banned LGBs from teaching on the basis of their morally corrupting influence. The headline-grabbing political "moral majority" began to put antigay ordinances on ballots in municipalities across the United States—and won. In this increasingly imperiled climate, LGB activists began to pivot to tolerance as a rights strategy. Lesbians, gays, and bisexuals were repositioned as no threat to the American way of life; they were rule-following, law-abiding citizens asking merely to be tolerated. Tolerance was recuperative: gay rights are as American as apple pie—after all, aren't tolerance for difference and freedom of expression the cornerstones of the liberal democracy on which the nation was built? In this reframing, it is the Religious Right that is marked as intolerant and therefore *un*-American, out of step with the fantasy of US sexual exceptionalism.

However savvy and successful a strategy of rights seeking may be, it necessarily limits future social movement possibilities. Etymologically, tolerance's association with endurance and fortitude implicitly positions the object of toleration as negative. Tolerance implies the ability to withstand something objectively odious; it strips away the joy and the defiance of gay identity, the queerness in which activists reveled throughout the 1970s. The "tolerance trap," as Susanna Walters deemed it, painted the movement into a corner. Gay rights meant settling for passive indifference over riskier but more exciting and expansive possibilities.[20]

Certainly positioning tolerance as the only reasonable and civil approach to difference makes LGB inclusion more palatable for the wary. For example, April said she put it to work in a discussion with a flight doctor who griped, "I shouldn't have to accept other people's lifestyles that fundamentally go against my beliefs, I'm so sick of people talking about acceptance, acceptance, acceptance." April remembered that she countered, "That's a very good point, sir, but we're not always talking about acceptance. . . . [Y]ou do have to at least tolerate these people." She told the doctor that LGBs "are human beings, they are fighting alongside you, and you need to be able to be a human being to them." April told the story as an example of getting through to someone less tolerant than herself, paraphrasing the doctor's tentative agreement: "I can handle tolerance. I can tolerate people that serve with me that I don't like. But I'm not going to accept that their life choices (as he called them) are correct," she concluded. This distinction between tolerance and acceptance draws on discourses of US exceptionalism as a wedge: to tolerate is sacrosanct to the narrative of American democracy.

Tolerance discourse is a Western formation, posited as the enlightened solution to conflict since early modern Europe. Despite its associations with peace, civility, and nobility, political theorist Wendy Brown asks that we consider whether tolerance is actually an instrument of violence.[21] Tolerance requires intolerance as a foil in order to take shape. In the US military context, touting tolerance also suggests there are other parts of the world that are *intolerant* and need to be saved, taught a lesson, or eradicated. Such is the positioning of "Islamic extremism" and, by extension, most of the Middle East. This kind of martial tolerance, then, is both all too successful and all too dangerous. The threat of intolerance enlivens homonationalism, uniting both homopatriots and homophobes against a common threat in the form of the war on terror. The irony, as Brown clarifies, is that the tolerance/intolerance binary ultimately fails to redeem the tolerated in relation to the intolerant. Tolerance is a dual regulatory regime: it maintains the abjection of the tolerated by holding them at arm's length, even as they are deployed literally and figuratively against intolerance elsewhere.

Tolerance is the ultimate expression of military fealty: embracing uniformity and putting aside difference in the name of democracy and freedom *is* the job. In narrating his evolution from homophobia to tolerance, Kyle shared an evocative story. He began by saying that another veteran he knew "talked about this guy he served with in Vietnam who was gay," and how the friend said "we'd tease him about it and play tricks on him and was always kind of harassing him." In short, Kyle continued, "The guy did his job, and they trusted him to do his job, but when they weren't out in the field, he got some harassment." This dynamic came to a premature and tragic end that taught his friend, and Kyle by extension, a powerful lesson:

> [The gay servicemember] got killed in Vietnam. Killed in combat. My friend told me, he says, "You know, I've always regretted that [harassment]. I've always regretted doing that to him. And he died over there doing the exact same job I was doing." He said, "If we're truly a free nation, liberty has to be extended to everybody regardless." When I heard him say that, it definitely pulled me out of the homophobic closet and had me doubt my beliefs.

In military members' estimation, dying in combat is the ultimate sacrifice. In laying down his life to defend democracy, this gay servicemember led

Kyle and his fellow veteran to reexamine the depths of their own commitments to keeping America a truly free nation. The sacred concept of "liberty for all" was called into question through death, leading both to reaffirm a commitment to tolerance (at least for fellow soldiers).

The reverence expressed for tolerance in my interviews was frequently linked to appeals to diversity; as I asked about the repeal of DADT, many told me that tolerance had facilitated the military's transition into a more diverse, forward-looking workforce. Sabrina explained:

> It's definitely allowed us to recruit a more diverse younger force, which the military was lacking. It definitely needs more diversity and had trouble with recruiting, so being able to say that Don't Ask, Don't Tell has been repealed definitely widens the aperture a little for the ability for homosexuality to be prevalent and open in the military ranks.

By this inclusionary logic, the repeal benefits the institution doubly. First, it serves a practical purpose, solving a recruitment problem by bringing in new reserves of prospective entrants. Second, it gives the military cover in terms of its record on diversity, defined by Sabrina as historically lacking, possibly providing the military's detractors with a way to question the organization's reputation.

In the parlance of US exceptionalism, diversity is the outcome of the fabled multicultural "melting pot" said to make America unique. But when diversity discourse ignores the function of power and dominance, it can paradoxically reproduce the stratification it purports to challenge.[22] It can do so because diversity as a discursive good does not mandate social or institutional transformation, merely inclusion. Sara Ahmed writes that diversity is often conceptualized as adding color, in the literal and symbolic senses.[23] Diversity is the "spice of life"—an apt metaphor, given that diversity is often conceptualized as just a "dash" of racial/ethnic diversity that enlivens the otherwise bland essence of unspoken whiteness. Over time, diversity has eclipsed the institutional goals of equality or equity, which as legal concepts might implicate whiteness, maleness, straightness, and cisness as actionable sources of harm. By contrast, diversity is light and bright, an additive top note rather than punitive imposition.

Multiculturalism, the ideology that positions diversity as an institutional value-add, espouses the validity and importance of all viewpoints and actions. In a multicultural society, everyone should have equal access to expression as it relates to their beliefs or traditions. While this seems like a worthy goal on its face, it creates a false equivalence between those already holding power and the groups historically denied a share in that power. Multiculturalism's influence is felt everywhere, perhaps most troublingly in setting the terms of responsible public discourse as "hearing all sides" and respecting a "diversity of opinion," no matter how incorrect, reprehensible, or incendiary. For instance, white nationalism and its public menacing can be positioned as a positive reflection of the freedom of expression that makes the United States distinctive by its own exceptionalist lens.[24] Although calls for increased diversity originate in resistance to the gatekeeping of predominantly white (and male and straight and cis) institutions, diversity is increasingly redefined as "diversity of thought" by conservative tacticians struggling to refasten the latch on the gates to power.[25] Motivated by anxiety over the potential dismantling of their privilege, they use diversity of thought rhetoric as cover, glossing antigay (and anti-Black, anti-immigrant, anti-trans, etc.) animus with pedantic legitimacy.

In their discussions of the repeal, many of my respondents were quick to correct a misapprehension they believed civilians such as myself held about the military. Nate, a 19-year-old white cis straight man who joined the Army after the repeal, told me that I'd be "surprised by just how much diversity there was with sexuality. Especially when you always hear about how the Army is very antigay, how soldiers really won't be open about that." Per Justine, there is a common "[mis]conception that the military is sort of this Old Boys Club and kind of old fashioned." On the contrary, she asserted, "It's just a lot more diverse than people would think." April agreed: "We have an inclusive force. I mean, we've got some amazing, brilliant people out there that have all sorts of different genders and identities and beliefs and hobbies, and we shouldn't exclude anyone who can be an asset to our military."

Positioning gender and sexuality alongside beliefs and hobbies attests to the movement toward the "diversity of thought" frame as well as the inherent problem of equivalence. When she went to training camp, Cassie "wanted to make sure [she] wasn't going to get freaking killed" before she would allow herself to mention her partner in conversations with fellow cadets. When I asked why, given that she was out to everyone in her ROTC program, that was a concern at training camp, she explained that "you never know where someone is coming from in terms of religious diversity." The use of "religious diversity" here in place of, well, religiously informed homophobia, demonstrates the limitations of the diversity framework for redressing harm. Even though DADT had been repealed, Cassie understood she was at risk of homophobic violence in training camp because diversity, as it is deployed in contemporary discourse, holds a space for that, too.

Comparing appeals to professionalism, which stress uniformity, with appeals to diversity, which emphasize variation, spotlights an apparent contradiction in the overall logic of LGB inclusion. However, research participants insisted that uniformity and difference aren't mutually exclusive for many in the institution, despite what outsiders might believe. Uniformity, made literal through the military uniform, bridged this gap for some. Nate explained:

> A lot of people don't understand the diversity in [the military]. Yeah, it's unified. We wear the same uniform, we have the same haircut, but there's so many perspectives and everyone has a different reason they joined, a different reason they're in it, and different expectations. . . . It's not cookie cutter.

As I show in part 2, this emphasis on uniforms and uniformity took on a different meaning in the context of gender integration, but as it pertains to sexuality, visual similarity and sexual difference were presented as happily coexistent. In fact, gay ROTC cadet Thomas found the uniformity freeing:

> For me, it's like—when you put on the uniform, you *are* the uniform. You're not who's underneath the uniform. It's not that it's repressive, but it's the opposite. You're free to be who you are underneath that uniform. When you put on that uniform, you're expected to live up to a certain standard of behavior, a certain standard of your own actions. You're supposed to be honest and have integrity . . . that leadership acronym. Have you heard that? [*CC: No, I don't think I have heard an acronym about that.*] There's Army values, the acronym for it is l-d-r-s-h-i-p and it stands for Loyalty, Duty, Respect of Service, Honor, Integrity, and Personal Courage. Those are the values that you're expected to live up to as a soldier, as long as you can do that, then you're a soldier. There's nothing in that acronym that says, "by the way—you can't be gay, lesbian, or bi."

This interpretation of uniformity as freedom to "be who you are" is a fascinating juxtaposition. In the military, the uniform represents shared values (loyalty, duty, etc.) that cover the potential disunity threatened by individual differences.[26] It is a site within which Thomas can incorporate two of his core identities—gay and solider—into a cohesive, Army-issued whole.

Still, Jude (34, biracial trans queer man, Navy veteran) had a very different perspective on the military's ability to provide conditions of freedom for LGBTs. He was kicked out under DADT. It was very early in his military career, he told me, adding that "the military really is all about conformity. . . . [Y]ou can't color outside the lines, it's not allowed." By contrast, he said wistfully, "One of the beautiful things about being queer or trans is that we *do* color outside the lines." Jude said he would hate to see a queer or trans person "dimming their light" for the military: "It would break my heart." As Jude attests, not everyone could (or is willing to) accomplish the project of merging uniformity and difference within a totalizing institution.

"The Snowball of Civil Rights"

As one might expect, framing the repeal as an act of diversity promotion very commonly drew on racial analogies, including in the CRWG report that ultimately recommended repeal.[27] Jesse (22, white straight cis man, Army ROTC) placed responsibility for DADT's prolonged tenure outside the institution itself, saying, "I find it funny that the people making the biggest stink out of [repealing] it weren't in the military and have nothing to do with the military." DADT, he said "wasn't necessarily something organic to the military itself." On the contrary, Jesse argued, the military was a leader in inclusivity: "If I have to equate it or relate it to anything else, I think of 194[8], when the military was integrated and Blacks and whites served alongside each other. What better way to start the snowball of a civil rights movement than to integrate the military?" This story—that social change often begins within or is accelerated through the US military—was a fairly common one.

For example, Fiona Dawson, the director of *TransMilitary*, a documentary about transgender service, offered, "If you look back in time, the military has actually led the way on social change. African American people could serve in the military before the Civil Rights Act of 1964. Women . . . get paid equal within the military, and yet [a woman's labor is] worth 79 cents to every [man's] dollar in [civilian] society." Dawson was in no way naïve about the military's discriminatory elements, as her film makes clear. Instead, she believed the military's reputation as a politically conservative but meritocratic institution, one willing to bend to meet its own standards of equity, made it a compelling vehicle for changing the minds of more conservative Americans. Dawson used the military's record to point to the compatibility of military readiness and inclusion. She and others described the military as more like a slingshot of social change: first, tension and resistance until the point of change, then an exponentially more powerful trajectory forward. April drew a similar comparison:

> Even though the military seems like it's the most conservative, restrictive environment, we were the first to desegregate African Americans. We were the first to allow women. We were the first to allow gays to serve openly and even define policies so that they could be married, you know, and now we're going to be the first to deal with the transgender issue. You know, some people are kind of sick of that, like, "we're sick of being the social experiment," but at the same time I'm really proud that the military as an organization, we have—the way we're set up, you can kind of force people to shut the fuck up and let it happen. Whereas a lot of civilian organizations, they can't force people to step in line, in the military we can, and then we can prove the concept, because no one's really fighting it, you know, unless it doesn't work.

The military's culture of deference to authority, that is, allows the institution to enforce compliance with progressive changes in a way that other employers might not be able to. Jesse explained, "You know if they say, 'women are going in combat' or 'gays are allowed to serve openly,' it's, 'Yes sir, yes ma'am. Roger.' I've got to support it and work with it regardless." For those unwilling to, in April's words, "shut the fuck up and let it happen," be it racial, gender, or sexuality integration, the military can be quick to reprimand.

Kyle's description of reactions to Clinton's promise to repeal the gay ban functioned similarly:

> [Older generations] were angry, because the old soldiers thought that President Clinton was allowing the gays and lesbians in the Navy. All that, "It's just going to open the door for them! Next thing you know, it's going to be all these homosexuals can come bug you because you're heterosexual!" . . . It's like when the Navy integrated Blacks. A lot of people quit because of

> that. . . . It was just kind of another culling that happens in the evolution of the Navy.

Like pruning trees and plants to encourage new growth, culling those who could not be tolerant in the service of the nation was necessary to the long-term health of the institution, Kyle figured. Laura, a 21-year-old white cis straight woman in Army ROTC, offered another explanation for why the military was uniquely suited to integration under protest: "A lot of times, I feel like when you're in a danger situation with somebody you normally would have some type of discriminatory belief against—whether it's a woman, a Black person, or a gay person—those types of experience wipe away any prejudices you have." Harkening back to the idea that when you're under fire, you don't care who's fighting next to you, Laura reiterated the common theme running through both logics of inclusion: the mission takes precedence over politics, including sexual politics.

As I have written elsewhere, such "like race" comparisons are common meaning-making tools in the narration of gay rights across domains.[28] It is a common strategy in the litigation of sexuality-based rights—see, for example, the characterization of DOMA as the "Queer *Loving [v. Virginia]*" in marriage equality advocacy.[29] Rhetorically effective, the equivalence language is nonetheless inaccurate and dangerous. It positions race and sexuality as parallel rather than intersectional and mutually constituted. The scientific classification of bodies by race, sex, and sexuality were and *are* intersecting processes and technologies of domination. To understand homophobia as "like racism" is to miss how heteronormativity and homophobia are constituted through racism. Drawing a line connecting racial and sexual integration practices flattens complexity and contributes to post-racial mythologies that hide the ongoing operation of white supremacy. As gender and sexualities scholar Liz Montegary writes: "The repeal movement cordoned race off from sexuality to imagine a postracial present in which LGBT equality had become possible. With past racial discriminations resolved and the next frontier for justice identified, [race] has become irrelevant to a now 'color-blind' military."[30]

Over the course of my data collection for this project, the Army announced another diversity-driven policy change: permission for servicemembers to wear religiously prescribed facial hair and head coverings while in uniform. While this was framed as a race-neutral religious accommodation, the racialization of Sikhs and Muslims as brown in the racial landscape of the United States makes this policy relevant to this discussion of race and sexuality comparisons.[31] A few servicemembers raised this change as another example of the military's commitment to diversity, usually characterizing it as a welcome step that would strengthen the institution. Christopher, however, strenuously objected to these uniform accommodations. The growing demand for the military to welcome diversity, he believed, tipped the balance too far away from the crucial "oneness" of the military identity.

Regarding DADT, Christopher expressed concerns that open service would degrade the "integrity of the unit" because being "obviously gay, and telling people you're obviously gay" creates distinctions, and distinctions are the enemy of lethal, mission-first unity. Similarly, turbans and other religious head coverings posed a problem, because "we all need to look like one Army'" He continued, "One Army is going to war, and one Army has to kill our enemies. We cannot make each person different. I think we allow turbans now in military uniforms . . . that bothers the hell out of me." When I asked, "Because then everyone doesn't look the same?" he replied, "Exactly. We are all the same." Without prompting, Christopher then pivoted back to sexuality: "I don't care who you are sleeping with. I know that when you show up . . . we all look the same. We all have our standards we all follow." Our conversation continued as I nudged:

CC: Just to play devil's advocate about the turban issue, why does it matter what uniform you have on if you're all doing your job?

CHRISTOPHER: Because the Army is all about uniformity and uniform. I cannot wear anything but the hat they issued me, which has nothing to do with religion. It has nothing to do with family history. It has nothing to do with [anything] except the soldier that died yesterday was wearing it. The soldier that is going to die tomorrow is wearing it, and we all look the same. Once you start letting in personal things like that, that means they think that they now have a *choice*. "Oh no, Sargent. I'm not going to shoot that guy because he's wearing a hat like mine." Or whatever it is. No. We're all the same. It's an issued uniform. That's why they call it a uniform. It's the same as everybody else.

If "being obviously gay" was a threat, being obviously Sikh and Muslim was even more so for this veteran. Turbans, in this telling, not only made difference visible within the US military, they made similarity with the "enemy" more visible, too. What if soldiers who wear turbans end up identifying with those they are supposed to fight, shoot, and kill? The ability exercised by the military to dictate who lives and who dies is part of what Achille Mbembe calls "necropolitics."[32] For Christopher, wearing the same "hat" as the enemy disrupts (necro)politics as usual.[33] It blurs the line between the valorized and the expendable, the valuable and the pathological.

The Islamophobia that animates the continued war on terror plays a crucial role in the symbolic boundary making between "us" and "them." Building on the work of gender and sexuality scholar Sherene Razack, Inderpal Grewal argues that it is this kind of racialization and abjection of Muslims that has cast them out of neoliberal citizenship: "What is foreclosed for Muslims in the decade since 9/11 in the contemporary United States is even the *opportunity* to become the exception, the neoliberal economic citizen-subject . . . who takes responsibility for saving the security state."[34] While I agree with Grewal's assessment, I also read the military's religious accommodation as a dangling promise of repatriation. Like the homopatriot, some are offered an opportunity for "exceptional citizenship," as Grewal calls it, via their willingness to deploy Islamophobic violence on behalf of the security state.

More commonly, my respondents positioned diversity and inclusion as a boon to the military's ability to carry out its necropolitical agenda, rather than the threat suggested by Christopher. The DOD has a web page dedicated to lethality, or the servicemember's preparedness to enact lethal force. Its strategies to improve lethality are written in oddly cheerful language and framed by beautifully composed and colorful photographs of bombs, tanks, and explosions. What keeps the military lethal, the website says, is "modernizing the force, thinking ahead, being more flexible with our capabilities, and having the best and brightest on our side."[35] Repeal advocates explicitly appealed to the DOD on these grounds, arguing forcefully that neither readiness nor lethality was diminished by open service. Their strategy was effective in that it dovetailed with the military's use of diversity discourse to "moderniz[e]" the force by increasing capacity to recruit "the best and brightest" to "our" side. In discussions of the repeal, sexuality, race, and religion are posited as separate and equivalent expressions of multiculturalism, each making the military a more diverse—and more efficient—lethal force and distracting from any examination of the rightness of that lethality or its role in the maintenance of sexual, racial, and religious conflicts across the globe.

CONCLUSION

Contrary to what many imagined, the repeal of DADT didn't turn out to be a radical adjustment for the military. Instead, for many it felt like a policy that merely put on paper what was already happening: the relatively peaceful coexistence of straight and LGB servicemembers. A select few pined for the "discretion" of those bygone days, sure, but the vast majority welcomed open service. They narrated the repeal as the only reasonable outcome for a professionalized and diverse twenty-first-century force. The homonormative bargain facilitated LGB incorporation into these logics by converting homosexuality into a private pursuit. Privacy, patriotism, and gender normativity enabled some to offload the stigma of perversion, pushing them off onto queer Others, including those whose gender and racialization, rather than sexuality, marked them as queer.

Military service may have made some LGB lives in the United States more livable, but it has had the opposite effect for many Muslims, especially those living in Muslim-majority countries made queer by homonationalism. The expansion of the "life world" of LGB US citizens has come at the cost of an equal and opposite expansion of the "death world" of war, torture, and invasion.[36] These queer necropolitics are not the exclusive provenance of the military; they also contribute to the more mundane, everyday death worlds of mass incarceration, poverty, interpersonal violence, and other deadly implements.

Rather than challenge the rationale that sustained DADT for so many years—to be effective, the military must not tolerate femininity—the repeal largely recruited new populations into new forms of intolerance. Homosexuality may have shaken off the contaminating effect of effeminacy enough be folded into the culture of martial masculinity, but inclusion of this sort maintained the rejection of femininity and gender nonconformity. Without sexuality-based bans to keep those dangers away, the production of such abjection shifted into a process exacted through informal modes of punishment and surveillance. Sexuality is no longer a formal barrier to entry, yet it is not immaterial to post-inclusion treatment. So too, we shall see, is the continued queerness of femininity in the military, which has redoubling effects for women, trans women in particular.

3 "He Acts Straight but He Has This One Thing . . ."

OPEN LGB SERVICE AND QUEER SOCIAL CONTROL

In the 1943 film adaptation of Irving Berlin's musical *This Is the Army*, soldiers in drag perform as the "ladies of the chorus," beseeching an audience of their peers, "Don't we look lovely, my dears? / In corsets and dresses / and cute golden tresses / to hide the dirt behind our ears?" They trace suggestive curves with their hands, singing "We're here to romance with / to sing and do dance with / a bunch of dirty guys like these" as a group of servicemen enter stage left. The servicemen partner up with the drag chorus, dancing across the stage, and we see an audience member in black tie nudge the man next to him. Excitedly, he points and exclaims, "That's my son, the fourth from the left!" The camera closes in on a soldier in drag as he's embraced from behind by an amorous suitor. The man next to him replies, "He's pretty, isn't he?," much to the father's amusement. In a later scene, the ladies of the chorus sing longingly of their desire to "do more for the boys" than simply sing and dance: "We're glad to be of service / but we could do much more!," a thinly disguised reference to sexual availability. Unfortunately, they opine, "We don't get too far / the rules and regulations are / we musn't be seen / outside the canteen / with a soldier." They continue, "We must resist / we take a vow when we enlist, / to never be found / canoodling around / with a soldier."

This performance is called a pony ballet, a form of drag in which hairy, muscular men perform exaggerated, over-the-top femininity; it was a popular art form during World War II. *This Is the Army* also included "female illusionists," acclaimed by reviewers from the *New York Post* to *Newsweek*, who praised their fetching seductions, especially a striptease by a soldier performing as Gypsy Rose Lee. Stagedoor suitors flocked to such drag performances, bringing flowers, praise, and propositions to the female illusionists who impersonated larger than life figures like Carmen Miranda, the Andrews Sisters, and Mae West.

These shows, writes historian Allen Bérubé, "inadvertently opened up a social space in which gay men expanded their own secret culture."[1] Ironically, it was the aggressively heteromasculine culture of the military that allowed such campy expressions of queerness to flourish: "The propaganda that portrayed soldier actors as masculine, combat ready, and essential to the war effort served as a camouflage that protected gay GI performers on the military stage, giving them greater freedom there than in other areas of military life to camp it up."[2] The prohibition on homosexuality enabled transgressive performances because everyone in the military was presumed straight. Dressing in drag, at least for the stage, was just good old-fashioned heterosexual boisterousness.

Looking back from the twenty-first century, it can be hard to fathom that soldiers' drag performances like the ones in *This Is the Army* were once considered necessary morale-boosting and camaraderie-making tools. Throughout the military's history, drag, camp, and queerness have been used to promote unit cohesion and solidarity, not only through drag performances but also through initiation rituals such as the Navy's "crossing the line" ceremonies, many of which have included men in drag, dancing naked, and simulating or engaging in same-sex erotic acts.[3] Treating queerness as a glue binding troops together feels like an odd fit with the logic that sustained DADT: that homosexuality is corrosive to unit cohesion. However, it was the covering of overt homosexuality through the range of prohibitive policies that gave such rituals their transgressive power. In this chapter, I ask: How are homoeroticism and gender transgression managed in the post-DADT context?

We saw in chapter 2 that the vast majority of my research participants accepted the repeal and open LGB service, as well as the strings attached to that inclusion. In the absence of a formal social control mechanism (i.e., a ban on LGBT service), informal structures of queer social control compel LGBT servicemembers to closely constrain queerer presentations of self and reminds them that their inclusion is highly conditional. Queer social control, as a concept, captures the distinct but interrelated phenomena of heteronormativity, homonormativity, and femmephobia (and, as we will see later in the book, it is inflected with cisnormativity and transmisogyny). It shows how these forms of discrimination are obscured by the performance of inclusivity in the era of the "gay-friendly" institution.[4] Queer social control is the mechanism that allows the logics of professionalism, tolerance, and diversity to define open LGB service; without it, LGB servicemembers are illegible as professionals and marked as "too much" diversity.

In the name of professionalism, LGB servicemembers are expected to keep their private lives private, remaining silent about their sexual lives and preferences. They must not mention same-sex partners or flirt (especially if the targets of their flirtation are straight), lest they be considered sexual harassers—a form of gay panic that steals focus from the military's most common perpetrators of sexual harassment and assault: cisgender, heterosexual men. Under the homonormative bargain, gender nonconformity, especially in men, is closely surveilled and judged against the systematic devaluation of femininity.[5] As a result, gay and bisexual men withstand intense gender scrutiny in this hypermasculine context. When asked to reflect on similarities and differences between the treatment of gay and bisexual men versus lesbian and bisexual women, most research participants assumed that women did not experience gender policing, yet data tell a different story. Just as gay and bisexual men experience the consequences of femmephobia, lesbian and bisexual women experience the consequences of lesbophobia. For Black women, this lesbophobia interacts with what Moya Bailey calls misogynoir, "the uniquely co-constitutive racialized and sexist violence that befalls Black women as a result of their simultaneous and interlocking oppression at the intersection of racial and gender marginalization."[6]

In the rebranded military, straight servicemembers hold up their end of the homonormative bargain by suppressing more obvious expressions of homophobia. To compensate, queer social control processes offer a release valve in the form of teasing and humor that communicate the "dos" and "don'ts" of LGB comportment without violating the terms of the bargain. Geographers Catherine Nash and Kath Browne coined the term "hetero-activism" to refer to these more subtle and nuanced forms of resistance to sexual and gender inequalities in the gay-friendly era.[7] Per Nash and Browne, heteroactivism is both an ideological system and a set of practices; here I propose that teasing is one such practice, moving the disciplinary power of homophobia just off the radar of nondiscrimination policy and diversity discourse.

In my previous book, I documented the production of "gay-friendly schools" through the suppression of queerness on campus.[8] In that project, the most common entry point for comingling LGB identity with the professional identity of teacher was through the performance of the "good gay role model," an achievement made possible through monogamous partnership, the suppression of sexual expression, and the appearance of gender normativity. The good gay role model, I found, was tightly circumscribed by fears about the corrupting influence of queerness on children. Here, I find that LGB servicemembers are constrained to contain the corrupting influence of queerness on the masculine security state. They navigate femmephobia and lesbophobia, engaging in what sociologist Erving Goffman calls "impression management" by muting sexual discussion and performing gender normativity.[9] In this way, they mitigate perceived dissonances, downplaying their LGB identities in favor of their servicemember identities. The institutionally specific instantiations of queer social control in this chapter cannot be removed from their place within the broader network of institutions and institutional actors who police and criminalize gender nonconformity and queer expression. The accounts here are not apart from, but a part of, what sociologist Brandon Robinson calls the "queer control complex."[10]

MANAGING QUEER CONTAGION

In the previous chapter, I noted that sociologist Shawn Trivette argues that the silencing of homosexuality enforced by DADT actually created queer space within the military.[11] The prohibition on asking and telling did not *eliminate* homosexuality; instead, it created the peculiar paradoxes of glass closets and queer communities hiding in plain sight. As if to compensate for the lack of physical privacy in military life and push off the growing visibility of homosexuality outside it, DADT manifested as a compulsory policy of "identity privacy." In the conditions described by old-timers like Christopher and Cal through their anti-repeal comments, open service threatened to force straight servicemembers to acknowledge the erotics of group showers and other potential sexual spaces; the identity privacy foisted upon LGB servicemembers by DADT protected their homophobic peers.

In fact, heteromasculinity can—and does—contain forms of queerness itself.[12] Prior to open service, sexual encounters between men or between women were surprisingly commonplace in the space of the military.[13] Historical accounts of World War II service document the unexceptional nature of same-sex sexual contact, coded as natural expressions of boyish exuberance or especially close female friendships.[14] These intimacies were even institutionally encouraged through a "buddy system" that placed same-sex servicemembers in intimate contexts, including shared beds.[15] Mutual masturbation, manual stimulation, and even oral and anal sex were coded as fairly unremarkable (and heterosexual) encounters in the context of sex-segregated living. Gender and sexuality scholar Jane Ward points out that these "heteroexceptionalist" encounters (especially those between men) were explained away as the outcomes of loneliness and the isolation of long stretches of deployment.[16] The presence of slang phrases, including "it's not gay if it's underway" or "it's only queer if you're tied to the pier," evidence the ubiquity of heteroexceptionalist qualifiers: sex between people of the same gender during war and deployment could be laughed off with a little doggerel.[17] These discourses of heteroexceptionalism enabled queer sexual encounters that maintain the mutual straightness of men engaging in sex with other men, so long as the heterosexuality of both parties is presupposed. Various iterations of the gay ban, including DADT, maintained the crucial presupposition that everyone in the military was, in fact, heterosexual.

There is also ample anthropological documentation of the various "queen for a day" rituals and traditions of cross-dressing, queer flirtations, and simulated or real sexual acts between men in the military.[18] Like the performers in *This Is the Army*, The Amputettes, a troupe of disabled drag queens who lost limbs at war, were wildly popular with military audiences in the 1940s.[19] Crossing the line ceremonies on Navy ships feature King Neptune and his cross-dressing queen presiding over bawdy performances of simulated sex acts, including sucking off rubber hoses and feigned analingus between soldiers.[20] Other initiation rites in military academies, boot camp, and specialized training programs routinely involve nudity, genital contact, and various forms of sexual humiliation. Analyzing these rituals "make[s] visible the mechanisms by which certain queer acts gain tacit heterosexual approval."[21] Most analyses suggest that these queer performances provide a release valve for deep-seated anxieties about service, like becoming disabled or developing gendered and sexual "perversions" when consigned to sex-segregated living.[22] In these sometimes sexually violent initiation rituals, the ability to engage in and withstand queer contact, paradoxically, reinforces one's innate heterosexuality.

The forced feminization and homoerotics of this pageantry are rooted in misogynist and femmephobic ideologies. Being made to be "like a woman" is the ultimate humiliation; therefore enduring this humiliation proves a man so quintessentially heteromasculine as to be worthy of the sacred fraternal society of "true" soldiers, sailors, airmen, Marines, and so forth. Ward posits that these "erotic spectacles of repulsion" continue, in part, because of the interplay of arousal and disgust; participants withstand but are also excited by the humiliation, in such an irresistible way as to overcome widespread prohibitions on hazing in the twenty-first century.[23] The beginnings of such practices—be they in the military, the fraternity house, or the boarding school—almost always trace to a history of exclusive institutional whiteness through racial segregation. What's more, they are commonly coded in the symbolic language of masters and slaves, conquerors and conquered. Again, Ward demonstrates that these rituals use abjection of the feminine, the perverse, and the animalistic (all three, as you'll recall, are frequently attributed to the "enemy" in the form of the queered Muslim terrorist in the modern US military) to reassert the supremacies of whiteness and heterosexual masculinity.

Nothing could more abruptly or thoroughly deflate the bubbling, heteromasculine excitement of violating taboos than an earnest declaration of homosexuality. Just a few simple words could lay bare the potential realness of the performance. In *Excitable Speech*, Judith Butler argues that military regulations on the utterance of "I am a homosexual" position homosexuality as a contagion.[24] Sexual acts between men or between women are held at a protective remove, preventing the transmission of that contagion by either avoiding or parodying that fateful utterance. In this regard, DADT did double duty. Not only did it cover such homoerotic spectacles with a protective coat of heterosexuality, it also enabled the use of lesbian and gay baiting to threaten and expel LGBs unwilling to go along with the harassment and abuse used to keep them in their place.[25] Now that the declaration "I am gay/lesbian/bisexual" is permissible, how is queer contagion managed? The answer, I argue, lies in the informal, interactional practices of queer social control.

Weapons of Mass Seduction

"People thought just because it was being repealed that now you have to wear a sign that says, 'Hi, I'm airman so-and-so, and I'm gay,'" laughed Hank (30, Black trans straight man, Air Force) when I asked about disclosures after the DADT repeal. Removing the threat of discharge, it seemed, wasn't the same as encouraging open service. Ben (35, white cis gay man, Air Force) hinted this was part of the mandate for professionalism and the "mission first" ethos:

> I don't want to sound like I'm bashing myself or anyone else for choosing the way they live—that's their life, their choice. But someone comes up to me, they don't say "Hi, I'm so-and-so; I'm straight." So I don't really feel a need to go up to someone and say, "Hey, I'm [Ben]; I'm gay." That's just not who I am. Even though I'm gay, I've lived a very straight life, I guess, is the best way to put it.

Choosing not to disclose is one thing, but the social expectation that LGB servicemembers, as a group, will choose not to disclose their sexuality is another. Maryann, a 31-year-old white cis straight woman in the Navy, offered some typical advice for her LGB colleagues: "What you do off the ship is your choice, but when you're on the ship you need to focus on your job, focus on the team, and focus on the mission." Asked to elaborate, Maryann added: "Come to work to work, then go home and be home.

I think it kind of sounds like 'don't be yourself,' but I don't feel like anybody was really themselves when they came to work. . . . [P]retty much just like, don't try to out yourself." Another straight white cis woman, Lily (Army, no age given), said she had "no issues with homosexuals in the military," though she was also quick to offer examples of her issues with open service. In chapter 2, for instance, she told me that, without DADT, "now you can talk about it all you want" and "that's uncomfortable." Lily was fine with LGBs serving "until it affects me personally," which included the post-repeal reality that "people can just say right to your face, 'Yes, I like women.'"

Respondents' wariness about coming out (their own or others') was embedded in discomfort about introducing sexual tension into unit dynamics. Under DADT and similar homophobic policies, LGB servicemembers became well-versed in what psychologist Lois Shawver calls the "etiquette of disregard," which allowed them to go unnoticed and unharassed in the intimate spaces of bathrooms, locker rooms, dressing rooms, and dorms or barracks.[26] The open acknowledgment of LGB service heightened the stakes of violating these informal rules. Lily, for instance, thought DADT kept group showers a "safe space" and admitted she would interpret another woman's sexual interest, but not a man's, as a reportable instance of sexual harassment. In her words:

> Another female hits on me, that would make me very uncomfortable. You would sooner see me report *that* than a male who said something inappropriate, because I would just respond to him with a "don't ever say that to me again." Whereas a female, I think I would just be—I would be mortified. I'm not going to lie. I would probably report that, say, "No, I can't have this." I don't know why there's a difference there, but there is, to me.

Post-DADT, there remains a stark difference in the consequences of expressing romantic or sexual interest, with LGB advances seen as particularly disruptive and upsetting—though few were as explicitly willing to own up to their discomfort with the possibility. Lily's repeated use of the word "uncomfortable" alongside her threats to mobilize disciplinary structures against a hypothetically flirtatious woman indicate how carefully LGB servicemembers must thread the needle in order to be "good," presentationally asexual gays.

None of the straight men I interviewed outright admitted fear about men's sexual advances. They did, however, illustrate this taboo, often through anecdotes about *other* men's discomfort. Christopher offered a particularly colorful story starring the quintessential roughneck Army soldier: "I'm thinking of one guy. . . . Neanderthal, 6'6", 200 pounds, built of steel, 'go-in-a-barroom-and-beat-up-seven-people-just because-he-can' kind of guy," he began. "He was a great soldier, but he was a Neanderthal. You can't be gay, you believe in God" and so forth. "He knew we had gays and lesbians, but it never bothered him," Christopher insisted, then, in the next breath mused, "If one came over and touched him . . . if a male came over and touched him on the thigh or something, he'd probably just kill him. He was that tightly wrapped." I was momentarily stunned at Christopher's light, upbeat delivery of this violently homophobic fantasy.

Laura (21, white cis straight woman, Army ROTC) and Alyssa (34, cis straight woman, Air Force, race not given) seemed to grasp the double standard their peers imposed on LGB, but not straight, servicemembers. Laura noted that the readiness argument was durable: "I mean, there's always been the belief that [open service] will ruin the continuity, the unity, the readiness. Guys who are straight are going to feel uncomfortable . . . [at the thought that] guys are going to hit on them." Alyssa shared that, among her peers, "homosexuality is [thought of as] a sex-based thing. . . . [P]eople default to heterosexuality and don't think about that person having sex." She continued, "If you're uncomfortable with homosexuality, I think you might be thinking about [their sexual practices] more and thinking about it being abhorrent." "It would make you uncomfortable," Alyssa concluded, "because you feel like you know this really personal thing about them, even though it's actually the same thing to know personally about a heterosexual person." Even in the absence of any sexual overtures or homosexual behaviors, LGB servicemembers are always already sexualized in the minds of those who find their identities "abhorrent."

Maryann, the Navy officer, characterized the reactions to open LGB service within her unit:

> I did hear some people say, "Doesn't matter to me. I don't care as long as they don't try to hit on me." . . . I think on a ship and submarines, in those close quarters, where everybody is sleeping next to each other—very close quarters, communal showers kind of stuff—that probably caused some

> angst, but as an officer, it's hard to say if it did or didn't because I was separated from it. I did hear, "As long as they don't check me out, as long as they don't hit on me, I don't care." That was what I kept hearing, but not a whole lot of people talk about it. It was one of those things that not a whole lot of people talked about. . . . That's why the talk was, "as long as you don't hit on me, as long as you don't stare at me, we're going to be fine."

Joseph (35, Latino cis straight man, Marine veteran) traced this homophobia to the demands of a hypermasculine institution and its femmephobia. He related a story in which Marine Corps Commandant James Conway visited his base overseas. In a town-hall style meeting, Conway was polling Marines about their comfort level with an openly gay Marine in increasingly intimate order: on base, in their unit, in their platoon, on their team, then finally in the same barracks. The initial question was met with "a couple thousand" raised hands, indicating the Marines felt fairly comfortable having openly gay servicemembers on their base. But with each subsequent question, fewer and fewer hands remained in the air. (A year later, Conway would float the idea of creating "gay barracks," saying, "I would not ask our Marines to live with someone who is homosexual if we can possibly avoid it. And to me that means we have to build BEQs [bachelor enlisted quarters] and have single rooms.")[27] Joseph remembered asking his friends about their hesitation with sharing housing with gay and bisexual Marines. He paraphrased their responses thus:

> Well, once this passes, what are we going to have? Pride parades on bases? Does that mean sexual harassment is going to go up because now they can act as they want? If they're attracted to another man, they can also just go off on that feeling or urges to want to either talk to or hit on another man.

In response, Joseph felt that "your hesitation and your worry is what women worry about in the military: sexual harassment, rape, not being able to just walk down the street because they don't want to be sexually harassed at night." At its core, Joseph believed their real fear was that such flirting or harassment would feminize them—a fate worse than death for some hypermasculine Marines.

Brian (40, white cis straight man, Navy) tentatively assessed the post-DADT atmosphere, telling me, "I think there's still some level of—as much as people have grown to be more accepting of gay folks, I think there's probably more men, like junior enlisted men in the military, who are still somewhat suspicious." He imagined them thinking, "This gay guy, is he going to want to hit on me?" Ultimately, like Joseph, he figured this homophobia was not pure intolerance, but "it's more so that they're afraid." It's useful to step back here and note that each of these examples overlooked the rampant harassment and violence deployed against LGBT servicemembers, solely framing the "gays in the military issue" as a threat to straight servicemembers.[28] The rhetorical reversal perpetuates predacious myths about homosexuality.

Elise, a 23-year-old white cis lesbian woman in ROTC, said an openly gay cadet in her program was generally accepted, but still inspired "comments . . . just stupid locker room talk." And, of course, "they would take [that talk] out of the locker room and say how they got scared [he] was trying to catch a glimpse of them topless." So it wasn't really just locker room talk—and it wasn't limited to cadets. April (40, white cis straight woman, Air Force) thought straight men in the Air Force, with "their own insecurities and their own egos," had an attitude like "I don't want to have to go into the men's locker room and think I'm going to be hit on by one of my peers." To her, "It's like, 'Dude, really? You think that someone's going to come out as gay and hit on you?'" Returning to the logic of professionalism and evoking the words of earlier respondents, she dismissed these anxieties bluntly: "Dude, if you're in a foxhole together, the last thing either of you are going to be thinking about is sex, I guarantee it. So *really*?"

Like Joseph, Justine (33, white cis lesbian, Army) summarized this phenomenon in a particularly poignant and sobering way: "I think there's this kind of fear of gay men, like, 'Ooh, they're going to sexually assault me, they're going to whatever—treat me the way I treat women.'" In these few words, Justine perfectly captured how the heterosexual matrix has compensated to survive the destabilizing threat of increased LGB inclusion: expressions of queerness must be tightly controlled in the context of gay visibility. Anything otherwise would force straight men to confront how their own gender and sexuality (which, if they consider it at all, they see as inherently biological rather than social), is constructed through dominance over women. Homonormativity omits such overt confrontations, asking LGBs to self-regulate queerness to avoid forcing heterosexuals to confront how gender inequality shapes their sexuality.

"Outrageously Flamboyant and Risqué"

The homonormative bargain severely limits gender nonconformity, particularly in its tacit encouragement of femmephobia. Femmephobia intersects with but is distinct from the concepts of homo- and transphobia; it specifically targets those who embody "inappropriate" femininities, many of whom may be gay or trans, and in a manner that perpetuates misogyny as much as it does antigay and anti-trans animus. Femmephobia is fundamentally anti-queer; gay rights progress has relied on the systematic suppression of queerness to assert itself.

Kyle, the Navy veteran (51, white cis straight man) who spoke of transcending his homophobia after a peer relayed a tragic war story, said that the "public stuff" of gay visibility "made me hold onto that homophobia a lot longer." Though "he didn't really care that people were gay and lesbian and they loved each other," it "turned [him off]" when he was "seeing gays and lesbians in parades. . . . [T]hey were just very, very outrageously flamboyant and risqué and stuff like that in public. That made me uncomfortable." Kyle also remembered a fellow sailor on his first ship, a man who was "very, very effeminate." "I mean, everybody knew that he was probably gay, and a lot of people harassed him about that: . . . His last name was [Romo], so they all called him ['Juan Homo'] instead."

"I think it's hard to be a gay man in the military," Justine commented. "You know, people see [homosexuality] as, you know, very sissy." Army ROTC cadets Christian (20, white cis straight man) and Sean (20, white cis straight man) spoke of an initial disjuncture between their mental image of a gay and bisexual man and those they encountered in ROTC. When I asked Christian, for instance, if he was surprised to meet gay cadets, he replied, "Not really. Well, it did come as a surprise, but only because they didn't *seem* homosexual" (emphasis added). Sean, too, remembered that encountering his gay peers "didn't necessarily surprise" him, except that they were indistinguishable from their straight counterparts. "Two of the guys, they're very gung-ho, typical Army Ranger [types] and everything," he noted, contrasting them with the "few openly gay people in high school, all of whom were very flamboyant individuals."

Travis (20, white cis straight man, Army ROTC) acknowledged that the Army "tends to have this macho thing," but argued the hypermasculine culture didn't affect the gay cadets in this program because they are "probably the most macho guys I know." That the "macho" behavior might be mandated—a social condition of inclusion for gay servicemembers—by the hypermasculinity went unremarked upon in Travis's account, though Zach (20, white cis straight man, Army ROTC) connected the two. Avoiding discrimination, Zach thought, all "depends on personality": "If you're gay and you're doing more pushups than everybody," he explained, "if you're 'Beast Mode'ing and being in the front of the pack, [you won't experience discrimination]. Versus if you're complaining, I think people treat you differently." Gay servicemembers needed to outperform the masculine accomplishments of straight servicemembers to retain tenuous inclusion. More directly, many straight participants suggested LGB participants should consciously hold themselves to homonormative standards; Maryann advised a hypothetical gay soldier to "try to keep any gestures, anything that might separate you from the pack—just try to keep those at bay."

Those "gestures," of course, included any visible signifiers of queerness. Christopher thought a solider with "I don't know how to say it . . . [gay] mannerisms . . . that might reflect a woman" would struggle to succeed in the Army. I asked whether he meant effeminate mannerisms, and he replied: "Yes, something like that could be hurtful in a military unit, especially a combat unit." Again, I probed: "Even after the repeal?" "Absolutely after the repeal," he confirmed. "It's going to get worse before it gets better." "These 17-year-olds, 19-year-olds, full of piss and vinegar, being brainwashed by Army standards and want to kill, kill, kill—they're the ones that are going to have a harder time convincing, and they're the ones that are going to go up against someone that is effeminate." Just as he had with the hypothetical turban-wearing soldier (see chapter 2), Christopher appealed to necropolitics as constitutive for military identity and readiness. To incite young soldiers to "kill, kill, kill," the military must inculcate them into a "piss and vinegar" heteromasculinity constructed through homophobia and the abjection of the feminine. He concluded, "If [a gay soldier] walks in in a dress and ballet shoes, and I know I'm being a jerk when I say it that way, but to make my point understood—*that*, I think, is going to cause a problem."

Joseph also observed necropolitical motivations behind his friends' resistance to open service in the Marines. As the repeal approached, he recalled hearing:

> "How are we going to be feared going down in battle and then someone comes up with a Pride flag? How are other nations going to fear us?" The statement in itself is ridiculous, but I think that it is a genuine concern: how does this impact our ability to conduct warfare? . . . A Pride flag being flown in combat says that we're not that fierce fighting machine. That's what the Marine Corps is known for: "First to fight, first in and last out" mentality. It's a "kill first, ask questions later" thought process, which also needs to change, but things like that, I think that there's a concern over how we're viewed and how the legacy of the Marine Corps is viewed.

Like the symbol of a Pride flag, just seeing "a man show up in uniform . . . with his husband or boyfriend" felt like a potentially provocative situation to some.[29] Nate (19, white cis straight man, Army ROTC) imagined the response to such a soldier:

> "Are you sure this person is fit to be in this position? That's a lot of responsibility." It's a very physical job. It's very tough. [You have to be like,] "Don't be soft on me because I'm gay." [*CC: Have you seen any of that personally in the ROTC program?*] I have not, but only because all the cadets we have who are gay—well, all the *male* cadets we have who are gay . . . had already proved that they were tough; they were there to hack it and stuff. . . . I can see people from the outside looking in have that mentality I talked about earlier of, "Is he too soft to be in this position? He's gay. Is he going to be able to perform?"

Nate's comments suggest that "failure" to contain expressions of homosexuality (defined here as simply bringing a partner to a uniformed event) triggers straight men's fears of femininity, "softness," and a cadet's potential inability to "hack it" when it comes to the dirty work of war. Here we see that containment of sexual expression and maintenance of gender normativity are deeply intertwined expectations. Failure in one domain is seen as failure in both.

All this keeps queerness in check even though open service is now formal military policy. The particularly gendered pressure on gay and bisexual men to self-police queerness in the form of any hint of femininity perpetuates an individualizing "agency myth" that blames these men for their own harassment and obscures the cultural processes through which queerness is maintained as an abject status.[30] Cassie (22, white cis lesbian woman, Army ROTC), like other ROTC cadets, noted that gay men seemed particularly likely to lean into masculine swagger, but connected it to their attempts to deal with the cultural processes of containment:

> There's this one guy . . . he's in my grade, he's gay but he's open. He also overcompensates with the macho-ness to try to compensate for that fact that he's gay. It's funny because he could be a really nice guy, but he's so busy trying to be an asshole. . . . I feel really bad because the guys have it really hard. I can just totally be myself and it's fine. The guys have it really hard. [*CC: In your program, you think that it is different with lesbians versus gay men?*] Yes. [*CC: Have there been instances where you've seen that in action?*] Just the general approach to leadership. There's another gay guy in our group and they kind of feed off each other in that way. It's like they've got to prove something.

Brit (21, Asian cis straight woman, Army ROTC) shared her observations: "I feel like my gay friend [in ROTC], he has to be more masculine than he is normally, especially during ROTC events where we're with other people." In a near-identical quote to Cassie's, Brit continued, "I definitely think he becomes more masculine, like, he tries to emulate more . . . well, that might just be his leadership style, but I definitely know him on a personal level and he's different."

Certainly for some gay and bisexual servicemembers, like Ben, proximity to heterosexuality feels organic ("I've lived a very straight life"), but the expectation to disprove stereotypes nonetheless encourages (if not requires) it. Ben explained that "people have preconceived notions of what a gay guy or a lesbian is going to be like," and he said proudly that when he comes out to others, "It's always the same reaction: 'Wow, we have a notion of what a gay guy will be like and that's not you at *all*, that's crazy.'" Others owned up to consciously manipulating their gendered presentation to find approval. Michael (22, white cis gay man, Army ROTC) explained:

> Especially because the military is a hypermasculine organization, . . . it's very competitive. You go into that, and you know [that], "Well, I'm already disadvantaged, so I need to really kick it into gear. I need to prove myself. I need to do this and this and this in order to be better than other people." And show them that. That I am competent. That [my sexuality] doesn't matter. . . . People are a lot more willing to accept me than they would a flamboyant male. . . . They can deal with me. "He acts straight but he has

> this one thing" [versus] "Oh, this guy acts fruity and he acts *that* way." Now we have somebody that they just completely don't understand.

There was another gay cadet in Michael's program who he said was similarly masculine, or straight-but-for-this-one-thing, as he would put it. Behind closed doors, when the two were alone, Michael said they both relaxed their performance of hypermasculinity. Occasionally, they would even engage in campy banter in front of others, doing "something a little effeminate or whatever" because "nobody would really challenge" them given their predominantly masculine gender presentations. I wondered aloud whether Michael thought he would feel as free in such low-key transgressions once he became an officer, prompting him to reply: "I've never really felt uncomfortable but yeah, I think if I was alone in a new unit . . ." He trailed off. Perhaps relaxing his hypermasculine front was only possible when his masculinity was simultaneously reinforced by the presence of a similarly gendered, equally respected gay man.

In sociological terms, Michael and others manipulated their gendered habitus to maintain their status as well-liked and well-respected. Pierre Bourdieu defines habitus as the dispositions (tastes, habits, styles) that become embodied through a practice of bodily hexis, the incorporation of social rules about class, race, gender, and sexuality that imprint in the ways we hold and move our bodies through the world.[31] Queer theorists like David Halperin argue a distinct "gay sensibility"—what sociologists might then call a gay or queer habitus—is being stamped out in the era of homonormativity.[32] This was borne out in my interviews; Michael, for instance, described a form of embodied code-switching in which he and his similarly macho gay friend occasionally slipped into a campy, queer habitus emboldened by their confidence that it wouldn't threaten the status they'd earned through their otherwise masculine performances. The way he trailed off when he considered his career beyond the small world of his ROTC program evinces a melancholy about the future: Michael understood that queer embodiment would have to be guarded even more carefully as he moved up the ranks.

Queer social control processes compel gay and bisexual men to engage in what legal scholar Ken Yoshino calls "covering." In the era of the homonormative bargain, "discrimination directs itself not against the entire group, but against the subset of the group that fails to assimilate to mainstream norms."[33] Yoshino continues, "This new form of discrimination targets minority cultures rather than minority persons. Outsiders are included, but only if we behave like insiders—that is, only if we cover." The problem with covering is that it "hurts not only our most vulnerable citizens but our most valuable commitments." Michael's wistfulness shows how even those who can convincingly cover their queerness experience grief at the hard bargain; he cannot expect his commitment to the military to be reciprocated should he fail to cover.

Because the discussions and debates around DADT and previous iterations of the military's gay exclusion were animated by femmephobia and fears of gay and bisexual men's inclusion, one could get the sense that women were and are largely untouched by military homophobia.[34] For example, when I asked Melanie (28, white cis lesbian woman, Army) if she saw a difference between the experiences of gay/bisexual men and lesbian/bisexual women servicemembers, she said definitively: "People tend to be more accepting of lesbians than gay men." This was especially true, she argued, for gay men who weren't hypermasculine. She said of a gay colleague, "I know he's been picked on a little because he's a little feminine, nothing really extreme. But they say mean things every once in a while, and we'd have to stick up for him."

Kyle argued that lesbians had more room to be gender transgressive than gay men: "The lesbians were much more outspoken, they were much more brazen when it came to their sexuality." "Men, on the other hand," he said, "They were very quiet about it. . . . They didn't flirt or flaunt it at all, because there's more acceptance, or at least less resistance among females with lesbians [than] there is with [straight] men and gay men." In this masculinist institution, some said, masculine women were fairly unremarkable. They didn't unsettle the culture quite as much as feminine men, perhaps because of a different set of gendered preconceptions. For example, Jesse (22, white cis straight man, Army ROTC) said: "I think it's easier for women to come out in the military because, again, there's the stereotype of the butch woman in the army [against] the stereotype with gay men, that they're effeminate or less manly, or tough." April said that lesbians and bisexual women have more freedom in the military because "it's easier to hide being gay than it is to hide being a lesbian." She continued:

> [Women in the military are] already considered to be a lesbian whether you are or not. . . . Our hair styles, in some ways, make us look like lesbians whether you are or not. You know, some of us prefer a shorter haircut that can look butch. . . . The assumption and the joke always tends to be more about women in the military being lesbians already. [By contrast,] gay men don't join the military, gay men are fashion designers. My perception is when lesbians come out, most people are like, "Yeah, no kidding, we already knew that, whatever." . . . I just think for [straight] men, the gay man is more threatening than the lesbian woman.

For April, the perception that women who would want to join the military must be lesbians or lesbians-in-waiting could cushion a woman's disclosure. But under the gay ban, this perception actually put women at *greater* risk of sexuality-related discharge than men. Men may have been at the discursive center of the DADT debates, yet women were targeted under the policies. As I outlined earlier, under the DOD directive that preceded DADT, women were 10 percent of the force yet comprised 25 percent of homosexuality-based discharges. Throughout the DADT era, when women comprised 14 percent of the force, they accounted for 30 percent of the sexuality-related discharges, a number that rose to 39 percent in the last year before the repeal.[35]

The overrepresentation of women among DADT discharges reflects its use as a mechanism of punishing women and maintaining their subordination.[36] Femmephobia may drive the queer social control experiences of men, but lesbophobia—the intersecting dynamics of homophobia and misogyny—drives women's. Contrary to April's assertion, scholars of military gender politics argue that women in the military must walk a careful high wire because of the presumption of their potential lesbianism. Sociologist Francine Banner explains: "Military women must balance, on the one hand, being masculine enough to conform to the ideal soldier paradigm and to be accepted as a colleague or superior by peers, and, on the other hand, being feminine enough to avoid the pejorative label of lesbian."[37] Before and during the DADT era, lesbian baiting was a pervasive enforcing mechanism.[38]

Comparing uniform and grooming regulations demonstrates the active work put into feminizing women's appearance and maintaining visual distinctions between men and women in the military.[39] Jude (34, biracial trans queer man, Navy veteran) inadvertently ran afoul of the dress code during the DADT era:

> I was still—I did not transition, had not transitioned then. I was still identifying as a lesbian and I was very, very masculine, very butch in my presentation. [In basic training], I had a friend who was also a lesbian. We both joined at the same time. We ended up being roomed together. . . . The men were on the third floor, and the women were on the second floor. Our recruiters, before they dropped us off at the hotel room, [had accidentally given us the uniform] caps for men. We were walking around wearing them . . . and my head was bald, completely bald at the time. We're hanging out, outside the hotel room with the hats on. Hanging out chatting, and these guys walk by and they were also recruits, and they were like "Are those guys on the second floor? Why're y'all with all the women?" We were like, "Are they talking about us?" Then they were like, "No wait, that's a bunch of fucking dykes." I was like "shit." [When the recruiters first gave me the hat], I didn't think it was a big deal. I was like, "a hat is a hat." I didn't really think about what it meant at the time. Afterward, I realized I was going to be in some big trouble. I mean, before I had shaved my hair, my recruiter, when I told him I was going to do it, he actually was like "please don't do that."

Gender policing and the careful management of the appearance of heterosexual femininity were even more crucial in the accounts of Black women, who data have shown were discharged under DADT even more disproportionately than other groups of women.[40] Shannon (45, Black cis lesbian woman, Navy) and Courtney (44, Black cis lesbian woman, Navy veteran) both invented boyfriends and made a point to be seen with men, buttressing their "cover" because they understood their Blackness contributed to their heightened surveillance. Growing up, Shannon remembered, her mother allowed her to be "free to do what [she] wanted to," including "run[ning] around with my shirt off, play[ing] basketball. But "being Black and female" impinged on those freedoms as she grew older and when she joined the Navy. Suddenly she was put into "this little mold" and told, "'Hey, this is what you're supposed to do. . . . You're not supposed to do that, you're supposed to act this way.'" When I asked Courtney how being both Black and a lesbian shaped her experiences, she answered that these intersecting disadvantages made it so that she "didn't want anyone to know" that she was gay. "Even after I got out [of the service], I didn't want to associate myself with that title," she said, meaning lesbian. Later in our interview, she described enduring a supervisor's racist discrimination. Because Courtney was five feet nine and Black, she said her embodiment could "be intimidating for some people—my height and stuff is a little intimidating sometimes." Thus her fear of being found out as a lesbian was informed by her mistreatment as a Black woman. Shannon's and Courtney's experiences demonstrate how misogynoir exaggerates gender panic around Black lesbian and bisexual women compared to their white peers.[41]

Black women experience gender and its consequences in the world differently than non-Black women. In particular, whiteness grants white women automatic status as feminine until proven otherwise. This is not to say that white women do not experience lesbophobic treatment, but that racism intersects with lesbophobia to create different patterns of disadvantage for Black women and other women of color. White lesbian and bisexual women experience harassment and assault for especially egregious violations of the expectation of femininity because such transgressions threaten the foundations of white supremacy, in which white women are assigned the role of keepers of virtuous domesticity in the service of white cis men's patriarchal authority. Racial and gender domination require the maintenance of hegemonic masculinity, the system through which masculinity and femininity are given meaning and through which cisgender men maintain power over women.[42] Hegemonic masculinity's relational nature is racialized, in that white femininity requires the subjugation of Black women (just as masculinity demands the subjugation of femininity). White women may be punished for rejecting their naturalized feminine status, but Black women are always already masculinized. Slavery dehumanized and defined Blackness through "monstrous" physicality.[43] Because the economy of slavery was reliant on both white women's domesticity and Black women's labor, Black women's embodiment was classified as excessive, fearsome, and perverse. This legacy contributes to the circulation of controlling images of Black women as aggressive and intimidating that perpetuate racist treatment of Black women regardless of sexuality.[44]

The intersectional process of racialized gendering put Shannon and Courtney at heightened risk of discharge under DADT. Their stories bring vivid detail to the statistically established facts of Black women's vulnerability to DADT discharges. Because of structures of white supremacy,

Shannon and Courtney had to take additional precautions and engage in "deep cover," bound by racist and sexist tropes, including the "angry Black woman," which biased how others perceived them. Courtney had to tread carefully with her supervisor, understanding that in a conflict between a white woman and a Black woman, she was likely to be seen as the aggressor. As an interviewer, I cannot make claims about what Courtney's supervisor was "really" thinking, but the endless scroll of news stories about white people calling police or enacting violence on Black people for daring to presume access to "their" spaces (parks, stores, neighborhoods, and public pools) affirms this perspective. We have ample evidence that the social pattern of racial bias and perceived threats has devastating consequences for people of color, especially Black people. In the military, specifically, the compounding effects of race and gender discrimination are well documented.[45] If Courtney's supervisor felt overly threatened—or even simply weary of her—DADT gave her a way to get rid of her, which in turn led Courtney to feel even more pressure to perform heterosexuality.

The repeal of DADT may have taken that option away, but some scholars argue that the specifics of the repeal have maintained lesbophobia.[46] The working group report that supported the repeal recommended against adding sexuality to the nondiscrimination statute in the UCMJ; it drew on the gay rights discourse of homonormativity in insisting that the gender presentation of LGB servicemembers was no different than that of straight servicemembers. Accordingly, the repeal should "minimize differences among service members based on sexual orientation and disabuse Service members of any notion that, with repeal, gay and lesbian service members will be afforded some kind of special treatment."[47] That translated, in practice, to LGB servicemembers bearing the onerous task of "minimizing difference" between themselves and straight servicemembers in order to avoid any appearance of receiving special treatment.

Cassie, the 22-year-old Army ROTC member, shared a glaring example of these forces at work:

> Most people were okay with [my sexuality]. . . . [However,] one of the guys was like, "When you and your fiancé want kids, I'll come fuck her for you." [*CC: How did you react?*] . . . What was I going to say? "You're a fucking asshole?" I didn't want to lose my military bearing because somebody [else] couldn't keep theirs. Also, I wasn't there to promote gay rights; in order to

> be treated like a normal couple, I guess you have to act like a normal couple. [Although] if another male told another male they were going to fuck their wife, I guess they'd hit them. Military bearing. Got to be better than them.

As she dealt with overt lesbophobic harassment, Cassie realized it was up to her to manage it—in fact, to dismiss it in order to get along, to show that she was "normal" and not there to "promote gay rights" or otherwise distract from the mission at hand. Cassie recognized the double standard: a man in her shoes would have social permission to respond with force, whereas she had to maintain her "military bearing" and be "better than them." Carefully muted responses to harassment were among a range of strategic responses LGBT servicemembers cultivated for instances of interpersonal homophobia and transphobia. Many felt they had to be exceptionally good natured about anti-LGBT comments, jokes, and harassment as a way to assure their peers that open service would not dampen the esprit de corps or dislodge the practice of bonding over "casual" sexism, homophobia, transphobia, and femmephobia.

As with the cis gay and bisexual men who manipulated their gendered habitus to manage stigma, so too did ciswomen, as well as the trans men who were officially classified as female at the time of their service. Chase, a 33-year-old Latinx trans man and Air Force veteran, said he used "pretty privilege" to avoid harassment during his service, when he was classified as female. Though "at the time" he was "more tomboy" looking than others, "people would say that I was cute because I'm short and I have long hair. And so I felt I had this kind of pretty privilege—just, cute privilege—where I could get away with appearing straight." Even still, Chase said, sometimes "people did question my sexuality based on what I wore that day or because sometimes I'll get my hair braided." Chase felt his cuteness or pretty privilege protected him most of the time, but for others, "the more butch, the ones people would deem as maybe not so attractive" that was a harder task. Harassment befell those who were deemed "not pretty, or not behav[ing] in certain ways that a woman even in uniform should."

Twenty-eight-year-old white cis lesbian Army veteran Lorna's feminine appearance gave her cover of the kind Chase described. She explained, "I didn't look like your stereotypical butch lesbian or whatever you want to call it, I had more of a feminine appearance." But being attractively feminine and presenting gender conformity was no real protection for her. Hewing to the dictates of professionalism, she made sure "my personal life is my personal life," yet her boss found out about her girlfriend through social networks. After that, "he made me feel very, very highly uncomfortable because the more he talked about it, the more straight that I had to pretend that I was." In this post-repeal moment, Lorna's boss couldn't use DADT to push her out of the service, but he could apply pressure to disprove the stereotype of lesbians as butch or otherwise deviant. She said she felt she had to "outwork every one of" her colleagues to "prove to them" that her being a lesbian "didn't matter in the end."

The culture of misogyny that maintains feminine abjection in the form of femmephobia for men has its effects on women, too. The repeal's reinscription of "traditional" military values like bravery, courage, and fearlessness, each implicitly coded as masculine, contributes to the continued subordination of feminine cis men, cis women, and, as I show in greater detail in part 3, transgender servicemembers.[48] Gay and lesbian baiting and blackmailing might have lost steam under the conditions of open service, but these interviews suggest that queer social control maintains a hostile context for LGB servicemembers despite their official incorporation.

Just Messing Around

As policy changes made it less acceptable to espouse more explicitly homophobic beliefs, jokes and teasing took on heightened significance as mechanisms of queer social control within the military. Before the repeal, Brian said, the phrase Don't Ask, Don't Tell "was another kind of 'hilarious' thing to make jokes about. . . . If somebody did something—like if a guy liked a 'chick flick' movie," for instance, others might shout "'Don't Ask, Don't Tell! I'm not going to ask you anything about that!' You know, like a joking thing." Post-repeal, the jokes changed. For instance, under open service, sexual harassment and assault briefings can be more transparent about same-sex incidents. But when I asked Cassie whether her ROTC commander addressed same-sex sexual harassment, she said he did it "in a joking way." As an example, she said the commander chose two men to roleplay a harassment scenario. As he directed the scene, "He was talking about it in a way that it would be hilarious and ridiculous if they were gay." "If you're somebody who is afraid of coming out," she continued, "that would make you stay in the closet."

Fellow Army ROTC member Julie (20, white cis queer woman) witnessed the same training. She corroborated: "He made up this scenario and he used two guys, which I thought was pretty indicative of his mind[set]." According to her account of the event, the commander nudged one of the men to say, "Oh, you have really nice legs, man." She continued, "It was a little problematic, people were laughing." If done differently, she thought the roleplay could be useful. But here it was not, "Because I know you're homophobic, [I know] you're using two guys because you think it's funny." By her interpretation, the skit positioned the hypothetical harasser as gay and the harassed as straight, further conveying the harmful notion that "the guy who's gay is more apt to commit sexual assault."

SHARP is the acronym used for military sexual harassment and assault response and prevention training. Brian recalled a senior admiral asking a group of sailors what they thought of the training's use of a green/yellow/red light metaphor for acceptable, borderline, and unacceptable interactions. "Everybody used to make fun of it, everybody used to make jokes about that. If you accidentally brushed against somebody, [you'd joke], 'Yellow light!'" Similarly, Sean said, "We'll catch ourselves, whenever we're in uniform at an ROTC event, we'll say some joke—I've got a buddy of mine, I'll smack him on the ass, like, 'good job, buddy' and then we'll all yell SHARP! as a joke. It's among friends, it's a joke." As a lesbian, Elise (23, white cis lesbian woman, Army ROTC) experienced such jokes differently: as hints that undermined the seriousness of sexual harassment and assault, including same-sex incidents. When treated "like a joke," she said, it becomes clear that "it's not anything anyone takes seriously." Elise was in a different program, yet the same joke circulated in her program: "You walk past someone and if your shoulder brushed them, they'll be like, 'SHARP, ha ha ha.' And I'm like [*deadpan voice*] 'Yeah, that's hilarious, great.'"

The majority of research participants were skeptical about the effectiveness of sexual harassment and assault prevention modules, which were both too cursory and too flippant. Some facilitators, like Cassie and Julie's commander, used same-sex examples, but because they relied on homophobic and heteronormative tropes, same-sex sexual harassment was presented as a joke. Across my interviews, I found very few who had experienced training that took the issue of homophobia and transphobia in the military seriously and recognized how it puts LGBT servicemembers at risk for sexual harassment and assault. Instead, open service allowed facilitators to turn vignettes and role plays into opportunities for comedy, which in turn emboldened cadets and servicemembers to make light of same-sex sexual harassment. As Elise's comments demonstrate, the treatment of same-sex sexual harassment as an opportunity for frivolity can have a chilling effect for LGB servicemembers who hear that their sexual subjectivities and their experiences of harassment and assault are funny, not to be taken seriously or reported. Not only are such approaches ineffective, they can actually give rise to the very harassment they are intended to prevent.

As we discussed the informal mechanisms of queer social control they had experienced and witnessed, participants offered ample evidence of what sociologists Candace West and Don Zimmerman call "accountability structures," the interactive exchanges that uphold the gender binary in everyday talk.[49] For example, I asked Michael if he ever was teased for being gay despite his popular status. "They throw jokes out," he acknowledged. But he claimed, "I appreciate that! If you can joke about it." What did he mean, I prompted, by "jokes"? "Oh, they'd be like, 'Oh, that's gay—that as gay as [Michael]!'" He added that he tried to respond with nonchalance: "Like yeah, duh!" This was "partially me trying to normalize the situation, but also it made me feel comfortable." From his perspective, "I can be the brunt of the joke, just like they're the brunt of the joke sometimes. You accept your share of it." Other LGB cadets might say, "'Well, that's offensive and insulting', but to me it's just like, 'Oh, they accept me.' That's what it means." Michael said he was glad that his sexuality was not treated with kid gloves. He interpreted jokes as signs of acceptance, given the prevalence of teasing as a communication and bonding device. This would be a theme throughout many subsequent interviews: accepting as routine the jokes and teasing laden with racialized, gendered, and sexualized slights, even calling them fun.

Laura (21, white cis straight woman, Army ROTC), for example, said that "there is a lot of fag discourse" in ROTC, but she didn't consider it homophobic. "It's based more on the masculinity portion, not the sexuality portion. If anyone makes stupid homophobic jokes, it's [a gay cadet] who is just being dumb." Laura, who had taken a gender and sexuality course prior to our conversation, drew on sociologist C. J. Pascoe's concept of "fag discourse" to explain how effeminacy remained the butt of the joke under the conditions of open service, but she insisted its use was tongue-in-cheek.[50] This interpretation runs contrary to Pascoe and other scholars of masculinity, who argue that heteromasculine accomplishment and feminine abjection are two sides of the same coin. Pascoe defines fag discourse as the "jokes, taunts, imitations and threats through which boys publicly signal their rejection of that which is considered feminine."[51] By distancing themselves from the specter of effeminacy, men who participate in fag discourse implicitly endorse homophobia and misogyny, and the homonormative bargain compels *all* men, regardless of sexual identity, to participate in fag discourse as a strategy of protection.

In one of his stories, Christopher demonstrated the ubiquity of fag discourse and the attendant nonchalance regarding its effects. Recently, he said, he'd found a voice memo on his computer. "I push the little arrow that says 'start,' and it says 'Lieutenant [Smith] likes to suck big dicks.'" He offered this as an example of hazing, then paradoxically insisted, "There was no hazing, they were just harassing me. I find it funny! . . . It wasn't to insult me, it wasn't to hurt me." While he presented this "fun" homophobia as normal, boys-will-be-boys stuff, I read the event as a subtle reminder to men that engaging in oral sex with each other is so abhorrent that the very thought of it is hilarious. The prank only works because it assumes that both parties share that interpretation; these kinds of jokes reinforce homophobia even in the era of so-called tolerance and inclusion.[52]

Tony (20, Asian cis straight man, Army ROTC) was the butt of more than one racialized and sexualized joke—which he presented as relatively harmless—as a cadet:

> I remember one instance. We were doing a urinalysis and you have—under the watch of someone—[to] pee into a cup. [The supervising advisor] . . . was making comments like, because I'm Asian that I have a small penis and whatnot. He's joking around and trying to tell the other advisers. . . . He's like, "don't miss the cup because you have a small penis!"

This "joking" was not explicitly homophobic, but it was about a repudiation of queerness, in the sense of being on the wrong side of relations of power.[53] It drew on racist stereotypes about Asian masculinity and embodiment in order to uphold a racialized hierarchy of heteromasculinities in which Asian men, even when straight, are positioned as dangerously proximate to femininity.[54]

Another ROTC advisor Tony remembered would make similar homophobic jokes targeting straight men:

> Sometimes you'd have one of the male advisers make just—very off the cuff homoerotic jokes. They were never offensive or derogatory, just kind of like. . . . I don't know. For example, we'd be all sleeping outside [during a training exercise] and it would be like, "We should all get naked and cuddle with each other or something. Don't be afraid to shower together, you need help, scrub each other."

When I asked if he considered such "jokes" to be derogatory, Tony replied, "Absolutely not . . . not necessarily homophobic, but sort of drawing on the idea that it would be funny if you were gay. . . . But I can't think of any instances where there was an example of derogatory comments toward gay personnel in our unit." By Tony's reckoning, offensive comments directed toward specific LGBs might be offensive, but homophobic teasing directed at cadets who are presumed straight in this telling was a bit of harmless fun. Even when I prompted Tony to consider the possibility that such jokes could constitute anti-queerness or create a hostile climate for LGB cadets, he stood by the exculpatory interpretation.

It's interesting to consider that Tony may have, in this anecdote, been referencing the same commander who made homophobic jokes out of sexual harassment trainings. In that case, we might wonder what homoerotic interest might lie behind this advisor's preoccupation with the sexual bodies of men. Regardless of the presence of latent desire, same-sex eroticism is treated as comic relief here, reinforcing the superiority of heterosexual masculinity. Like Michael, Sean, and Christopher, Tony excused the homophobic implications of such "comedy" in the name of brotherly camaraderie. This is part of what Lorraine Bayard de Volo and Lynn Hall call the "gendered continuum of violence" in the military, which ranges from "quotidian harassment often misrecognized as harmless" to legally actionable and legible forms of harassment and assault.[55]

Jokes and teasing exploit a sort of loophole in the post-DADT policy context, communicating the "Dos" and "Don'ts" of inclusion without explicitly violating nondiscrimination and anti-harassment policies. Their harm is minimized, including by some LGB servicemembers, in the name of building and maintaining the much-vaunted military esprit de corps. I argue that the centrality of the unit cohesion argument in debates for and against the repeal created a climate of ostensibly open service in which LGB servicemembers are expected to police their gender presentation, silence their sexual selves, and downplay any harassment (including in the form of "jokes") used to enforce both. They are expected to "take it like a [cisgender heterosexual] man" to prove their worthiness for inclusion in this masculinist institution—to demonstrate that they're one of the "good gays" rather than a threat to the status quo.

In "Notes on a Sociology of Bullying," C. J. Pascoe writes that our conceptualization of bullying is inadequate for capturing how power and inequality structure interactions.[56] The bullying narrative individualizes: the bully is to blame, rather than a set of social conditions that make bullies or structure patterns of who is bullied. In addition, bullying discourse frames this as a primary and secondary school problem, something that may be harmful, but that young people will grow out of. The gendered and sexualized teasing that is prevalent in the military is, I argue, a form of harassment that does not fit this bullying narrative and therefore evades attention and critique.

The "teasing" practices I describe here are characteristic of masculinist institutions like the military, where they are given sacred status as bonding mechanisms that will facilitate cohesion and ultimately, lethality. The misogyny that informs them—and all of the mechanisms of queer social control—is imprinted and enacted early, through what we recognize as childhood bullying, later given cover under the more trivializing label of joking. Yet "just messing around" maintains the femmephobic and lesbophobic hostility implicated in the racialized, gendered organization of the military.

CONCLUSION

Despite their avowed support for open service, research participants frequently described engaging in interactive practices that regulate queerness. There are implicit messages of queer social control—don't act "too" gay, and certainly don't flirt, or touch, or shower near, or even stand too close to cisgender and straight servicemembers; don't react to or report harassment if you want to be accepted; and don't put a damper on the camaraderie established via boisterous enthusiasm for gendered and sexual teasing. In small and not-so-small ways, queer social control processes make it clear that LGB participation may be tolerated, but violations of the homonormative bargain will not.

The normalizing politics of gay rights, with their insistence on the separation of LGB sexual identity from gender transgression, have been all too successful. The homosexual body, once considered the site of gender confusion, is no longer *inherently* queer. This de-somatization allows homosexuality to float freely, unmoored from the associations of gender aberration, yet ultimately constrained by the imperatives of gender conformity and sexual respectability. Because the homonormative bargain sensitized heterosexuals to the possibility of the "normal gay," it solidified and narrowed the coercive conditions under which LGB servicemembers might be granted provisional acceptance.[57]

It is *not,* in this light, strange that the same military personnel who told me they approved of the DADT repeal also held antigay attitudes. Servicemembers are more apt to internalize institutional policy as part of their identity than are workers in many other occupational categories, and support for the repeal asks only their tolerance (revocable should their continued fixation on "professionalism" reveal any violations).[58] Keeping queerness at bay through informal queer social control further neutralizes inclusion for those who otherwise have moral objections to homosexuality. As will become all the more evident in Parts 2 and 3 of the book however, the same logics disappear when it comes to respondents' attitudes toward gender integration. Why, if people can make a distinction between their moral distaste for queerness and their support for the repeal policy, do they so vigorously argue against the DOD's move to repeal combat exclusion for women and the exclusion of trans servicemembers generally?

We can make sense of the positive reception of the DADT repeal as reliant on a narrow interpretation of inclusion that uses discourses of professionalism, tolerance, and diversity to carve out a conditional form of acceptance for *some* LGBs, usually at the expense of others. Shifting to policies on women in combat and trans inclusion in parts 2 and 3 reveals that some changes are a bridge too far for the tolerant modern military. Servicemembers and veterans remain heavily invested in the preservation of a military "way of life" that denigrates women and femininities and upholds binary notions of sex even as the sharp edges of the homo/hetero binary are slowly filed down.

PART 2 Ending Combat Exclusion

4 "When You Want to Create a Group of Male Killers, You Kill the Woman in Them"

FEMININE ABJECTION AND THE IMPOSSIBILITY OF WOMEN WARRIORS

During his tenure at the Pentagon, Lieutenant Colonel Greg Brown worked on both the DADT repeal and the removal of restrictions on transgender service. In both cases, he said, the Office of Military Personnel Policy's research followed the evidence all the way to the conclusion that the policies' underlying rationales were outdated and inaccurate. LGBT open service was entirely untested in the US armed forces, but servicemembers' opinions largely agreed, as we have seen in part 1, that the DADT repeal caused none of the upheaval its detractors had predicted.

Meanwhile, research regarding ending the combat exclusion for women came to the same conclusion—it was an outdated policy—backed up by real-world evidence. Despite formal prohibitions, women had already been proving themselves in combat for decades.[1] In fact, throughout the wars in Iraq and Afghanistan, the need for frontline servicemembers led military leadership to exploit bureaucratic loopholes, bringing women to battlefields by designating them as "attached" rather than "assigned" to combat.[2] Women served alongside men in the region for a decade, yet when women's combat exclusion was officially rescinded, the backlash was swift.

Why was the reaction to the DADT repeal so different than the reaction to the end of women's combat exclusion? Brown told me he had contemplated this many times himself, ultimately concluding that, though he doesn't understand why exactly, the issues are "apples and oranges":

> [My wife and I] have a friend who you would swear is just this modern, well-read, liberally minded guy, [but] will just go up and down about it, that women just don't belong in combat. I can't quite figure it out. It doesn't surprise me—I think we have struggled so much more with women in the military. . . . In fact, many, many a [straight] woman has approached me after Don't Ask, Don't Tell was repealed to say, "You know that the GLB community is now in a better place than we [women in general] are in the military?" [And I say,] "Yes, you're absolutely right." There's something else going on, and whatever it is that leads us to misogyny is so different than homophobia. There is just something else going on there. . . . I was asked, "How did we get [LGB service] so right when we get women in the military so wrong?" The only conclusion I had was that they are apples and oranges. It is just different, and I don't know why.

To answer his question requires taking what we've learned in part 1 and using it to look at the layers of history, policy, and gendered expectations that inform contemporary understandings about women's military roles.

The first section of this book, to recap only broadly, established that the military is a deeply gendered institution in which the virtues of the "good soldier" are inextricable from a specifically white, straight, cisgender masculinity. Deviations, such as gay masculinities and non-white masculinities, are disadvantaged, regulated, and punished. Women can and do perform masculinity, though they hardly benefit from its successful performance, least of all within this totalizing institution. In fact, women servicemembers are often penalized for violating the military norms specific to femininity. Lesbian and bisexual cisgender women, trans women, and women of color of all sexualities face harsher sanctions, and women who overlap in these domains exponentially more. To succeed as a woman in the institution is to walk the thinnest of tightropes: masculine enough to earn respect, but feminine enough to meet the standards of comportment befitting a woman in the military. Despite its stated purpose of sidestepping sexuality-based discrimination and harassment through enforced silence, DADT allowed assumptions relating sexuality to embodied gender performance to justify discharge, a cudgel that helped keep nonnormative femininities tightly controlled.[3]

The inextricability of the virtues of the ideal soldier from masculinity, in other words, put women in what social scientists often refer to as a double bind. The woman servicemember can be a good warrior *or* a good woman, but never both simultaneously.[4] Drawing on transnational feminist insights, this chapter critiques both the misogyny that sustained women's exclusion as well as the imperial ambitions of "security feminism," the incorporation of militarism and securitization into the project of gender equality, and patriotic paternalism, the social forces that resisted women's incorporation into the military at every step.[5]

In this critical history, I show how both the misogyny of military culture and the liberal feminist response to it ultimately sustain global patterns of raced, gendered, and sexual violence. Against cultural scripts in which women are supposed to be the beneficiaries, not the heroes, of military-maintained freedom, liberal feminists attempted to reframe women's service. In resisting the paternalist frame, however, they made a bargain not unlike the homonormative bargain: to gain inclusion, they declined to critique the patriotic half of patriotic paternalism and left behind many of the radical, intersectional possibilities of feminist critique. The result has meant embedding the language of women's empowerment—particularly white women's empowerment—within the logics and strategies of US imperialism. To be sure, recent research suggests that a younger generation of security feminists is pushing back on the racism and xenophobia implicit in securitization, but as long as women's participation in counterterrorism is held up as a feminist project, such attempts will be limited.[6]

BRAVE MEN, GOOD WOMEN

The exclusion of women, first from service and later from combat, has always been a constitutive property of the military as an institution. Despite the gradual eradication of formal prohibitions on women's service, the "woman soldier" remains, at least symbolically, an oxymoron for some. Indeed, the military, a proving ground for masculine bona fides, was long considered a homosocial safe haven from the feminizing influence of women.[7] Marines were once taught that they must "kill the woman in them" to become good warriors; the archetypical servicemember was constructed in direct opposition to womanhood and femininity.[8]

With the gendered tropes of "brave men" and "good women" integral to the very logic of war, the US military successfully prohibited women from *any* kind of sanctioned service, combat or otherwise, for over a century. And yet they served. Like LGB servicemembers, women were among the ranks well before their formal inclusion date. Tens of thousands of women participated in combat during the Revolutionary War and the Civil War, and the Army and Navy established a nurse corps of (mostly white) women in the early 1900s (Black women weren't admitted into the nurse corps until 1947).[9] In World War I, women were nurses, yeomen, clerks, and telephone operators. They filled any number of duties (classified as "support roles") that freed up male servicemembers to fight on the front lines. As the nation belatedly joined World War II, the Army and Navy officially formed "women's battalions": the Women's Army Auxiliary Corps (WAAC, later renamed WAC) and Women Accepted for Voluntary Emergency Services (WAVES). Both branches initially intended to disband the women's battalions after the war, but the 1948 Women's Armed Forces Integration Act created permanent, even peacetime service positions for women. Given the gender order of the era, which required a certain postwar reinscription of women's "appropriate" social position, women's permanent participation in the military posed a visible, unsettling social threat, even above and beyond the threat to the institution's vaunted masculine esprit de corps. Hence, a number of measures were put in place to minimize any "gender trouble" that women's inclusion might cause.[10]

Most apparent were the ways the military took great pains to distinguish WACs from "real" soldiers or sailors. Women were explicitly reminded that their role was to "supplement and complement" men's role in the military, *not* replace it.[11] They were largely consigned to clerical and administrative work, subject to strict rules of comportment, and demarcated through uniforms and housing. Women's uniforms established an easily visible line of demarcation; quite obviously, the skirts, stockings, heeled shoes, and tailoring that emphasized women's breasts and waists held no functional or safety rationale, nor did the guidance on hair styles, makeup, and skin care offered by WAC training manuals and films. These rules instead reminded women—and reassured men—of their subordinate, contingent inclusion.

The military's second set of measures to tamp down gender trouble incorporated and built a rationale around the first. The midcentury military undertook an in loco parentis approach to its new women servicemembers, an intensive, inward-looking paternalism. This involved a significant investment in protecting (and surveilling) women's femininity and sexual propriety (conveniently sidestepping any responsibility to address commonplace sexual harassment or its perpetrators). Women were expected to retain their femininity and their training commonly included formal lessons in makeup, feminine comportment, and etiquette—a bulwark against the loss of feminine graces within the masculine space of the military.[12] Curfews and strict sexual supervision reflected a wider moral panic over women's sexuality. In one 1942 slander campaign dripping with double standards and unfounded rumor, male soldiers accused members of a WAC battalion of "drinking too much, picking up men in bars, and having sexual relations under trees and bushes in public parks; there were also rumors that the local military hospital was overflowing with maternity and venereal diseases."[13]

Upholding sexual morality, of course, included rooting out homosexuals among women servicemembers. As discussed in chapter 1, this was also the era of mass lesbian purges. The investigations into alleged lesbian activities focused not just on sexual acts or gender deviance, but on all aspects of women's culture and friendships. Women were subject to deep surveillance tactics:

> [Agents] conducted "shakedowns" of the barracks, searching for letters, photographs, and books with lesbian themes. They set up wiretaps and took polygraphs. Investigators planted informants within units to report on the complicated textures of women's lives together. . . . They knew which soldiers did not date the men on base, they kept a record of which women gave each other gifts, shared a bank account, participated in a business venture, traveled together, or did each other's grocery shopping. "They knew the times I was [with a lover], the buses that I took, how long I stayed, my mode of transportation home, and what I wore," one woman in the Air Force recalls of the painful investigation she experienced. "They knew every damn move I made. It was mind shattering."[14]

Allegations of homosexuality among men were not nearly as invasive or extensive; such inquiries were much more focused on straightforward acts. Even women's career aspirations were considered signs of lesbian tendencies, thereby tempering their ambition and keeping them lower down the ranks. Terrorizing women, regardless of sexuality, seemed to be the point of this surveillance effort. "Women's integration, in short, did not neuter the tradition of martial citizenship, which remained male," Margot Canaday argues. "To preserve gender hierarchy in citizenship, though, the state needed to constitute lesbianism"—and, I would add, the licentiousness of heterosexual women.[15] Canaday notes, "The closer women moved to power, to first-class citizenship, the more homosexuality seemed to matter," within and beyond the military.[16]

Third and finally, the integration of women in 1948 came with quotas and combat rules meant to ensure that women's participation would remain exceptional, rather than acceptable. The Women's Armed Forces Integration Act specified that women would be capped at 2 percent of the overall force, and that no woman would hold any position that entailed holding command over men.[17] Relegated to roles and ranks often below their skill levels, women were explicitly forbidden from combat participation—they were excluded from service on or in any ship, plane, or ground unit that might potentially see combat.

A Crisis of Legitimacy

Military conscription, colloquially known as "the draft," came under mass criticism in the late 1960s, amid the controversial and casualty-strewn Vietnam War. Presidential hopeful Richard Nixon, not unlike Clinton in the 1990s, seized on the military as a political opportunity when millions took to the streets to protest the draft and the war. As part of his 1968 campaign, Nixon pledged massive military reform. Upon his election, he opened a commission on the possibility of moving to an all-volunteer force (AVF), and the policy was enacted in 1973 when Congress declined to extend the draft. By then, years of men publicly burning their draft cards as an act of civil disobedience had presented the public with a compelling alternative to martial masculinity: a protest-based masculinity that reversed the social meanings of the courage, valor, and honor long tied to service.[18] The

AVF was intended, in part, to help recuperate the reputation and reassert the importance of the armed forces.

The movement from an all-male conscription model to a gender-neutral volunteer force was an opening to de-gender the organization of military occupations. The strategy for rebuilding the ranks could have focused on marketing to and recruiting greater numbers of women, but in the midst of hegemonic masculinity's "crisis tendencies," the military was unwilling to destabilize the gendered order.[19] As a result, marketing around the AVF valorized martial masculinity by deploying the "band of brothers" trope to inspire men to service.[20] This led liberal feminists to use women's exclusion from combat and conscription as an example of sex segregation as they advocated for the ratification of the Equal Rights Amendment. The "right to fight" became a plank in the movement's platform, a way to resist the assumption of inherent sex/gender difference. Unfortunately, their strategic move would backfire, at least in terms of the ERA's adoption; in congressional hearings, the prospect of a "female draft" became a dissuasive scare tactic, helping to sideline the amendment as a whole.[21] Yet despite its masculine marketing, the AVF led to increasing numbers of women joining the service; throughout the late 1970s and early 1980s, various branches and ranks continued to slowly gender integrate.[22]

Despite—or perhaps because of—the changing gender composition of the force, policies "protecting" women from combat stubbornly evaded legal challenge. Like DADT and its predecessor policies against open service, gender exclusionist policy continued in various, sometimes overlapping configurations. In 1980, the US Supreme Court ruling in *Rostker v. Goldberg* upheld the constitutionality of excluding women from Selective Service registration. In 1988, the DOD reinforced the policy, adding a "risk rule" that excluded women from frontline work "if the risks of exposure to direct combat, hostile fire, or capture were equal to or greater than the risks in the combat units they supported."[23] The "risk rule" was rescinded in 1993 but replaced with the Direct Combat Exclusion Rule in 1994, which continued the exclusion of women from units whose "primary mission is to engage in direct combat on the ground."[24] In the Navy, women were wholly barred from serving on submarines, with leadership citing cost (by which they meant the cost of modifying facilities to accommodate sex segregation) and concerns about the likelihood of sexual misconduct in such close quarters. As in previous eras, women were the ones denied opportunities as a result of concerns about men's predilections for predation.

Surviving the Misogyny Paradox

Sexual harassment and assault are chronic plagues on women's service, both as actual occurrences and as rationales for women's exclusion. Research shows that as many as a third of all women servicemembers are sexually assaulted and up to three-quarters are sexually harassed during their military tenure.[25] What's more, women have frequently been blamed for their own victimization in the military. A 1992 letter to the *Navy Times* is typical: "So the US Navy is having a problem with sexual harassment. Well, what does anyone expect? When women go where they do not belong, sexual harassment is the logical result."[26]

Sexual violence is endemic to the culture and traditions of the military, an extension of the "fraternal state's" reliance on building male bonds through the domination of women.[27] Women in the first waves of integration—into service, into military academies, into specializations, and into combat—suffered for their violations of these fraternal spaces. Sue Fulton, introduced in earlier chapters, was among the first cohort of women admitted to West Point, the US Military Academy:

> I used to say, "West Point took 17-year-old boys and 17-year-old girls, and four years later, they graduated 17-year-old boys and 47-year-old women." It's a boys' school, and even the officers were opposed to us being there. There were some things about it that were wonderful when we were at West Point, but we were not welcome. When the upperclassman came back at the end of [first-year students'] Plebe Summer . . . many of the upperclassmen were genuinely astonished that there were still women there, because they were convinced that "Beast Barracks" would drive the women out, that the women wouldn't be able to handle it. And look, some women didn't. Over the four years, we lost half of the women. [Half of us made it], but it was just constant nastiness. It's very interesting to be around the women in my class [now], because over time, I recognize that some of us show signs of trauma. And I can look back and realize there were signs of trauma then. There were signs of trauma right after. It's just, PTSD wasn't a thing back then. . . . It's just very deeply rooted: join the Army and be a man.

The "Beast Barracks" refers to West Point's infamously brutal summer initiation program, replete with gendered and sexual hazing. Long after women's formal incorporation, military academies remain fertile ground for the inculcation of misogyny and sexual violence.[28] The US Air Force Academy was the site of a major sexual assault scandal in 2003, for instance, when sixty-one women cadets reported they had been sexually assaulted. Subsequent investigations found that sexually violent language and traditions were ubiquitous at the academy, where one familiar jodie (a call and response chant that coordinates marching) included the line: "I wish all the ladies were holes in the road, and I was the dump truck, I'd fill them with my load."[29] Though these jodies are officially prohibited, they are deeply institutionalized; a cadet's refusal to join in could be considered insubordination by cadre leaders. Scholar Jane Ward notes this as but one example of the "misogyny paradox" endemic to military culture, wherein expressions of desire for women are simultaneously wrapped in hatred for them. The misogyny paradox crops up time and again, as women Marines (WMs) are said to be "Walking Mattresses" and "Wastes of Money," the Women's Air Force (WAF) is resignified as "We All Fuck," women in the Navy are "Women Used By All" (WUBA), girlfriends back home are cheating "Susie Rottencrotches," and so on.[30] Women who are sexually unavailable or who resist and report harassing language are deemed humorless scolds or lesbians (both of whom need to be put in their place). The gendered continuum of violence categorizes women as "one of three things in the military—a bitch, a whore, or a dyke."[31] To survive, women learn that "camouflage isn't only for combat"; the camouflage of gender presentation and emotion management are necessary strategies of survival in this virulently hostile work environment.[32]

Navigating these minefields is difficult business. A woman in the service is expected to "manage her physicality, sexuality, and femininity adeptly to achieve the trust and confidence" of her colleagues.[33] A woman can never be "as good as a man," but "if she possesses sufficient physical strength, keeps sexuality out of the workplace, and conducts herself professionally," "she need not be his equal as his equivalent, a respected peer in a familial relationship."[34] But in the military family, discussed in greater detail in chapter 1, "good" women—those who survive the gauntlet of harassment, insults, and abuse, anyway—can only really rank, in the best case, as mother figures or little sisters. In the past decade, the professionalizing discourse that increasingly discourages overtly misogynistic treatment has made a little more room for some exceptional women to become "one of the boys," earning "honorary man" status.[35] That is a tenuous accomplishment, though, and it can be rescinded at any moment. Even in death, women are grievable only as "good soldiers" or "good women" because "good women soldiers" remain socially and politically unintelligible.[36]

Women, the Secret Weapon

Combat exclusion remained on the books, yet the wars in Iraq and Afghanistan blurred the lines between combat and noncombat work, bringing more and more women to the front lines.[37] Operation Enduring Freedom and Operation Iraqi Freedom involved women in a number of de facto combat positions.[38] With the AVF stretched thin by the ongoing, expansive war on terror, the troops were increasingly replenished through a combination of creative role interpretation and bureaucratic trickery. As the *New York Times* (2011) reported:

> Women . . . can serve as machine gunners on Humvees but cannot operate Bradleys, the Army's armored fighting vehicle. They can work with some long-range artillery but not short-range ones. Women can walk Iraq's dangerous streets as members of the military police but not as members of the infantry. . . . They can lead combat engineers in war zones as officers, but cannot serve among them. . . . On paper, [one unit commander] followed military policy. The women [he commanded] were technically assigned to a separate chemical company of the division. In reality, they were core members of his field artillery battalion. "We had to take everybody," [the commander said]. "Nobody could be spared to do something like support."[39]

As with the gay ban, combat exclusion was conveniently overlooked when the mission demanded. And in fact, women "proved indispensable in their ability to interact with and search Iraqi and Afghan women for weapons, a job men cannot do for cultural reasons. The Marine Corps created revolving units of 'lionesses' dedicated to just this task."[40]

It became harder to pretend women were excluded from the front lines as they began receiving commendations for their combat service.[41] The formal policy nonetheless precluded the creation of any policies to address the new, twin problem of women experiencing simultaneous sexual violence and combat trauma during this era.[42] Still, in this tenuous moment, there seemed to be no putting this toothpaste back in the tube; now that women were visible as successful combatants, keeping them out was a losing proposition.

PATRIOTIC PATERNALISM IN THE COMBAT DEBATES

Academic and legal analyses of the DADT repeal asked whether the end of combat exclusion was sure to follow.[43] In many ways, the debates over these policies' repeals were similar. As they had with regard to DADT, advocates used empirical evidence to debunk long-held assertions about its "dangers" for unit cohesion, morale, and readiness. Even the tension between radical, liberal, and transnational feminist readings of military inclusion mirrored the ones that roiled among liberationist, homonormative, and queer readings of DADT. The crucial difference, looking back on these debates, is that combat exclusion protectionists explicitly emphasized women's embodied deficiencies and the need to "protect" women from overestimating their fitness for combat.

This difference, I argue, is an outcome of the homonormative bargain, which did the work of de-somatizing homosexuality by moving it away from embodied gender difference and leaving the military's inherent femmephobia unquestioned. When liberal feminist activists attempted to rhetorically ungender military service, their bargain meant co-opting, rather than resisting, militarism to argue that women were every bit as capable as men of doing the maiming, torturing, and murdering work of the war on terror.[44] This strategy was successful in moving the military toward combat inclusion. Yet the rank and file remained unconvinced. For decades, women had performed these jobs from which they were formally barred, but when the rules changed, servicemembers were far less receptive than they had been at the end of DADT. The distinction, as the next chapter explores more fully, hinges on the persistent, near unassailable belief of women's embodied and psychological deficiencies and similarly biologized beliefs about men's instinct to protect them.

To begin, we must tease out the core elements of the policy fight, organized around cohesion and morale, readiness, fitness, and protecting women from the brutal reality of combat service. Unit cohesion did a lot of heavy lifting for defenders of combat exclusion, as it had for DADT's supporters. The "band of brothers" mythology rests on the belief that "male bonding" is an exceptional, essential element of winning warfare. A 2018 survey about the gender integration of combat quoted a servicemember: "As far as combat arms units go, [gender integration] would [have] an extremely negative effect within units which are traditionally male. The things that go on there, the bonds, would be damaged.... *I would almost rather die before changing my demeanor within my unit* [emphasis added]."[45]

In his book *Deadly Consequences: How Cowards Are Pushing Women into Combat*, retired Lieutenant Colonel Robert Maginnis argued that "feminizing our ground combat forces" by allowing women to serve "threatens to destroy the warrior spirit, that masculine mindset that glues fighters together and fuels their aggression to kill our enemies. Damage that spirit and you condemn our military to defeat."[46] Others suggested it was "sexual tension" that would ruin unit cohesion. "Women have done wonderful jobs in the military in many things. I just don't think they are necessary in the infantry," began Naval War College professor Mac Owens in an NPR interview.[47] The reason, he said, was their potential to undermine cohesion, which is based on "mutual trust" and unlikely to survive "sexual tensions and things like that" (that cohesion could have so fragile a linchpin went unaddressed). Even more flippantly, a *Washington Post* opinion writer quipped that though "sexual tension is a most delightful distraction in civilian life," it has no place in combat.[48]

Given the misogyny documented thus far in this book, it makes sense that gender integration would impact unit cohesion and morale to some degree. However, those in favor of gender integration turned, like the repeal advocates had, to social science for evidence that might disprove the idea. They found a considerable body of work showing that in noncombat positions, the entrance of women had no negative effect on unit cohesion (more than occasionally, their incorporation improved cohesion).[49] Particularly hypermasculine and male-dominated specializations, researchers found, did see some lowering of cohesion following gender integration; however, that research also showed that such disruption can be mitigated by strong leadership and tends to diminish over time.[50] Retired two-star Major General Kathy Frost argued, in the same NPR piece featuring Mac Owens, that relegating women to combat support positions fomented resentment and lowered cohesion:

> Giving men a disproportionate responsibility for assignment in these units by denying women the opportunity and the responsibility of serving in these units is really going to cause resentment. . . . And that's going to really affect unit cohesion, force cohesion, and will cause long-term readiness problems and tremendous resentment among the men, and it's unfair.[51]

Frost flipped the unit cohesion argument to suggest continuing to deny women full access to combat roles was the more dangerous choice, another similarity to the DADT repeal playbook.

Military readiness is also measured by deployability. At any given time, things like illness, injury, and situational factors can take servicemembers out of the field, impeding both the deployability and the lethality of troops. Opponents of women in combat point to pregnancy and motherhood as particular hindrances to readiness. In the context of duty, the "personal choice" of pregnancy becomes a "public spectacle," a blatant refusal to make the sorts of sacrifices to autonomy the institution—and the mission—demands. According to critics, "physical competency and prowess are intrinsically tied" to leadership ability; therefore, "it logically follows" that a pregnant servicemember cannot be an "optimally successful leader."[52]

Critics even charge that women will "work the system" to avoid work, including by using pregnancy (real or faked) as an excuse to avoid doing their part. One woman Marine captain is quoted in a 2014 critique of combat inclusion as follows:

> There are some women that abuse their female-ness to get out of being a Marine and that's just not right. There are those who "have cramps" so they can't PT. There are those who "'surprisingly'" become pregnant so they can't deploy. There are those who "'can't find a [baby]sitter'" so they can't stand duty. . . . [W]omen [are] abusing their sex to get out of the duties and responsibilities that they agreed to perform when they signed that contract.[53]

In addition to pregnancy's effect on readiness, motherhood is assumed to quell the "killer instinct" that combat duty requires and to distract women from their duty.[54] Thus from the imagined inevitability of "sexual tension" comes the inevitability of sex comes the inevitability of pregnancy and motherhood: women's sexuality is positioned as a security threat at every stage. Advocates of gender integration rebut these arguments with data showing that men's substance use and on-the-job injuries are far more detrimental to deployability than pregnancies, though the latter retain a mythical status that's tough to dislodge with data.[55]

This brings us directly to the third area of contention in these debates: women's overall fitness to serve. Combat exclusion advocates rely heavily on claims that women are not equipped, psychologically or physiologically, for the work of ground combat. The arguments run the gamut from claiming that women can't carry enough weight to be useful to insisting they have inferior hand-eye coordination skills; they are too conflict averse and peace oriented; they resent authority, shirk responsibility, they are "too hormonal" and therefore irrational; and their presence will result in the deaths of too many "good men."[56]

The idea of a "natural order" of sex/gender difference runs through claims that women aren't aggressive enough for combat; the implication is that their service will thwart and pervert the "true" nature of (cis)gender.[57] Feminist advocates make clear that this is faulty logic propped up by bad science, and that claims about men's rationality and women's emotionality are nothing more than smokescreens for hegemonic masculinity.[58] In other words, combat exclusion is fundamentally *not* about women. It is about men. It is about protecting and shoring up their fragile masculinity through women's exclusion, about retaining the band of brothers by denigrating would-be sisters and others. When women prove their fitness and receive commendations, misogynist rebuttals spring up like mushrooms: she was lying about her accomplishments, she was given special privileges, she didn't do *that* well (compared to men), the military is downgrading its standards for commendation.[59]

In 2013, the year that combat exclusion for women was rescinded, two Air Force women received Bronze Star medals for their service. Just as soon as the Air Force announced the commendations, the gendered online bullying began:

> "My brother in the Army was awarded the bronze star with valor," one person wrote. "If I showed him this I bet he'd give it back. I'm sad to be an

> airman right now." Some of the comments got nasty, accusing the Air Force of giving Gamez the award out of favoritism or because she is "a female or minority." . . . "I can only hope that she will take a trip up to Arlington and think long and hard [and] leave the medal there where it belongs and never wearing it because she realized it was not earned."[60]

In its most paternalistic iteration, opposition to women in combat urges that they be excluded for their own protection.[61] This rationale draws on the previous three (cohesion, readiness, and fitness) but wraps them in the guise of care. Clearly, such "benevolent sexism" fits with the discursive system of patriotic paternalism.[62] As it plays out in the context of the war on terror, patriotic paternalism centers on three groups of women in "need" of protection. There are the civilian mothers, wives, and daughters whose way of life is directly threatened by hell-bent forces of terror. Next, there are the Muslim women in the Middle East who need enlightened US liberators to save them from repressive religious and political regimes. And finally, there are the women servicemembers, who are to be commended for their commitment to the nation but have dangerously overestimated their abilities and must be protected from their irrational urge to engage in direct combat, where they endanger themselves as well as their units and the military mission writ large. Whether at home, in the field, or in the towns and villages of Afghanistan and elsewhere, women are in need of the (male) patriot's protection. Patriotic paternalism gives a moral weight to the continued incursion of the United States into the Middle East as well as the exclusion of women from its front lines.

The media coverage of Private First Class Jessica Lynch and Private Lynndie England is instructive insofar as it shows patriotic paternalism's acrobatic exploitation of any opportunity to assail women's fitness for service.[63] Whether the imperiled feminine captive Jessica Lynch or the monstrously masculine Abu Ghraib torturer Lynndie England, women are rendered *both* failed soldiers and failed women, regardless of their gender presentation. PFC Lynch survived an attack on a military convoy, then was captured and taken to a hospital in Nasiriyah by Iraqi soldiers. After nine days, a Joint Special Operations Task Force raided the hospital to extract Lynch. Helmet-mounted camera footage became inescapable as the media seized upon Lynch's capture and rescue. Reports emphasized Lynch's white femininity, describing her as beautiful, girly, delicate, and almost comically petite.[64] *Time* magazine, for example, described the soldier as "pale, skinny, with thin straight legs that look as if they would be easy to snap. Hardly ideal for surviving the deadliest ambush of the war."[65] The press often stripped away her rank and last name, instead referring to her as "Jessica" or even "Jessie," a childhood nickname. She was repeatedly infantilized and framed by tropes of innocence and helplessness.[66] A biographer notably described how Lynch's fatigues "swallowed her like a big frog. . . . She looked like a child who had sneaked into her daddy's closet and tried on a uniform to play soldier."[67] Her unfitness for combat, as it was conveyed in so many media descriptions, was made literal in her own biography: the uniform overwhelms her, she is quite literally *unable to fit*. Underscoring the point on ABC's *Primetime*, journalist Diane Sawyer claimed: "In her government issued glasses and huge hat, the 5′3″ Lynch *willed* herself through basic training."[68] This framing of Lynch, in which she is adorably committed to physical achievements despite a lack of inherent or embodied aptitude for combat—darkly hinting that her capture was all but inevitable and her rescue a distracting drain on military resources—is patriotic paternalism par excellence. So, too, is a story in the *Houston Chronicle*, which describes the soldier as "a sliver of a beam, 5′2 and 90-something pounds that made her seem as fragile as a glass figurine" before recounting a story of her youthful attempts to assert her baseball prowess: "In the box, her cap pulled low over those Bambi eyes, Jessie hacked and whacked at pitches, sometimes landing smack on her tush."[69]

In a sharp contrast, the special ops team that retrieved PFC Lynch was painted as a team of highly skilled warriors deployed to save both a woman in need and the reputation of the United States. *Newsweek* reported that the extraction mission "was a welcome reminder to Americans that their forces could strike almost at will in Iraq." Saving Lynch positioned them as ideal soldiers, thereby "preserv[ing] masculinity, power, and dominance, with women as the objects of their militaristic efforts."[70] The rescuers were heroic in their masculine dominance, while Lynch was heroic only for surviving in spite of her feminine weaknesses. In this way, patriotic paternalism operated in two registers: Lynch's story confirmed the need to rescue women from themselves and the need to rescue the United States from the potential emasculation of being bested by the enemy. Some more skeptical commentators noted that the "mythic quality" of the rescue, combined with testimony of hospital workers who said the facility had been unmanned, should raise our suspicions that the mission might not have been a real "rescue" at all but merely the performance of one.[71] Voyeuristic speculation and demand for information about Lynch's possible sexual assault during her captivity further underscores the mythic positioning of Lynch as the vulnerable woman in peril and the team as the defenders of her honor.[72]

Lynch's story has another wrinkle: she wasn't alone. In fact, three women survived the initial attack on the convoy. Along with Lynch, there were Specialist Shoshanna Nyree Johnson and Private Lori Piestewa. All three were captured and brought to the hospital, where Piestewa soon died. Lynch, who was held captive for nine days total, insisted that Piestewa was the real hero of the story and noted that Johnson was held for another thirteen days. Why aren't these women's names just as familiar as Lynch's? It is because while patriotic paternalism is ostensibly about gender, it is deeply inflected with race and racial meaning. Lynch was effectively portrayed as the "everywoman" and the "girl next door," characterizations made possible because of her race, class, and gender positionality. Her "embodiment of traditional notions of white, middle class femininity" made her the ideal damsel in distress.[73] Media scholar Deepa Kumar argues that "while the stories are similar, Johnson could not be Lynch. As a black woman with dreadlocks, she simply does not qualify for the status of 'girl next door.'"[74] And though Piestewa died in her service, ostensibly making her a better fit for the story of military sacrifice, she was also Native American. She and Johnson, when they were mentioned at all, were framed as "single mothers," a racialized status that evokes white anxieties about the uncontrollable fertility of women of color.[75] Political scientist Jennifer Lobasz explains the significance of retellings of the "Lynch rescue":

> The exclusive focus on the young, childless, and possibly raped Lynch carried echoes of the myth of virginal white women who need to be protected, especially from men of color. Women of color, such as single mothers Piestewa and Johnson, were seen as aggressive and sexually rapacious in this myth, and were not accorded the same protection. Black women in particular, whose brawn is mythologized in figures such as Sojourner Truth, are portrayed as towering pillars of strength who stand in stark, unfeminine, contrast to white women.[76]

These dynamics position women of color as less deserving of paternal protection. Johnson and Piestewa's femininity is suspect, only partially recuperated through mentions of their (still stigmatized) status as mothers. Much as research participants like Shannon and Courtney, featured in chapters 1 and 2, were more vulnerable to accusations of lesbianism by virtue of their Blackness, Johnson and Piestewa were made masculine by the implicit racism of patriotic paternalism.

Also positioned in stark contrast to Lynch is Private Lynndie England, infamous for torturing detainees at Abu Ghraib prison. The flip side of Lynch's cautionary tale was England's, who posed for photos with naked detainees: dragging one on a leash, smiling behind a human pyramid of others, cheerfully pointing at and giving a thumbs up to the penises of naked detainees with bags over their heads. If Lynch was a woman imperiled by her hapless femininity, England was a ruined woman whose femininity was corrupted by proximity to the masculine business of war.[77] Like Lynch, she became the singular stand-in for a high-profile military crisis involving multiple soldiers. However, whereas Lynch was girlish, pure, and virginal, England was mannish, corrupted, and sexually promiscuous.

Media references to England's appearance never failed to include her "short-cropped hair, a tight, muscular body and that don't-mess-with-me expression," calling her "homely," "ugly," and "tomboyish."[78] Where we read about "Jessie's" childhood innocence, England was depicted as having been a "wayward teenager sneaking out to have sex with her boyfriend."[79] Even references to her impending motherhood—England was eight months pregnant at her court martialing—were used to whip up scorn. Unmarried, pregnant with the child of the alleged ringleader of the torture, Charles Graner, England's visible maternity was used as a signifier of her sexual immorality, evidence of inappropriate femininity that attested to her more spectacular, if then still alleged, lapse in that area. Notably, England was not the only woman photographed engaging in torture at Abu Ghraib or elsewhere. However, her masculine appearance as well as her taboo pregnancy, the result of a sexual relationship with a military superior, made her a more appealing villain, much as Lynch was the more appealing heroine in her trio of survivors.[80] To the extent that anyone suggested England was redeemable, it was through paternalistic interpretations of her culpability, which was diminished by virtue of her victimhood and motherhood. The most generous framings presented England as a "naïve, pregnant, promiscuous child," misled, intimidated, coerced into posing with the detainees by her abusive older boyfriend.[81]

In both cases, the public was told that Lynch and England, led astray by the false promise of feminist empowerment, demonstrated women's inherent unfitness for combat. One columnist called Lynch a victim of feminist propaganda promoting the "absurd claim" that women can do anything men can.[82] A *Chicago Sun Times* editorial argued that the fate of future Jessica Lynches "can [also] be laid at the feet of feminists who want to use Lynch as the poster girl for the 'I can do anything better than you' feminized military."[83] In the *American Spectator*, a columnist argued that Lynndie England's behavior was the "cultural outgrowth of a feminist culture which encourages female barbarians."[84] "Conservatives were shouted down," the column continued, "when they warned that placing women in combat would not only expose them to abuse but could turn them into abusers."[85] And in the *Boston Globe*, a conservative commentator mused over whether it is "good for civilization and society to try to turn women into men and put them in the traditional role of the male warrior."[86]

Rather than refute this characterization, some liberal feminist commentators doubled down. They focused on drawing attention to the sexism inherent in expectations regarding the "fairer sex." In the *Atlanta Journal-Constitution*, the director of the Girls, Women, and Media Project was quoted as saying:

> It's actually sexist to think that somehow the bar is higher for women, that women in war have more of an obligation than men do to keep things as fair and humane as possible, and that seeing women break the rules of law and of dignity is more offensive than seeing men do it.[87]

In a commencement address at Barnard, reprinted in the *Los Angeles Times*, journalist Barbara Ehrenreich admitted that England's actions disappointed her, as she supported women's full opportunities in the military and had hoped that their increased incorporation would improve peacekeeping. In the images of England at Abu Ghraib, however, she saw "arrogance, sexual depravity . . . and gender equality." It was not the version of equality she had hoped for, she said glumly, but "if we believe in democracy, then we believe in a woman's right to do and achieve whatever men can do and achieve, even the bad things."[88]

Like gay liberation, the feminism of the late 1960s and early 1970s was staunchly antiwar. Radical feminists of the era considered warfare an outcome of the inherently aggressive and violent "male style." And like the move from gay liberation to rights, the ascendance of liberal and later neoliberal feminism moved away from resistance and separatism and toward assimilation and inclusion. Liberal feminism emphasized sameness between men and women and the primacy of equal opportunity, including in military participation. Security feminism, ascendant since 9/11, solidified this shift, replacing the radical declaration that "war is a feminist issue" with the notion that "national security is a feminist issue." The security feminist, per Grewal (see the introduction for more), is the "liberal, white, and patriotic feminist working for the state and the military."[89] In a recent analysis, anthropologist Negar Razavi identifies two strands of "NatSec feminism" in Washington, D.C.:

> The first has appropriated the goals and language of the global women, peace, and security (WPS) agenda to serve the US counterterror project. The second strand, which I term the "gender equity movement," aims to bring more women into national security spaces, aligning clearly with the figure of the "security feminist" critically examined by Grewal and others.[90]

The first strand of NatSec feminism can be seen in efforts by organizations like the National Organization for Women (NOW) and The Feminist Majority to position Afghan women as "in need of feminist rescue." This work revives "older forms of colonialist missionary feminist projects,"[91] by adding white women to the ranks of "white men saving brown women from brown men," as Gayatri Spivak famously characterized it.[92] The second strand is found nested in the feminist emphasis on the value of "female counterinsurgents,"[93] an iteration that "individuates women's ability to succeed in the military while simultaneously capitalizing on what women's gender difference can offer to military campaigns reliant on infiltrating civilian spaces"—for example, the Marines' "lionesses."[94] Similarly, organizations like #NatSecGirlSquad frame women's counterterrorism work as a form of "competent diversity" that creates a "more resilient, capable, and agile national security and defense workforce."[95]

In chapter 2 I critique the appeals to diversity participants used to narrate their support of the repeal, which treated LGB servicemembers as potential value-adds to the institution while ignoring the institutional power structures that banned gay servicemembers in the first place. Applying that critique here, we can point to the relentless positivity of diversity discourse surrounding combat integration for its erasure of institutionalized misogyny and femmephobia. It also commodifies and contains difference, packaged into appealing expansion packs for the white, straight, male servicemember base model in the game of international aggression.

Referring to an organization called the Service Women's Action Network, American studies scholar Elizabeth Mesok explains that it

> argues that a "diverse military is a strong military," a logic in line with the military's own "new diversity vision," which claims that all differences—including racial, gender, ethnic, and national—should be viewed as potential commodities to be leveraged in order to militarily engage civilian landscapes on a global scale. Diversity is viewed as a "combat multiplier," or a factor that would significantly influence combat abilities or effectiveness. As one officer told me, having more women and more people of color allows the military to better "blend in" in urban warfare where engaging the population is necessary.[96]

NatSec feminism is, of course, not a monolith. Razavi's fieldwork uncovered a younger generation of immigrant women and women of color importing a thicker, more substantive understanding of intersectionality to questions of security policy and gender, sometimes directly critiquing imperialist US foreign policy.[97] Razavi holds cautious hope that these women may create change from within the military, while Mesok's read of security feminism remains pessimistic. "Movements that seek equality and justice from a nation-state responsible for perpetual global violence," Mesok writes, "but that do not critique the structures that facilitate unchecked state and military power are limited in their potential."[98] What's more:

> This strategy of advocating for women's incorporation into the military institution while eliding any critique of US militarism, or even acknowledging the global victims of US sexual and imperial violence, perpetuates the myth of the military as an institution capable of justice, both for its US enlistees and the civilians it "helps" across the globe.

Security feminist challenges to patriotic paternalism resist the framing of US women as in need of protection without wholly divesting from the inherent patriotic paternalism of the self-styled global protector state. Further, in this approach to the problem of misogynist subjugation, the patriotic half of patriotic paternalism remains entirely untouched. To the extent that this strategy has made a dent in attitudes about women's physical and psychological aptitudes for war (and, as the coming chapter shows, that dent is minor at best), it has been by laminating white American feminism onto the same old masculine militarism, co-opting women into the work of exploitative exceptionalism.

CONCLUSION

In 2013, Secretary of Defense Leon Panetta rescinded the combat exclusion rule for all branches of the armed forces. Each branch was tasked with assessing the feasibility of opening all positions to women by 2015, at which point Panetta's successor, Ashton Carter, announced the official implementation of gender-neutral accession standards. Carter said with an air of triumph that women would now "be able to serve as Army Ranger and Green Berets, Navy SEALs, Marine Corps infantry, Air Force parajumpers and everything else that was previously open only to men."[99] Indeed, in the following years, women began entering (and passing) the Marines infantry officer course, the Navy's SEAL officer screening, the Air Force's Special Forces training, and Ranger School, the Army's elite tactical training program.[100] The Navy even moved to gender-neutral uniform regulations, removing some of the symbolic demarcation of women as "women sailors" rather than sailors, full stop.

The story of women's incorporation closely mirrors many aspects of the movement toward open LGB service. In both cases, martial masculinity enforced virulent resistance to their incorporation for over a century. In both cases, assimilationist strategies carried the day. In both cases, policy advocates deflated exclusionary arguments about unit cohesion, morale, and readiness through updated social science research. In turn, both leveraged professionalism and diversity discourses, succeeding within years of the other. Yet as the next chapter shows, the *reception* of these policies has differed dramatically. As I will demonstrate, much of the divergence traces to the concessions of the homonormative bargain. Giving up on the gender liberation embedded in gay liberation's ethos thwarted any meaningful challenge to misogyny, because the de-somatization of homosexuality excised rather than embraced effeminacy. As a result, some normatively gendered gay and bisexual men were released from assumptions of their embodied deficiency, but in the military and other spheres, underlying beliefs about the inherent inferiority of embodied femininity and womanhood marched on.

5 "My Problem's Not That I'm Gay; My Problem Is That I'm a Woman"

THE PATRIOTIC PATERNALISM OF COMBAT EXCLUSION

The issue with combat exclusion, former secretary of the Army Eric Fanning explained in our interview, is "not just about women wanting to be in combat." The military's transparent promotion and pay grade structures mean that it generally does better than the civilian labor market on the issue of equal pay for equal work. But the principle of "equal pay for equal work" assumes equal *access* to work through equitable promotion processes; women's exclusion from combat has been a key factor in the military's enduring gender wage gap. That's because rising through the ranks of infantry, compared to other specializations, increases the likelihood of moving into higher rank, higher paying, and higher prestige positions; prohibiting women from infantry positions has thus thwarted their career ambitions and achievements.[1] Indeed, data show that women in the military are less likely to be promoted and retained, and they have lower lifetime career earnings than their male colleagues.[2] Women advocating for combat access are, in effect, arguing for equal opportunity in more ways than one.

Fanning noted that other exclusions, like being shut out of all-male training programs like Ranger School, negatively impact women's career outcomes in the armed forces:

> In the Army, for example, women were kept out of Ranger School. You really can't be the Chief of Staff of the Army if you don't have a Ranger tab on. It is, more than anything, a leadership school. If you want to attain leadership positions and rank in the Army, you're much more advantaged if you have a Ranger tab than if you don't. If women want to make a career of the military and want to achieve leadership positions, they realized they've got to do these things too, or it will hurt their chances as they rise up the ladder.

It's a commonsense argument, but when the Army opened Ranger School, its elite tactical and leadership course, to women in 2015, it was met with swift public rebuke. That summer, I was conducting interviews with ROTC cadets. Elise (23, white cis lesbian woman, Army ROTC) filled me in:

> There's definitely this idea that women in the military are a lot weaker than the men in the military. Right now, they have women going to Ranger School. There's nineteen of them out of twenty that started; they're still there. If you go on the Fort Benning website or the Fort Benning Facebook page—which is where Ranger School is—or on the Ranger Battalion Facebook page and look at the comments from a lot of the men, it's so agitating to read them that I just unfollowed it completely. I can't even look at the site anymore, it's so annoying. They say things like [*mocking tone to indicate immaturity*] "I hope they bring their tampons to Ranger School" and "Since when did we lower the standard for women?"

By August that year, two women had successfully finished Ranger School, an impressive feat given the program's notoriously slim completion rate. In their moment of achievement, though, they were inundated with online harassment and death threats. The accusations flew: supervisors must have inflated the women's marks, they had secretly been allowed to redo the course, their packs were lightened, or they cheated their way through. Training brigade leader Major Jim Hathaway, on his own public Facebook page, dispelled each rumor about unfair advantages individually, then wrote:[3]

> No matter what we at Ranger School say, the nonbelievers will still be nonbelievers. We could have invited each of you to guest walk the entire course, and you would not believe; we could have video recorded every patrol and you would still say that we "gave" it away. Nothing we say will change your opinion.

A fellow soldier chimed in, attesting that he was in the same Ranger class with the women graduates and penning an online essay refuting the accusations of preferential treatment.[4] The Army's chief of public affairs also issued a strong denial of the accusations. In spite of this, and as Major Hathaway predicted, outlets as disparate as the *New York Times* and *People Magazine* continued to report the rumors as facts. As of March 2022, one hundred women had completed Army Ranger training, yet public reactions remain skeptical, if not outright disbelieving. No woman, it seems, could *possibly* pass this physically and psychologically grueling course on her own merit.

This incredulity threaded through my discussions with research participants, as they, too, wondered whether women could make it through Ranger School, Navy SEAL training, infantry training, and the like. I argue that such comments are tinged with deep-seated anxiety about how women's inclusion and performance might upend beliefs about the inflexible and absolute embodied differences between (cis) men and (cis) women. Interviewees, including those who supported the DADT repeal and even those who had already worked with women on the front lines, spoke with a sense of doom and described the impending "disaster" of women's entry into combat roles. The diversity value-add that they celebrated in their responses about open LGB service was tossed aside, and sudden cynicism about the motivations behind diversity efforts came rushing into their narratives. Repeatedly, I heard that ending women's combat exclusion was a *very bad idea*—it was costly, risky, and illogical, political correctness run amok.

Women servicemembers, who personally battled sexist assumptions about their inferiority for service throughout their careers, were about as likely as men to oppose women in combat, largely reproducing the gendered rhetoric of exclusion. In conversations about the DADT repeal, not a single LGB cadet, servicemember, or veteran believed homosexuality was a reasonable disqualifier for service. Yet here I met women cheerfully enumerating the reasons they were unqualified for combat.

In this chapter, I show how the same misogyny and femmephobia that serve as guardrails against the potential "problems" of open LGB service are revealed in the ongoing horror with which women's combat service is regarded. Gender normativity can help some gay and bisexual men reach enough escape velocity to overcome femmephobia, but women cannot use that strategy. In fact, many participants dropped the logics of inclusion they used to support open LGB service when it came to the combat question. Their logics of *exclusion* centered on biologically determinist explanations of sex and gender and on concerns that political correctness was a dangerous disruption to the necropolitical order of the US military.[5] These explanations are driven by patriotic paternalism, the ideological system that leverages imperialism, militarism, and male dominance in the name of protecting women, calling on women themselves to acknowledge that their natural inferiorities would prove disastrous—even deadly—to their fellow servicemembers, to the military's might and repute, and to the security of the United States.

Liberal feminist activism, as we saw in the last chapter, has largely responded to patriotic paternalism by challenging only the element of male dominance, leaving the rest unquestioned. What's more, the homonormative bargain has rendered gay rights complicit with this system, foreclosing possibilities of coalitional resistance to the militarization of LGBT and feminist politics. In what follows, I analyze patriotic paternalism's effects on women's service experiences and on the ways servicemembers narrate their resistance to combat inclusion. Before delving deeper, a caution: unlike with the DADT repeal (in part 1) and transgender military eligibility (in part 3), I was not able to interview any direct beneficiaries of this policy change. That is, I did not speak with any women who have chosen to serve in newly opened combat roles. My analysis is only able to assess the meaning-making process of those who had not (at least, had not *yet*) seized the opportunity made possible by women's combat integration.

"IT'S STILL THE GOOD OL' BOYS GAME"

As one of the first women out of West Point, an out lesbian veteran, and a key organizer in the fight for trans inclusion, Sue Fulton's experiences are a microcosm of the gender and sexuality transformations in the US military. We discussed the repeal at length, then our conversation turned to the question of women in combat. By this point in my research, I had heard from many respondents who were supportive of LGB inclusion but strongly opposed the end of combat exclusion. When I expressed my curiosity about her take on this contradiction, however, Fulton gently—and rightly—corrected my naïveté:

> It's a masculine culture. It's a misogynist culture, in many ways. . . . And you'll find it in LGBT veterans, too, the bias against women. It's just very deeply rooted. "Join the Army and be a man." I'm not a sociologist, but I have a lot of thoughts about it—yeah, that [contradiction you're hearing] doesn't surprise me. Listen, I've had women at West Point say to me, "Look. My problem isn't that I'm gay. My problem's that I'm a woman. I'm a woman in the Army." Women in the Army, women in the Marine Corps. "I don't have any problem being gay, nobody cares. What sucks is that I'm a woman."

I may have over two decades of sociological training, but Fulton had her own decades of experience. Her sociological analysis did what mine was struggling to do: identify misogyny and LGB acceptance not as a contradiction, but as the logical outcome of a bias against women so pervasive that it crosses the homo/hetero binary. Even under the mountain of evidence I'd been gathering on the operationalization of the homonormative bargain in military service, I had lost sight of the terms of that bargain: removing feminism (along with antiracism, anticapitalism, and antiwar views) from the agenda, reducing liberation for all to attenuated rights for some. Abhorrence for women and all things feminine was so essential, so inexorable, that aligning against it was understood as a losing battle. As documented in queer of color theorist Roderick Ferguson's history of gay liberation, the movement was actively severed from the civil rights and women's movements of the time.[6] White supremacy and male domination may rely on the suppression of homosexuality, but to the extent that white gay and bi cis men pitch in on efforts to suppress femininity, they have been allowed to join the party.

When Hank (30, Black trans straight man, veteran) served in the Air Force, he was, in his words, "female identified" within an organization of "mostly heterosexual white males—it's not the most diverse branch of them all, let's be honest." He continued, "Which is another reason why it's the 'elite' branch, because it's still the good ol' boys game." Homophobia was not at the top of the list in terms of what disadvantaged him in this context:

> I dealt with other issues—I guess there was really not even any time for it to be any LGBT issues, because I was having to deal with the fact that I was Black and female identified [at the time]. LGBT didn't even hit the surface,

> because that wasn't even what was the matter of focus. I think that's why I said that I didn't really have to deal with it like some other people did, because I had to work with a bunch of white guys all day. I had a different spin on things. Sometimes, I said, I'd almost rather I had to deal with some other LGBT issues versus some of what I had to deal with on a daily basis.

LGBT issues, by comparison, seemed like a luxurious form of discrimination to Hank. Black and classified as female, he was "always, always, always, always, always" assigned his unit's grunt work. When he came out of basic training, he went for "almost six months without a direct supervisor, because I was virtually invisible." But visibility, when it arrived, wasn't great, either: "I got into some trouble . . . because I was not taught what I was supposed to be doing." In the absence of direction from supervisors, his aimlessness attracted the angry attention of a high-ranking airman. Though a peer had made the "exact" mistake just a week before, "He was a white kid and didn't get in trouble, but I got in trouble for the same thing. It's crazy." Going before the squadron commander to plead his case, Hank was met with an "extremely angry" response when he revealed he didn't know who his supervisor was. He'd made the squad—and thereby, its commander—look bad. "It all went bad from there," he sighed as he recalled the backlash. "That was a very, very, very long six months." Even so, "I can only imagine how much worse it would have been if any LGBT issues would have been coupled with what I had to deal with on a day to day with that."

Sociologist Stephanie Bonnes calls experiences like Hank's a form of raced and gendered "bureaucratic harassment."[7] Per Bonnes, bureaucratic harassment attempts to derail or terminate women's military careers through the manipulation of administrative processes. By assigning Hank grunt work, leaving him unassigned, and punishing him unduly, institutional actors pushed him out of the service. Hank linked this treatment to racialized sexism; by comparison, homophobia and transphobia didn't even rate.

Degrading the Standards

As I conducted interviews, the end of combat exclusion had not materialized any changes to PT standards. On the contrary, the Army Combat Fitness Test, or ACFT, would go on to raise the readiness standards for all. Still, the possibility that including women would mean lowering standards was a common preoccupation. Cara (22, white cis straight woman, Army ROTC) was typical in this regard:

> My biggest concern with allowing [women in combat], especially with things like Ranger School and stuff, is I think there is a huge discrepancy between physical strength, male and female. . . . We already do adjust standards for things like the PT test and that sort of stuff, but if you're going to ask them to be in those roles, I think they have to rise up to the same standards as males, and they need to be treated 100 percent the same. I do think some females can do it. I think it's a very, very small percentage. I think it's costing a lot of time and resources to figure that out.

Nancy (59, white cis straight woman, Army) also made a cost-benefit analysis as she worried about the logistical expenses of gender integration in combat:

> If you're in the infantry, and you're out marching across the desert for hours on end, it's real easy for a guy to stop and take a leak, but it's not so easy for us to do that. It's the simple things in life like that that you've got to think about. . . . The logistics of it are hard—legally, you have to have different sleeping quarters, you have to have different bathrooms, you have to have different showers. Those are huge logistic things to try to figure out when you're up on the front line somewhere and you don't have a lot of room. . . . For the military to try to make it work and make it work the way it should, I think it would be very, very difficult.

To these respondents, it seemed nonsensical to devote scarce resources to accommodate a vanishingly small number of fully qualified women. Kyle (51, white straight cis man, Navy veteran) insisted, "I'm a pragmatic person. I think that if it works, it's right. If [a woman is] qualified to do it, she should be in it!" What worried him was, "If that unit's going to have a higher injury rate because of it, that's going to affect material readiness, operational readiness." I asked, "Are you worried that these changes will mean that unqualified women will be put in the position?" Kyle replied: "Not unqualified, but . . . less qualified, I suppose," then added, "the side effect or after effect could be one that affects operational readiness."

Holly (white cis straight woman, Army veteran, no age given) explained, "I think there's some things that women shouldn't really do. I think it's great that they can and were able to do it, but sometimes positions like the

Rangers or snipers are . . . it's hard for females to go into an environment like that." Cal (42, Black cis straight man, Marines veteran) hedged "personally, I wouldn't mind it, just to stay equal," but then said:

> It's not quite the same when you get out there and are physically doing it. Your mindset is a little different when you're in combat. If they're in a combat role and that role is to drive the truck to get the bullets for the front line and *that's* a combat role, okay. If that person's vehicle is destroyed and they have to fight their way out, yes that's a combat role, but to be part of a group kicking down doors, jumping over walls, maybe hand-to-hand combat with the enemy? I think those roles should remain male, in my opinion.

These last two comments are inflected with patriotic paternalism. Both Holly and Cal profess to support women in combat, but in terms that could be read as patronizing (e.g., "it's great that they can"). They use distancing language to avoid the appearance of sexism ("personally, I wouldn't mind it, just to stay equal") while also communicating women's unfitness ("there's just some things that women shouldn't really do"). As he did in the case of open LGB service, Cal preferred the compromise that preceded the policy change, as evidenced by his references to the hairsplitting over women's work on the front lines. Driving a supply truck was acceptable, for instance, maybe even dealing with that supply truck being attacked, but being a woman would be an obvious hindrance when it came to kicking down doors, jumping over walls, and hand-to-hand combat.

Melanie (28, white cis lesbian woman, Army) took a different tack, bringing up worries that combat integration would lead to women's conscription. Clearly, the same fears about drafting women that were used to kill the ERA in the late 1970s were still in play.

> The only problem I see . . . is stuff like females being forced to sign up for the draft. Because, I'm sure you can relate, where you've met some females that just totally—you would never see them in the military. The fact that you would have your life dependent on that person in wartime, I just don't like that.

The possibility that combat integration could result in drafting women for war was too dangerous for Melanie's taste. She solicited my agreement as someone who "can relate" to the unfathomability of putting American lives in the hands of "some females." In our discussion, she conceded that exceptional women who can meet the physical and mental standards of combat should be able to do so; the bigger problem for her was that opening combat would mean ungendering the draft (not used since 1973), and women *as a whole* aren't up to the job of warfare.

An Idea Whose Time Has Come

The more full-throated supporters of women's combat service emphasized, in their interviews, the past accomplishments of women in partially closed and formerly closed occupations. Amanda Simpson, former deputy assistant secretary of defense for operational energy and the first openly transgender presidential appointee, exclaimed, "Women have been going on combat tours, in 'noncombat roles' for the last ten years plus! . . . Just, wake up!" Sabrina (38, white cis straight woman, Air Force) agreed: "In my opinion, there's no line in the sand and in the wars that we're fighting today that say, 'Okay. Now, you're in combat. Okay. Now, you're not.' I mean, as time has proven, if you're driving a truck *anywhere* in Iraq, you're in the combat zone." Pamela (33, white straight cis woman, Navy veteran) enthused, "I think [it's] amazing. It's about time. Women have been allowed on submarines, I think, for the last five to six years, maybe longer." On the question of women in Ranger School, she added, "There are women that are going to go in there and they're going to kick butts, and those guys aren't going to know what to do with themselves."

Another supporter of integrated combat, Alyssa (34, cis straight woman, Air Force, race not given), simply objected to the arbitrary use of sex as a qualifying requirement:

> I am deeply of the belief that the best people for the job should be chosen and that "best" is not reliant on your genitalia. It's not reliant on whether you wear a skirt or pants. . . . I think that most of the reasons that have historically been given for keeping women out of combat roles are not good reasons. I think they are not valid reasons. I don't want to go into combat myself, but I didn't think the law should be what's telling me that I don't go into combat. I think that should be based on my own capability and my own wishes.

Regardless of their support or disapproval for the end of the combat exclusion, most of the women I interviewed were like Alyssa: they had no personal interest in serving in combat. There were only two exceptions, and they were on opposite ends of their career trajectories: Cassie (22, white cis lesbian woman, Army ROTC) was about to graduate and become an officer at the time of our interview, and Lily (white cis straight woman, Army, age not given) had recently become a reservist after fifteen years of active duty.

In their final year, ROTC cadets are evaluated and assigned to different "branches," or categories, of service types: infantry, armor, finance, transportation, and so forth. Cassie would have liked to have "branched infantry," but her graduation year was wedged between the announcement and the formal enactment of the end of combat exclusion. As a result, she found herself in the aggravating situation of having just missed her opportunity:

> I was a little frustrated. I wanted to branch infantry, but it's not open [to women yet]. There are men in my battalion here who got to branch infantry and they had a lower score [on their evaluations] than me, which is really frustrating. That means that we *don't* get spots by merit. . . . The first wave of females who go through are going to have a hell of time.

Cassie also raised the point that closed occupations limit women's earnings. She lamented, "Infantry servicemembers get promoted at a faster rate, so it is discrimination, because their possibility of being a general officer some day and mine, I'm definitely lower." Because Ranger School *was* now open to women, Cassie decided her best course was to enter Army service as an officer in a noncombat position, then apply to the highly competitive program. Excitedly, she told me, she planned to "beat all the boys to get in."

If Cassie was a little too early, Lily was a little too late. Lily said she had experienced a long career of sexist microaggressions and exclusion, but that the opportunity to complete Ranger School would have made it all worth it:

> If [the end of combat exclusion] happened ten years ago, I'd be the first to sign up for that. . . . All the bad things that I have to deal with on a day to day basis—people that don't want women around, people with bad attitudes, drama, whatever—it would be worth it to me to get to that end stage, to be able to complete one of those programs [like the Rangers].

LOGICS OF EXCLUSION

Their Bodies Are Not Built for It

Most who argued against combat inclusion underscored their belief that gender equality was, on the whole, a worthy goal. Their disapproval wasn't about discrimination, they said, but the biological "reality" of female bodies (which was interchangeable for them with "women," despite the reality of women with different embodiments than they imagined as female). Somewhat sheepishly, Jesse (22, white cis straight man Army ROTC) admitted, "I've gotten in a lot of arguments with people over it when I'd say, 'I do not think women should be in combat arms.'" He continued:

> The reason why is I think women are at a disadvantage—and it just sucks, but that's the way it is—you know, it's hard for *me* to load the Howitzer with the hundred pound shells and do fifteen per setting and stuff. It's just hard, and a lot of women, quite frankly, just can't do that. Their bodies are not built for it.

Laura (21, white cis straight woman, Army ROTC), too, "worr[ied] about the strength thing; a chick is not going to be able to carry a guy up a mountain with 100 pounds of body armor." To her, women are strong in *different* ways: "You'd be surprised how many men don't realize, oh yeah, like, women are strong in their hips and men are strong in their chest." Still, she doubted women could "meet the standard of helping some big dude if they got shot." Jackie (22, white straight cis woman, Marines) agreed: "I don't think women should be in the Infantry or Special Forces." It was "not that they can't hack it physically. . . . [T]here's definitely females out there who can do it," she said, but added:

> There's a lot who can't, because at the end of the day, our bodies are made differently. To get as much muscle as an average male, I have to work twice as hard as they would to build up as much muscle as them. Our bodies just aren't built the same.

It was curious to me that servicemembers like Jackie would support a blanket ban on women in combat even as they acknowledged that some women *can* meet the physical fitness standards demanded of infantry work. Jackie's admission that she could meet the standards if she was willing to "work twice as hard" as men implicitly acknowledged that sexed bodies are produced through social forces. They are made—and can be remade—through the repetition of movements and practices; these repertoires of movement are what produce "male" and "female" bodies.[8] Research has shown, for example, how transgender men use bodybuilding and weight training in self-remaking after lifetimes subject to the different bodily expectations associated with their sex assigned at birth.[9] Despite her implicit acknowledgment of the social construction of and malleability of sexed bodies, Jackie felt women were better off being excluded entirely.

Participants who used biology as a rationale for exclusion sometimes relied on science to legitimate their position, even if they did not actually know or accurately understand that science.[10] Michael (22, white cis gay man, Army ROTC) told me, for instance, that men "have the testosterone" and "various chemicals" that "make them stronger than women." The current science on testosterone shows that it is, at best, one small, relatively unimportant factor in the complex web of biological and cultural interactions that affect strength, yet its relevance to the popular imagination of dichotomous sex difference gave the mere word explanatory power.[11]

Even medical professionals like former doctor Edward (73, white cis straight man, Army veteran) spoke inaccurately about sex difference. For most jobs, he argued, it is fair to impose gendered fitness standards: "It's appropriate. If you're going to require everybody to do pushups, it is *fact* that women have less upper body strength and more lower body strength than men do; it's reasonable not to require as many pushups for Jane as for Joe across the forest." His invocation of "Jane and Joe across the forest" signaled some familiarity with pop evolutionary psychology explanations of male/female difference. Then, drawing on his authority as "both a clinician and a male," Edward outlined the different motivations women and men bring to their work as servicemembers:

> I do think that the role of intraspecies aggression—which is what the military is—has a different meaning for men and women. I think that [women's] decision[s] to be involved in the military revolve around either or both of [these two reasons]: one is, it made rational sense for their career, a very "left hemisphere" kind of decision, and the other is they desperately want to serve others, which is a wonderful reason to be involved. I think that for

> guys, both of those may be operative but I think there's a hormonal reason that is not there for the women. . . . I think that for a lot of [men], and I'm one of them, I'm going to be very, very honest, the concept of being in that role, that role play of the person who is carrying a weapon and is defending something, that's very hormonal for a lot of guys. I don't think it's as hormonal for as many of the women.

Edward believed women lack an evolutionary and hormonal instinct for aggression and protection. Women join because they "desperately want to serve others," as is befitting their supposed natural role as supporters and carers. Although he professed to believe women are equal (but different), Edward agreed with the "right-wing guys in the military" who "worry that the standard will be diluted" by gender integration.

The more unexpected use of biologically essentialist logics was when respondents described their opposition in terms of *men's* inability to work with women on the front lines. Men's inherent drive to protect women puts others in danger; their uncontrollable (hetero)sexual urges make them more easily distracted. Participants combined biological and sociological explanations, arguing that a combination of instincts and social experiences will lead men to neglect their assigned duties in the presence of women. Holly, for example, reported:

> [Women in combat] could be a distraction, it could be a danger, it could be anything. . . . It's always going to be a male reaction to try to protect the female, because it's always been like that. In a way, that can also be a distraction in the mission. . . . The female can probably do the job, it's more of—the male's going to want to protect the female because it's always been like that. They have a mom, they have a sister, they have a wife, daughters, whatever it is. It's always been like that. A male—it's always been—wants to protect the women.

In Holly's explanation, it's men, not women, who are incapable of putting the mission before their bodily or affective needs. Participants with diverse service and life experiences were united in the belief in cis men's instincts to protect women, either out of tradition or biological imperative. In addition to her skepticism about women's physical fitness, Nancy, who served for thirteen years, brought up "the mentality of the men," musing, "Are they going to be trying to protect the women amongst them, because that's what they're trained to do as a guy?" Meanwhile, officer-in-training Sean (20, white cis straight man, Army ROTC) called upon the evidence of his own so-called male instincts as evidence:

> Initially, they didn't have [gender integration] because they feared that, just, instinctually—say you're in a fire fight, and in your squad, the woman goes down, the military feared the men, instinctually, would go try to help the woman instead of focusing on the mission itself. Which, if it was a guy, you might react differently, which I understand. As a male, I understand why that might be a problem.

Patriotic paternalism didn't just position women as in need of protection on account of their sex, it positioned men as innately, constitutionally protective by virtue of theirs.

Another common lay interpretation of the evolutionary psychology of sex difference concerned the idea that men are driven to protect women in order to protect their access to sexual gratification from those women. Former Marine Cal said:

> You're depending on your other person to watch your back. Not to say that a female can't shoot a gun and watch your back, it's just the mindset of a guy who's been out in the field for two, three months out in the dirt, and the female is being shot at over here, and you need to be protecting the guy over here getting shot at, what's going to go through his mind is, "There's a female I can maybe get. . . ." I'm going to protect the female, because in my head that's what. . . . Basically, that's "my piece" that I'm protecting. . . . If you're stuck out in the bush, the dirt, for months on end. . . . Your mind's not the same, so you're thinking of where's my next chance, and if she's it, I'm going to protect her, because he's not my next chance. . . . I think the women would become a distraction.

Fellow Marine Jackie posited a similar hypothetical:

> If you're a woman in the field right now, you're one out of three hundred and, generally, I wish it wasn't this way, but it is. Men are going to fight over you and then, say you have sex with one and then have sex with another, and they start fighting and stuff, that's going to ruin my camaraderie. Those are the people who are going to war, who are getting shot at, getting killed and stuff, and you can't have that. At the end of the day, I'd like to be able to say that you can keep your personal and professional life different, but most of them can't. I think it will just cause problems and get people killed.

I will return to the idea that "most of them can't" separate their personal and professional lives, but for the moment, let's focus on the commodification suggested by this logic. In the classic feminist essay "The Traffic in Women," Gayle Rubin argues that the social construction of sex and gender established women's sexuality as a precious commodity, bought and sold through patriarchal kinship systems. "From the standpoint of the system," Rubin explains, "The preferred female sexuality would be one which responded to the desire of others, rather than one which actively desired and sought a response."[12] One year later, Dorothy Dinnerstein's *The Mermaid and the Minotaur* made a similar argument: the gendered division of reproductive labor gives rise to psychosexual dynamics that lead men to demand women's sexual exclusivity and women to mute their own sexual desires to meet men's.[13] These depictions of sex, gender, and power lend an eerie familiarity to Cal and Jackie's hypothetical scenarios, in which women are not desiring subjects; they are barely subjects at all. More accurately, they are sexual objects to men, nothing more than "my piece"—an odd counterpoint to Holly's notion that men are protective of women because they have moms, wives, and daughters, unless put in the context of commodification and transfer through male affordances.

This story, of course, involves the assumption of men's and women's innate heterosexuality, as well as the complete unwillingness to consider that not every straight man and straight woman actually want to have sex with each other (let alone during combat deployment). These kinds of hypotheticals rely on the "caveman mystique," a set of pop-Darwinian claims that both define and excuse men's behaviors as evolutionary holdovers.[14] Their irrepressible heterosexuality is at best misguided chivalry, if not an artifact of a cruder Cro-Magnon masculine instinct for which they can hardly be blamed. Cal and Jackie were far from alone in this particular dramatization of heterosexual dynamics; it is a common trope in arguments against women's combat service. You may recall from the previous chapter a *Washington Post* opinion piece critiquing the policy change, in which columnist Kathleen Parker called "sexual tension" a "most delightful distraction in civilian life."[15] She continued, in that piece, "But in close quarters, where men likely would vastly outnumber the few women who qualify for combat, other human emotions—envy, jealousy and resentment—enter into a fray that's already complicated enough." Parker allowed that women were "not to blame for men's weaknesses"; no, "both sexes are equally responsible for—or perhaps I should say, equally victims of—Nature's own agenda."

Unfortunately, it *is* the case that women are at heightened risk of sexual assault in the military, especially during deployments and in units where gender ratios are heavily skewed toward men.[16] This may mean that combat is a context of increased vulnerability to sexual assault for women. However, this is *not* the phenomenon that's being narrated here; in fact, these explanations contribute to rape culture, asserting that "men's weaknesses" aren't a matter of personal accountability but evidence of "nature's own agenda." The fixation on women's sexual availability does not protect women, but rather objectifies and disempowers them—they aren't servicemembers, they are door prizes.

In an even more egregious example, the president of the misleadingly named Center for Equal Opportunity, Linda Chavez, argued that the human rights violations at Abu Ghraib were the result of women's ill-advised presence. Political scientist Timothy Kaufman-Osborn wrote of her argument:

> Chavez suggested that [Lynndie] England's participation in the abuse at Abu Ghraib can be explained by the mounting "sexual tension" that has accompanied "the new sex-integrated military." Because that stress produces hormone-crazed soldiers, which "in turn undermines 'discipline and unit cohesion' (2004), we should not be unduly surprised when those in uniform occasionally release their pent-up passions by sexually abusing their captives."[17]

It is a painful irony that servicemembers demand that LGBs corral their sexual desires on the job, not even daring to *think* queerly, to return to an example from chapter 2. If straight men are unable to remain undistracted in life-or-death circumstances because of their uncontrollable sexual instincts, shouldn't *they* be restricted from combat? Why are women, by virtue of their assumed sexual availability, a threat to life, liberty, and the very project of American sovereignty?

Patriotic paternalism was also at play when respondents argued for exclusion on the grounds that women in combat would be uniquely vulnerable to an enemy's use of rape as a tool of war. "What if they're captured?" Nancy asked. "The things that are going to happen in captivity are probably a lot worse than even some of the things that would happen to the men, as far as rape and things like that." In point of fact, men do experience sexual violence as prisoners of war, though that reality is a poor fit for the women-in-peril, male-patriot-to-the-rescue narrative. Further, Nancy said, "The people fighting us [in the war on terror] have little regard for the women in their lives." That is, she invoked the geography of combat as an implicit shorthand for the imaginary of Muslim terror. Kathleen Parker's *Washington Post* column covered similar ground, with the provocative rhetorical question, "What happens to women when they're captured?"

> We know what happens. Will our men be able to withstand the screams of their female companions as they are raped and tortured? Eventually, we'll avert our eyes from footage of a young woman's tortured body—someone's wife, mother, daughter, sister, or lover—as she is crucified, burned, or beheaded in the name of God knows what. That will be a day no civilized nation should have invited upon itself.[18]

In this Orientalist fantasy of barbarism, the "civilized nation" of the United States has failed its women—and thereby its patriotic paternalist duties—by allowing them within arm's reach of those who would torture them "in the name of God knows what." In yet another moment of sickening irony, it must be acknowledged that women (and men) *were* tortured in the name of God knows what—at the US military's Abu Ghraib prison and elsewhere. Lynndie England, the former Army Reservist convicted, with ten other servicemembers, of war crimes in 2005, was released from incarceration in 2007. In 2009, she gave an interview that included the following:

> [*Did she see any women prisoners?*] "At one point, we had four. Oh my God, this one, she was crazy. They had to take her to the loony bin. We called her the wolf lady because she had all this hair." She starts laughing. "She was screaming and whatever." [*Did she see any photos with women prisoners in them?*] [Her lawyer] says, "The only thing I know is that someone got in trouble because he had had some contact with one of them." England snorts and says, "His *dick* had some contact."[19]

In discussions of the military's gender and sexual politics, homonationalist fantasies (see part 1) juxtapose US sexual exceptionalism against a projection of Muslim men's brutality, a wildly hypocritical projection in light of the facts. Saving women and homosexuals from the regressive cruelty they experience in the Middle East is a compelling and widely shared motivation for continued US military occupation.[20] Comingling this homonationalism with patriotic paternalist beliefs about American men's chivalrous, protective instincts and the imagined perversity of the Middle East has become a potent argument against women's combat inclusion. One need only point to a gut-wrenching, if wholly imagined, scenario in which a US patriot is distracted from his savior's mission by his instinct to protect wrong-headed, physically inferior women from sexual violence at the hands of the enemy, to unspeakably disastrous consequences.

The Dangerous Business of Political Correctness

Across the spectrum of interviewees' concerns, the prevailing sentiment was that in ending the combat exclusion, the military was bowing to the political "optics" of gender exclusion and, in the process, sacrificing operational readiness. Equality and readiness were treated as mutually exclusive goods; gender equality was a worthy (or at least acceptable) goal, but its cost was too steep to stomach. Like Jesse, Sean said that he'd "gotten into a lot of arguments with people" over his objection to women in combat: "I've had people accost me for it, but this is a matter of life and death for people. . . . The military is not some politician's social rights playground where they can try and earn points with special interest groups by advocating for policies that may end up getting people killed." Add Hank to the list of those who felt their reservations about women in combat made them unpopular: "I've been criticized by fellow trans individuals for being too old fashioned and misogynistic." His response? "I'm alright with that. I'm alright with certain things being traditional, because certain categories and certain roles were set in place for reasons, and that's all right. That's not saying that women are not as strong as men, but some things women just shouldn't do." The military, Hank believed, "is fishing for air, they're just swimming around in a pool with a weight on their leg." The weight, in this metaphor, is the belief that the military is too old fashioned and out of step with contemporary politics. As a result, he said, "they're just trying to find any point to, I guess, kind of stay relevant."

Because of this desperation to "stay relevant" and appear politically correct, some say, military officials are manipulated into relaxing standards for women servicemembers to keep up with political correctness.

Kyle recalled that in his day, sailors would grouse that "'In my Navy we—you know—'men were tough and they were on ships,' and blah blah blah. 'There's no way women can do my job.'" As he paraphrased his colleague's worldviews, Kyle adopted a mocking tone, employing a similar distancing strategy as others did when talking about sexist beliefs. Then, however, he pivoted to the first person:

> There *are* women out there who do justify that type of thought, too. I've met them. They try to get their male counterparts to do the heavy work for them so they don't have to. They bat their eyelashes and say, "You know, I'm just not feeling too well today. Could you pick up those 100 pound shells and carry them for me?" "Oh yeah, sure thing."

These opinions weren't the artifacts of a bygone generation; they were shared by even the youngest respondents within the sample. For example, ROTC cadet Jesse believed that women cadets manipulated the assessment system through flirtation and exploited men's fears about being accused of sexism. During exercises, he said, "The assessors were never there, and a lot of the girls who were just ditsy—not very good leaders at all—got some of the top marks because they bat their eyes and joke and be funny around the assessors." When the assessors were present, he said, "A lot of times I see men assessors fear giving a female cadet a bad rating," worried others might retort, "Well, you just think she's a bitch."

Cal used the same logic in explaining that political correctness was thwarting supervisors' abilities to correct women's mistakes, to the detriment of the military's standards:

> Policies have changed so much, so fast, that now if you're in the wrong and someone corrects you, the command is so scared of losing their jobs or being put in the spotlight or the news somehow that they're going to put the person who's correcting the problem under the microscope to make sure they're not doing something wrong. Basically, if you try to correct someone, now you've got to explain why. You've got to go through the whole system instead of just correcting and moving on. Now it's such a hassle that you don't want to correct anything. You just let things slide that you know you shouldn't

> because it's much easier. That's happening a lot. People aren't correcting the wrong because you're put in a situation as if you're in the wrong.

In her own hypothetical, Crystal (37, white cis straight woman, Air Force) positioned herself as the manipulator:

> Let's say I [signed up for Ranger School], go through the training, but I'm cut because I can't carry someone fifty yards or I'm not able to run with my gun and shoot at the same time. My feelings are hurt because I was cut. I start thinking, "Maybe they cut me because I'm a woman, not because I can't do this. Maybe I made someone upset. I have too many emotions for them. They don't like women who have their period on the fourth week of the calendar year." . . . Instead of maybe the person saying, "Okay, I legitimately could not do this," they make it the other person's fault. They start pointing fingers, instead of taking ownership.

In fretting that women might falsely lob accusations about sexism, Crystal leveraged sexist tropes about women as physically weak, overly emotional, irrational, and conniving. The precision of this example highlights its ridiculousness; women will use *anything* to point fingers and avoid taking ownership. Crystal's example suggests the deep internalization of misogyny, in that she positions herself as the blameworthy woman in her imagined scenario.

But where Crystal positioned herself as the manipulator, Christopher cast himself in the role of the aggrieved victim of women's exaggerated sensitivities. He said he was called to the carpet for telling a woman in his command, "You know, you can't drive like a girl, you got to beat the hell out of [the gearshift] to make it work for you." He continued, "Apparently, I hurt her feelings and she went to my leadership, who came back to me." Although he received only a slap on the wrist for this offense, later he believed it contributed to "a political move" in which he lost his position as team leader "for condoning sexual harassment in the battalion." Christopher thought it was a highly successful accusation "because [sexual harassment] is one of those taboo things that you can't touch" and leadership had become "afraid to take action against a woman." He explained, "The government says you have to connect and you can't discriminate, so people go overboard to not be in the 'line of fire.'" When a woman on his team could not meet PT standards, he said, Christopher asked that she not be deployed with his team, only to be told "You've got to live with it." Though Christopher remembered replying, "No sir, I don't want to live with it; she's going to get herself killed or someone else killed," he knew it was no use. "She was a woman. They're not going to go against a woman." As a result:

> The whole deployment, she was a pain in the neck. She was just smart talking, she was always out sick with injuries, I can't use her for missions, she's not reliable. I couldn't let her drive when I did use her for a mission because she'd always get in an accident. She shouldn't have been there. Had it been a man, I could get rid of her; because it had been a woman, it's like leadership was afraid to make the right decision.

The pressure to be politically correct, say such critics, creates an environment in which people are "afraid to do their job, afraid to be a leader, then that causes the problem." To Christopher, it was about the demand for diversity creating dangerous conditions—about advancing people on the basis of their race or gender rather than their excellence. In fact, he went on to share a story about an inept commissioned officer who was promoted, despite poor performance, because "he was Black or Islander, something like that" and leadership feared being accused of racism almost as much as they feared being labeled sexist.

KEEPING WOMEN IN LINE

In the previous chapter, I reviewed the literature documenting the no-win situations that arise as women servicemembers navigate the military's masculinist culture. My interviews confirmed and added evidence for this pattern. For example, Pamela (33, white cis straight woman, Army and Navy veteran) recalled that sexism in the early 2000s Army was "full blown, in your face," with commanders willing to openly say, "Oh, you can't be on the front lines because you're a woman. You can't do this because you're a woman. Oh, you can't do this." She continued, "Granted, I can't carry a fifty-pound pack on my back, I can't run at the same speeds," but "there are women that will take on a man any day of the week and will level them." Not that it did them any good; Pamela said the response to women who passed PT standards was, "You know what, you're just trying to outdo the guys, and you're not good enough anyway." Women who met the male PT standard were scorned as "trying to push [themselves] up" and "trying to be more manly than anything." Pamela concluded, "You can't win either way."

According to women still serving at the time of their interviews, it has become a little less socially acceptable to say such things directly to women servicemembers, though the beliefs are still there. Army reservist Lily said that no matter what women accomplish, "some males are unwilling to accept that information. In reality, they just will not chew it and swallow it. Just will not." The really tricky part, she said, was that now that it was frowned upon to say that out loud, women like Lily had to wonder about "what is said when I'm not in the room." For some men, "you can just see it, you can read it right on their faces," but it's the "little sleeper cells of misogyny that you have to look out for," she told me. These dynamics compel women to carefully manage any display of emotion on the job. For example, Maryann (31, white cis straight woman, Navy) explained she has to be strategic when her authority as an officer is threatened:

> I know that I'm a female, and a lot of people are going to be like—whether we like it or not, people are like, "Oh, females, when they get mad, they're just emotional." I knew that that was that kind of stigma, so I was like, I can't yell, scream, cry. I can't do any of that shit. I had to come about it very calm, cool, and collected.

Men can express anger openly, because it accords with martial masculinity, but according to Maryann, women cannot. Women's anger was too readily used to confirm demeaning sexist stereotypes.

In chapter 3, I discussed queer social control in the context of the DADT repeal, noting the processes by which LGB servicemembers are reminded that tolerance toward their sexuality is conditional. Women servicemembers experience gendered social control that takes similar forms, with conditions including constant emotional management and navigating processes aimed at keeping women in their place. Sexual harassment and assault are among this arsenal. For example, Holly filed a sexual harassment report after she "woke up [one night] and one of the sergeants was trying to rub my back." Although she "freaked out and jumped" out of bed, he continued to "make me put my cot—it had to be next to him." When her report was ignored, Holly said that "it sucked, because I didn't do anything wrong," but "I didn't care after a while; I'm like, 'Whatever, it's only a deployment, I'll end up going back home and back to my life.'" The routine mismanagement of sexual harassment reports normalized both sexual harassment and the overlooking of it as inevitable features of the institution: women needed to put up and shut up (or get out).[21]

The sexual culture of the military was shocking for Maryann when she joined her first ship. In accordance with a tradition of rating women's attractiveness with "ship scores," she recalled, "I would walk by and I would hear them go, 'Well, you know, dude—ship score, she's probably like a 7, but civilian score, she's like, a 4." She understood she was supposed to dismiss it: "I kind of chalked it up to 'guys are going to be guys.' They're probably saying shit behind my back. As long as they do their job, I don't really care. That was my mentality." In 2017, when Jackie was interviewed, the Marines United scandal had just broken. Jackie explained that Marines United was a private, men's only Facebook group where servicemembers would post "pictures of females they would get, nude photos and stuff, without their consent" and would write "dirty things about them or like 'Uh, this bitch, blah, blah, blah fucked this person, broke my heart'—basically it was like revenge porn, kind of." Other Marines and vets would comment under these posts with "really aggressive stuff like, 'I'd rape the shit out of her'; they were causing stalking problems, stuff like that." In her own experience, Jackie said, she proudly posted a photo of herself and a friend in uniform on her social media, only to see it copied and "posted to this Facebook Page called 'Wooks, Boots, and Pogs":

> Wooks [is] a dirty name for female Marines, Boots are new Marines, and Pogs are every Marine that's not an infantry or special forces Marine. There was someone who commented on [the picture]. A lot of stuff is mean, but someone commented, "This looks like a 140-pound box of rape, blah, blah." It's scary, and that happens a lot.

In another instance, Jackie's supervising officer, who she said "looked down on his females pretty hard," pulled her aside to chide her for behavior he saw as overly friendly with the men in her unit:

> He's like, "I don't know if you'd want my opinion or not?" I was like, "No, not really," and then he gave it anyway. He was like, "Well, it makes you look like a whore," blah, blah, blah, this, this and that. "Everybody's going to call you a whore."

Jackie said that the same officer scolded another woman for being friendly with a noncommissioned officer (NCO) of her same rank. "Other males in our shop would hang out with the Staff NCO male in our shop, and that wasn't a big deal," but when she hung out with an NCO who wasn't even in their shop, he asked her to stop "because it looks bad, it's all about perception." First, women are sexually objectified by their colleagues, then they are punished for their own objectification; friendships with men make them "look like whore[s]" because of the commodification of women's sexuality and the assumption that all women are sexually available to men.

April (40, white cis straight woman, Air Force) argued that this culture enabled not "just" sexual harassment, but also sexual assault:

> Intimidation is a form of violence. If you have a guy who's intimidating, and every supervisor just decides to deal with him until he becomes a colonel, now he's a real problem, you know? I experienced this firsthand myself. I was never, I've never been sexually assaulted, but I was very openly harassed by a subordinate, and as a young lieutenant—in my office, extremely lewd, horrible comments. I said, "No, thank you, get out of my office, and we're never talking about this again." I never mentioned it to anybody, because I was the officer, he was enlisted. We're always taught that we're the ones at fault regardless of what happens, or regardless of anything, at least at that time. So, I didn't say anything. I handled it. I told him a polite no, I don't want to talk about this anymore. Then, two years later, I was called to a court martial for him, because he had apparently assaulted . . . a number of girls in our unit . . . and the girls in our unit never said anything.

Between victim blaming and nonreporting, April felt that her unit—herself included—had perpetuated a culture of violence.

Courtney (44, Black cis lesbian woman), introduced in chapter 2, served in the Navy in the early 1990s. Once bullied in her unit for being a "tomboy," the veteran reported:

> I got sexually assaulted, twice. My first ship and bootcamp. . . . It is just fighting with all those demons and stuff, just different stuff you have to deal

> with. People who really know me, they were like, "You're different from when you went in to now." I have a friend who knew me before I went in. My best friend, we've been friends since we were six and she was like, "Yeah, you changed." I can only be around people who I really know, and that's when I can be myself. Because if you meet me right off the bat, you'll be like, "No. Just leave her alone." Quiet, until I'm around people who I really truly know, I can be myself. So it is what it is.

When I asked if she had reported the assaults, Courtney replied with an all-too-familiar refrain: "Who are you going to tell? You don't tell stuff like that. You don't tell stuff. I mean, there's a lot of stuff that happens, but you don't tell. For what? They're not going to believe you." This skepticism was amplified by her experiences of anti-Black racism and homophobia. And so she stayed quiet, and got quieter over time.

"My daughter's in the Army now and it's no different," Courtney continued. "I told my therapist, the biggest fear is for what happened to me to happen to her. And it did. The difference is my daughter is small, she's fair skinned, and she's a beautiful girl." Courtney's experience compared with her daughter's demonstrates the colorism of sexual violence motivated by misogynoir, which puts both darker- and lighter-complexioned women at risk.[22] Courtney's skin color and gender presentation made her a target; although her daughter was lighter skinned and more feminine, she was still targeted on the basis of her skin color and gender, just in a different way.

Courtney's daughter reported her assault, which returned to her some sense of control, but now she had to worry about retaliation. Her daughter moved out of the barracks after her attack. "Even though she's a sharpshooter," Courtney said. "She still has those fears that someone's going to try to come get her." When I commented, "That's what trauma does, right? It takes away that ability to feel safe and secure even in your own environment," she replied, "I mean . . . things happen to people. You just got to figure out how you're going to deal with it." She concluded, "You just got to be tough about it, but once you get out, you see how it affects everyday life, how it messed you up." Courtney, who lived in fear under DADT, said that although "you can be as gay as you want in the military now," being a Black woman remains as much of a risk as it was twenty or thirty years ago. Today's military, she thought, was "less homophobic," but her daughter's experience demonstrated that "it's no different" when it comes to sexual harassment: "You're sexually harassed from the time you get on board to the time you leave. It don't matter."

CONCLUSION

Continued opposition to women in combat, as this chapter has shown, transcends gender, age, sexual orientation, and military branches. To make sense of the tension between respondents' repeal support and disapproval for gender integration, I look again to the homonormative bargain: LGB inclusion, conditioned by homonormativity and homonationalism as described in part 1, is significantly less threatening than lifting gender-based restrictions, the prospect of which evokes sexist anxieties about fairness and standards. Even when participants framed their objections in pragmatic terms, resentments about women's entitlement simmered just below the surface. Patriotic paternalism made it impossible for some to see women as fit to serve, as demonstrated by suspicions that women were being coddled, protected, encouraged, and indulged in the name of political correctness and feminism gone awry. Because becoming a warrior requires deprivation, sacrifice, stoicism, and self-reliance, that (imagined) indulgence was incompatible with the military mythos. In other words, women must have manipulated their way into the ranks using their feminine wiles, because the possibility that women might invade the sacred all-male space of combat and succeed on their own merits is the ultimate threat to men's domination.

The normalization of LGB identity is the shaky ground underneath the sex/gender/sexuality regime that organizes social life. Now that some gay servicemembers have been repatriated into the masculine fold, they are no longer the problem—at least so long as they stay on the right side of feminine abjection. Under this compromise, femmephobia has gained relevance as its own axis of subordination. Femmephobia both punishes gender transgressive gay and bisexual men and redoubles the debasement of women, whether lesbian, bisexual, or straight. They are surveilled and manipulated through social control, especially in the form of sexual harassment and assault. The disparate responses to DADT's repeal compared to the end of combat exclusion might lead one to think of homophobia and misogyny as discrete domains, but this analysis demonstrates both are motivated by femmephobia. In part 3, I illustrate how the sexual logics of inclusion and the gender logics of exclusion, in turn, inform responses to transgender service. Through an analysis of the indeterminacy and in-betweenness of transness in the institution, I reveal the increasing incoherence of gender and sexuality as a unified package of political orientations and depositions.

PART 3 Removing Medical Restrictions on Transgender Service

6 "Once He Saw Them as Soldiers, I Knew We Had It"

THE TRANS BAN TUG OF WAR

Map Pesquiera had dreamt of joining the military since early childhood, even playing pretend in his backyard, eating MREs in between elaborately performed combat scenes.[1] At age 16, Map began taking testosterone, legally changed his name and gender markers, and set out to make his dreams come true: Secretary of Defense Ash Carter had just announced the rollout of transgender military inclusion. After the 2017 inauguration, the Trump administration attempted to reverse Carter's policy and reinstate the trans ban, but the process was slowed by court injunctions, and Map entered the University of Texas as a freshman and an ROTC cadet in 2018.[2] By spring 2019, Map's sophomore year, a US Supreme Court ruling had upended his plans, lifting the injunction on a 5–4 decision.

Under the newly enacted "Mattis plan" (named for its author, Secretary of Defense James Mattis), Map was disqualified for future service. Ostensibly, this wasn't because he was trans; the Mattis plan was not, the administration insisted, a trans ban, but a narrowing of the accession standards for all would-be servicemembers.[3] Instead, Map was disqualified because of the medical diagnosis of gender dysphoria that allowed him to access hormones and gender marker changes.[4] The Mattis accession policy allowed trans recruits to enter only if they had "lived in" their birth-assigned sex for at least three years prior, and only if they were willing to serve according to the regulations associated with said birth-assigned sex, which affect housing, uniform and grooming standards, PT testing, healthcare, and a host of other regulations. While technically these standards did not constitute an outright ban, in effect they functioned as one.

Anxious, Map contacted his ROTC advisor and the DOD to request a medical waiver that would allow him to continue in ROTC and, later, into active service. After months of silence, he received a terse notification: his ROTC scholarship was voided on the basis of medical disqualifications barring him from commissioning upon graduation.[5] A DOD spokesperson said while his gender identity did not determine his ROTC status, his "scholarship offer was contingent upon meeting the standards required of all prospective recruits, which he did not meet."[6] In subsequent media interviews, Map described how he initially blamed himself: "Why did I start transitioning? . . . I should have thought about it and put my transition on hold to make sure I would be able to go into the military and serve my country."[7] He continued:

> I started thinking this is my fault. This is my fault that I'm like this, I don't want to be like this. If I were just cisgender, I wouldn't have to deal with this—and why couldn't I have been born like this? Why did I have to be born trans?

With his scholarship revoked, Map's ability to stay in college was under threat. He started a GoFundMe to cover his tuition and was later presented with a $25,000 check from trans celebrity Caitlin Jenner.[8] Map raised enough money to continue at UT and, in July 2019, reenrolled in ROTC, crossing his fingers that, by the time he graduated, the policies would change and he could commission after all. As of January 2021, Map was still attending UT and serving as a student ambassador for GLAAD.

Map's predicament was shared by many transgender people caught in the space between the Carter and Mattis plans. And this is not a small group: research suggests that trans people are especially inclined toward military service and tend to serve at up to twice the rates of their cisgender counterparts.[9] With the exception of those who were admitted or retained in the very brief window between policies, the return of the ban forced many to serve in silence, with significant costs to their health, mental health, and safety.[10] Those who would not (or could not) were separated from the military for being trans, though a survey indicated the majority still said they would consider returning if the ban was again lifted.[11] Today, an estimated 15,500 trans people are currently serving, both openly and not, and analyses of military attitudes show some movement toward acceptance, especially among soon-to-be officers in ROTC programs.[12]

In this chapter, I trace the history of transgender service. Prior to the Carter plan, the military excluded transgender servicemembers as mentally and physically unfit,[13] an idea both out of step with civilian medical protocols and previously debunked in the specific context of military service.[14] Shortly after the DADT repeal, LGBT policy advocates turned their attention to crafting and delivering trans-inclusive policy changes.[15] The strategy of using social science to disprove gatekeepers' claims in the DADT repeal effort was undertaken with regard to claims about trans people and their medical fitness. That research showed the dangers to trans people of serving in silence, confirmed that they are entirely fit to serve, and provided evidence of their successful open service in other countries' armed forces.[16] Unlike the cases of LGB and cisgender women's service, there are comparatively few histories of trans service in the United States.[17] In the following pages, then, I use interviews with key trans inclusion advocates, trans servicemembers, and trans veterans to recount that history, incorporating the published accounts, DOD transcripts and memos, and news records that have begun to shed light on the rocky, switch-backed path to open transgender service.

Like parts 1 and 2, part 3 also considers the broader social movement strategies and discourses that shaped the possibilities, process, and politics of trans service. In particular, I interrogate transnormativity and its relationship to homonormativity and LGBT politics.[18] The forces of militarism, securitization, and assimilation that marked feminist and gay rights responses to military service also play out in trans politics. Concomitant with the expansion of gay rights, increased transgender visibility and mainstreaming have been achieved through normative politics, but whereas the de-somatization of homosexualities carved a path to acceptance for LGB people in the military, transnormativity has not brought about a de-somatization of transness. If anything, it has done the opposite, solidifying the idea of transness as an embodied condition in need of remedy.[19] Further, trans inclusion represents a more potent threat than LGB sexuality to the heterosexual matrix. As established in part 1, the uncoupling of gender and sexuality achieved through homonormativity did little to destabilize the power of the heterosexual matrix; it instead neutralized the potential gender trouble that increased LGB representation might have brought with it. By contrast, gender self-determination shatters the assumed coherence between sex and gender, leading to forms of gender panic within and well beyond the military. The virulence of specifically anti-trans discourse and policy over the past few years demonstrates the gender panic induced by even modest increases in trans visibility.[20] The similarities and differences between homonormativity and transnormativity have produced different outcomes for those who dream or dare to serve openly.

FROM BOMBS TO BOMBSHELL

"Ex-GI Becomes Blonde Beauty," blared the front page of the *Daily News* in 1952; almost overnight, Christine Jorgenson became the first modern transgender celebrity in the United States.[21] "She represented, in some ways, a figure of the United States," explains gender studies scholar Susan Stryker. "She exemplified the triumph of technology . . . this belief in the power of science to do almost anything. US science can make anything happen, from atomic bombs to so-called 'turning a man into a woman.'"[22] Jorgenson's transition from thoroughly masculine American "G.I. Joe" to glamorous and ultrafeminine "blonde bombshell" captivated the midcentury public, and she was, on the whole, celebrated and sought after. But Jorgensen's popularity was an order of magnitude above "exceptional": her whiteness, middle-class status, and feminine beauty helped the World War II veteran transcend the stigma otherwise attached to transgender people.[23] So, too, did her careful distancing from potential misrecognition as a homosexual or any other type of sexual "deviant." Jorgensen "epitomized something about the United States," according to historian Jules Gill-Peterson, by virtue of "having been at war and by having travelled to Europe and come back as a glamorous bombshell."[24]

Meanwhile, other trans people, especially Black trans women, knew the near-impossibility of approximating the raced and classed "American ideals" that Jorgensen embodied. Indeed, a comparative reading of Jorgensen's press coverage with that of working-class trans women and trans women of color during the 1950s reveals the enormous gulf between their representations.[25] Just two years after Jorgensen's debut, fellow vets Charlotte McLeod and Tamara Rees made headlines for their own gender transitions. Instead of being celebrated as miracles of the atomic age, however, McLeod and Rees were pathologized and sidelined. McLeod's narrative largely matched Jorgensen's, but her lack of middle-class decorum and less-glamorized gender presentation violated the emerging norms around the "good transsexual"; as a result, the media punished her through portrayals in which she was both a failed soldier and a failed woman. Rees, too, attempted to assert herself as a "patriotic domestic woman," but the way she framed her military service—as an attempt to prove herself as a "real man" before accepting her womanhood—made her suspect, something less than a "real veteran," "real man," or "real woman":

> The fact that she was able to succeed at the most "masculine" activities—such as paratrooping—suggested that even the most seemingly "masculine" men might secretly hold cross gender identifications. Jorgensen and McLeod, on the other hand, claimed white womanhood by not only asserting their heterosexuality but also by simultaneously participating in the hegemonic discourse that pathologized homosexuality and gender variance, a strategy that was apparently more palatable to the U.S. mainstream.[26]

Taken together, Jorgensen's, McLeod's, and Rees's media representations are illustrative of the complex interrelationships between whiteness, class habitus, homosexuality, transsexuality, and militarism in the mid-twentieth century.

Accounts of servicemembers assigned female at birth who served as men are sprinkled throughout the late eighteenth- and early nineteenth-century histories of US and European militaries.[27] Nearly always, the revelation of "cross-gender" service resulted in expulsion, but the DOD only officially committed to a policy on transgender service in 1963, a relatively late codification owing to the unsettled definitions around sex, gender, and sexuality in the early twentieth century. As discussed in part 1, the lines between the pervert, the homosexual, and the transsexual were only beginning to emerge in medical discourse. Military screenings for sexual deviance effectively marked all three as unfit for service, although, as previously mentioned, such screenings were selectively and irregularly enforced.[28] Even after Army Regulation 40-501 (1963) defined *transvestism* as a disqualifying "condition," it was not always treated as such. In 1976, Sergeant Joanna Clark was knowingly reenlisted after returning from gender-affirming surgery. An administrator at the Army Reserve Center later told reporters, "I'm the one who enlisted her, and she made absolutely no attempt to hide her background. . . . It didn't bother me one bit. She was the person qualified to do the job we needed done."[29] Clark served another eighteen months before she was discharged, the Army stating that "it is the Department of the Army Policy not to waive this disqualification due to the requirement for continuing maintenance therapy and the high incidence of psychological problems associated with the condition."[30]

In 1983, the medical regulations laid out in Department of Defense Instruction (DODI) 6130.03, *Medical Standards for Appointment, Enlistment, or Induction in the Military*, made the first specific reference to transsexual prohibitions. (The 1963 Army prohibitions on crossdressing were, in effect, the same prohibition, but 1983 marks the shift to regulations that explicitly named a transgender subject.) DODI 6130.03 disqualified potential servicemembers on the basis of "abnormalities or defects of the genitalia, including but not limited to *change of sex*, hermaphroditism, psuedohermaphroditism, or pure gonadal dysgenis" as well as "current or history of psychosexual conditions, including but not limited to *transsexualism*, exhibitionism, transvestism, voyeurism, and other paraphilias [emphasis added]." Later, DODI 1332.14, *Enlisted Administrative Separations*, would identify "sexual gender and identity disorders" as grounds for separation.[31] Similar to DADT, separation for transgender servicemembers included both acts ("changes of sex") and identities ("sexual gender and identity disorders"). The medical regulations of the individual branches of the armed forces followed suit with DODI 6130.02 and 1332.14.

In a review of the regulations used to prohibit transgender service, Elders and colleagues summarized:

> The regulations appear to be justified by notions that (1) transgender personnel are too prone to mental illness to serve, (2) cross-sex hormone therapy is too risky for medical personnel to administer and monitor, (3) gender-confirming surgery is too complex and too prone to postoperative complica-

> tions to permit, and (4) transgender personnel are not medically capable of deploying safely.... Unlike other medical disqualifications,... which are based on the latest medical expertise and military experience, it is the transgender ban itself that is inconsistent with current medical understanding and is based on standards that are decades out-of-date.[32]

As was once the case with LGB exclusion, trans exclusionary regulations relied on a medical model that presumed inherent mental and physical unfitness. However, whereas the medicalization of homosexuality lost credence with its removal from the *Diagnostic and Statistical Manual* (DSM-II) in 1973, transgender was remedicalized through its own series of DSM revisions. In 1980, the DSM-III introduced "gender identity disorder," also called "transexualism," which was itself replaced by "gender dysphoria" in the 2013 edition, DSM-V. Transgender *status* was no longer a mental illness, the handbook revisions indicated. Instead, the disjuncture between birth-assigned sex and gender identity could, under social conditions in which they are expected to be congruent, cause transgender patients to experience psychological distress. Thus transgender remains a medicalized status, even if destigmatized through the move to gender dysphoria diagnosis.

Following the demedicalization of homosexuality, antigay activists and policy makers had been forced to pivot from LGB service objections on the grounds of mental unfitness to objections framed around threats to military readiness and unit cohesion. Those who would prohibit transgender service need not make such a heel turn; the legitimacy of medical regulations excluding trans service was shored up in a series of court cases, including *Doe v Alexander*, *Leyland v Orr*, and *DeGroat v Townsand*, each of which upheld that transition-related healthcare (including administering hormones, gender affirming surgeries and aftercare, and psychological support services) would be too expensive, prohibitive to deployment or stationing away from qualified medical centers, and result in too much lost duty time.[33] The Carter plan introduced late in the Obama administration acknowledged that earlier assessments of the costs of trans healthcare and its effects on deployability were overblown, and it argued forcefully against the anachronistic pathologization of trans people encoded in the exclusionary regulations. Yet soon the Mattis plan would reverse course, returning to these empirically false, transphobic claims.

"WE'RE NOT IN THE POSITION TO DO ANYTHING FOR YOU"

After the repeal of DADT, the push to repeal anti-trans medical regulations accelerated rapidly, led by a small team of dedicated reformers. Because the DADT repeal was hailed as an "LGBT" victory, few (including some trans servicemembers) seemed to notice that the repeal actually had nothing to do with trans people—it did not remove medical prohibitions on transgender service. It is the case that some transgender people were erroneously discharged under DADT, but the policy's end did not mean the advent of open trans service. Sue Fulton, who played a central role in the fight for trans inclusion, explained: "To allow gays and lesbians to serve, what you needed was a repeal of Don't Ask, Don't Tell—a repeal of law. [But] what we needed for transgender service was a change of medical policy. Those are two entirely different paths . . . and [different] people you have to influence." Additionally, the range of sex-based policy details that trans inclusion would need to address was more complicated: "There were no elements of berthing and facilities and medical support [with the DADT repeal]; those things didn't exist for LGB people the way they exist for trans people. It's just completely different issues." Nonetheless, Fulton was determined to capitalize on the DADT repeal. As others asked, "Okay, if we get Don't Ask, Don't Tell [repealed], how many more years before we get trans inclusion?" Fulton recalled, "Most people said it'll be another seventeen years. Almost everybody said it's going to be another ten or twenty years. I was the only person—and you can ask some of the other folks!—I was the only person that said five years. We're going to get this in five years. And nobody believed it. Nobody believed it."

Amanda Simpson, former deputy assistant secretary of defense for operational energy and the first openly transgender presidential appointee, was also eager to keep the momentum going:

> I certainly knew going in that Don't Ask, Don't Tell only affected the Congressionally mandated law, which was about sexual orientation, and that transgender issues were not in *law*, they were in *policy*. So, actually, we literally left the press room [after the signing of the repeal], walked across the hall, and had a little party, reception kind of thing. And we're all like, "Ok, great. What's next?" And I said, "We need to do something about the transgender prohibition." And literally, within a week, . . . a small group of

> civilians at the Pentagon, we got together and said, "So, how do we address removing the prohibition on transgender service? . . . We spent almost the better part of the year putting this together—what are all the [issues], who's responsible for [them], who can change [the ban], what's in the medical regs—it went on and on.

Trans service advocates like Fulton and Simpson hoped that organizations like OutServe-SLDN (the merger of two advocacy groups, OutServe and the Servicemembers Legal Defense Network) would join in; those groups instead applied their post-DADT energies to lobbying for a repeal of the Defense of Marriage Act (DOMA). Brynn Tannehill, a trans open service advocate and member of OutServe-SLDN's advisory board, recalls, "We were pressing them, what's your plan for us? Don't Ask, Don't Tell's over, and by the way—you're giving up on this the week after DOMA gets overturned? You just won your big victory! So, what are you going to do for us?" She said the answer was, "'We're not in the position to do anything for you for at least nine months, and we have no idea what to do.'" Blake Dremann, a trans servicemember on the core organizing team, concurred: "OutServe did not feel that the repeal of the trans ban was a priority." Typical of the homonormative bargain, almost $20 million was spent on the DADT repeal in 2010 alone,[34] and hundreds of millions of dollars were dedicated to the national fight for marriage equality, while the total funding available to trans service advocates was closer to a couple million (primarily from one source, wealthy trans philanthropist and retired Army lieutenant colonel Jennifer Pritzker).[35] The most visible LGBT lobbying organization in the country, the Human Rights Campaign, would later apologize for and begin to address its overall deprioritization of trans rights, but they and others also pushed trans-specific needs to the bottom of their legislative "wish lists" during this period.[36]

In August 2013, a critical mass of open trans service proponents defected from OutServe-SLDN, starting their own advocacy organization for transgender servicemembers, veterans, and their families: SPARTA.[37] Sue Fulton was among its founders, and, true to form, she framed her participation in terms of military-bred ethics:

> I felt this, we had this obligation. There were a number of transgender veterans who fought really hard to get Don't Ask, Don't Tell overturned. Paula Neira at SLDN, Autumn Sandeen chained herself to the White House fence!

> Allyson Robinson at HRC. There are all these transgender veterans fighting to repeal Don't Ask, Don't Tell. We don't leave somebody behind. We don't leave anybody behind. We don't leave our comrades behind. And it just was really important to me, and I couldn't understand why it wasn't important to other people, but there you have it.

According to Brynn, SPARTA's successes depended on having Fulton onboard for the battle:

> [Sue Fulton] was instrumental in everything we did because of her connections and because of her experience with Don't Ask, Don't Tell; she knew how to do everything. She was literally—anytime we walked into a situation, she might not have the academic credentials [that others there had], but she was the smartest motherfucker in the room. . . . I can't say enough good things about her as the one crucial ally who threw her lot in with us. We could not have done it without her, absolutely no freaking way—none. So, if history wants to remember who our allies were, she's somebody . . . [who was] both crucial and somebody who really didn't have a dog in the fight, other than she's not leaving anybody behind. I can't say enough good things about her.

Allyson Robinson, OutServe-SLDN's former executive director, joined forces with SPARTA to push in earnest toward trans inclusion. At the same time, Aaron Belkin of the Palm Center enlisted the help of Lieutenant Colonel Greg Brown, who you'll recall from chapter 1 worked on the DADT repeal for the DOD. Brown fondly remembered, "Transgender inclusion. . . . [N]ot many people at the Pentagon get to inherit a project from the beginning, see it through to the end, and get to do a touchdown dance. [This was] my favorite experience of my military career."

Brown acknowledged, in our conversation, that when Belkin called for his advice about transgender inclusion, he responded by saying something like:

> "I have not formed my opinion on it yet, because this is an entirely different matter [than DADT]. Black people in the military are different than women in the military are different than gays in the military are different from transgender people in the military. I have an open mind, I am a sponge for research and experiences and talking to people. I have yet to form my opinion, but when I do, I will let you know. If you still want me [after that] we can make it work." . . . It did not take long to realize that the Defense

> Department's transgender policies were based on 1950s science and medicine, on 1950s thinking and prejudices.

Compared to both DADT and the combat exclusion rule, few outlets played out the debates on transgender inclusion. Supporters of the ban (both the initial ban and the Mattis plan) cited psychological unfitness; transition-related medical costs; and of course, threats to unit cohesion, readiness, and lethality, yet much like pro-LGBT organizations, the anti-LGBT lobby must have regarded the possibility of open trans service as truly remote. It languished at the bottom of their priority lists, too, well below the fights over marriage equality and LGB military service. Mainstream media and politics paid only minimal attention to transgender rights well into the first half of the 2010s. In this period, there was a relative vacuum of thought leaders organized against open trans service; the Palm Center began publishing a flurry of papers debunking the anticipated objections it knew would get louder once the lobbying got underway.[38] Once again, the research showed that any negative consequences for unit cohesion, operational effectiveness, and readiness would be, as they were after DADT's repeal, negligible.[39] This research, like that cited in the Carter plan, detailed the reasons the current regulations were out of date, including changing medical standards of transgender care and the minimal cost of adding trans-inclusive healthcare,[40] estimated to involve adding just 1/100th of 1 percent to the overall military healthcare budget.[41]

Proponents of trans inclusion argued it would be mutually beneficial for the armed forces and trans people interested in service. The change would, they argued, make the military stronger by improving the health and wellness of the approximately fifteen thousand serving in silence.[42] Transgender veterans, whose barriers to healthcare include the limits of veterans' benefits and the inexperience of veterans' hospitals with caring for aging trans patients as well as high rates of homelessness and high rates of family rejection, would benefit enormously.[43] In fact, supporters argued, it would provide improved health and economic well-being for a broad swath of trans people otherwise denied opportunities to maintain either. It would help affirm the gender identity of trans servicemembers, especially trans men; for example, Adam Yerke and Valory Mitchell posited that service may provide trans men a venue in which to explore, accept, and celebrate their masculinity.[44] And finally, they argued, it would go a long way toward the social legitimization of trans identities, affirming transgender lives and rights to exist as they choose, well beyond the confines of the military.[45]

IF THEY DON'T KILL, THEY DON'T COUNT

During Obama's second presidential term, key stakeholders began meeting on the issue of trans military inclusion. They needed to plan their attack. In 2013, Fulton recalled, "[We] laid out a plan. . . . As our first assumption: if we're going to get this done, we need to get it done before Obama leaves office." From there, the team, Fulton said, "did a timeline and backed into, okay, we need the Secretary of Defense to announce a working group by August of 2015, or we don't get it done." In early 2014, a friend at the White House working on LGBT policy reached out to Fulton, offering to collaborate. That unnamed friend then "helped facilitate pulling together a small group of very influential people inside the government" for a private meeting in which Fulton and Allyson Robinson pitched their plan. Fulton's previous work on the DADT repeal proved invaluable; during the repeal fight, for instance, she and LGB servicemembers had met with Obama advisor Valerie Jarrett, who was so moved by their testimonies that she would later describe the encounter in a speech at the inaugural Pentagon Pride reception in 2016. What Fulton learned in that process was the importance of testimony; to successfully make the case for transgender inclusion, they needed to, once again, appeal to hearts and minds.

The SPARTA team had, at this point, drafted a 148-page document laying out "the recommended policy changes" and the information "you would need to manage every possible detail—medical, berthing, facilities, physical fitness testing, everything." The report included detailed appendices, including case studies of other countries' processes when it came to trans inclusion in their armies. Based on her experience, though, Fulton "knew that [alone] wouldn't do the job." Greg Brown, too, suspected that comparative military data from New Zealand, Canada, and so on would be insufficient to convince skeptics. Bluntly, he said, "If they don't kill, they don't count," meaning that data from smaller, less lethal militaries were likely to be dismissed. Addressing potential repercussions for military lethality was as important as readiness or cohesion to the decision-making process.[46] "What we needed to do was to have them meet trans servicemembers"; "where [else] are they going to meet transgender servicemembers?" Sue wondered. "They might meet a transgender veteran or two, but likely, that person didn't transition on duty." However, the SPARTA team did include transgender personnel who were currently serving.

Next, the SPARTA team parlayed personal connections into an audience with Brad Carson, then undersecretary of the Army (later undersecretary of defense for personnel and readiness). Though he was "definitely a skeptic," Fulton said, remembering that he would say, "'I just don't see how you get this done,'" eventually "he agreed that he would meet with some servicemembers." To prepare, Fulton and the SPARTA organizers "worked with the servicemembers for a while":

> I worked with them on the phone, I worked with them online, and then we brought them in two days early. We spent a lot of time rehearsing their stories, preparing them.... I always had in the back of mind, "What's our ideal outcome?"... My dream, when I rehearsed it in my head, was that when he hears the stories, Brad turns to his chief of staff and says, "You know who else needs to hear this?" And then we get two more meetings, three more meetings, four more meetings out of it. We get to come back. That's my dream: We get to come back.

The day of the meeting, a snowstorm brought D.C. to a standstill. Getting to the Pentagon was slow going, including for Carson. Ultimately, "The good news [was]... [even though] the Pentagon doesn't take snow days, a lot of meetings got cancelled because a lot of people couldn't get in," and Carson's afternoon schedule had opened up enough to accommodate a later meeting. There was ample time for Carson to learn from their first-hand experiences, Fulton said:

> He gave us our full amount of time. And then after everybody spoke, he was incredibly gracious and thanked them. I thought they were all going to cry [because they thought], "Somebody actually thanked me for being me and having the courage."... And then he turns to his chief of staff, and he says,

> "Is Eric [Fanning] in today? What about Laura [Junor]?" And he huddles with her and writes down the names of people. He turns and says, "Do you guys have anywhere else you need to be?" and I said, "Nowhere but here." And he literally—we had two more meetings that day with the undersecretary of the Air Force and with the acting undersecretary of defense for personnel and readiness, which was huge. It was huge.

In Fulton's assessment, the trans servicemembers' testimonies took Carson "from a skeptic to, honestly, an advocate on our behalf, we worked really hard." Buoyed by the emotional impact of the snowbound day of meetings, the SPARTA report gained interest and circulation within the Pentagon.

In February 2015, Ash Carter became Obama's new secretary of defense; just five days later, he made a decision that opened up a clear and immediate path to trans inclusion. During a town hall with troops in Kandahar, Afghanistan, Carter took questions from the audience. The following exchange ensued:

> *Lieutenant Commander Jesse Ehrenfeld*: Quick question for you. What are your thoughts on transgender service members serving in austere environments like this here in Kandahar?
> *Secretary of Defense Ash Carter:* I come at that from a fundamental starting point—It's not something I've studied a lot since I became Secretary of Defense. But I come at this kind of question from a fundamental starting point, which is that we want to make our conditions and experience of service as attractive as possible to our best people in our country. And I'm very open-minded about what their personal lives and proclivities are, provided they can do what we need them to do for us. That's the important criteria: are they going to be excellent service members? And I don't think anything but their suitability for service should preclude them.[47]

As it happened, Lt. Commander Ehrenfeld was the doctor who had treated Staff Sergeant Logan Ireland, a trans servicemember, for a deployment-related injury at the Kandahar station. During deployment, Ireland was able to keep knowledge of his transgender status to only a select few and was able to dress, berth, and serve according to his gender rather than birth-assigned sex. In the documentary *TransMilitary*, Ehrenfeld explained, "As I was sitting there listening to the Secretary of Defense deliver his update, I couldn't get away from this idea in my mind that there was the perfect opportunity to ask him a question about transgender service." Ehrenfeld asked Ireland what he would ask if he could, then posed Ireland's question to Carter.

Asked and answered, it was clear this was going to make it into press accounts of the town hall. Ehrenfeld "knew there was no turning back" from this question, nor from the possibility it could lead to Ireland being outed or having his service record jeopardized. Instead, Carter's answer, assiduously reported by the rather surprised press corps, would be a major victory for Ireland and the trans inclusion team. Ireland recounted, "Everyone in the room looked over [at Ehrenfeld and Carter] and every camera was going nuts!" After the press conference, Ireland had the opportunity to introduce himself to Carter as "one of the 15,000 transgender actively service transgender members in the military." In response, Ireland remembered, Carter said, "This is incredible; thank you for your service and for having the integrity to tell me that," then presented the servicemember with a "challenge coin," a token of esteem given only by high-ranking members of the military and DOD.

Eric Fanning, who at the time was Carter's chief of staff, remembered that critical moment just as clearly. "The talking points would have just had him answer it as a medical question," but instead, "He just said, 'if you can do the job, you should be able to serve,' and boom, off we went!" Recalling the moment as a jolt of electricity, Fanning continued, "That got a lot of people's attention. I was exhausted, propped up in the back of the room, and I heard that and I was like, 'Well, here [we] go!'"

One person who said she wasn't taken off guard by Carter's public claim of support so soon into his tenure as secretary of defense was Amanda Simpson:

> Secretary Carter, first week overseas, the question from the audience. I was not involved in setting that up, I didn't know if it was going to happen until after it happened. Of course, you talk to Eric [Fanning] and he'll tell you that he was caught off-guard, people were like, "Woah, why did Ash respond the way he did?" [But] I had now been working with Ash Carter for three and a half years, in various capacities. I had briefed him on technical issues, he knew me, he knew my background. All the joint chiefs knew who I was. I was the only out trans person at the Pentagon.

The day after the town hall event, Obama's press secretary announced that the president agreed with "the sentiment that *all* Americans qualified to serve should be able to serve, and for that reason, we here at the White

House welcome the comments from the Secretary of Defense." On July 13, 2015, Carter issued a press release announcing a new working group to consider policy and readiness implications of open transgender service.[48] "At my direction," he wrote, "the working group will start with the presumption that transgender persons can serve openly without adverse impact on military effectiveness and readiness, unless and except where objective, practical impediments are identified." Evoking diversity rhetoric, he concluded:

> As I've said before, we must ensure that everyone who's able and willing to serve has the full and equal opportunity to do so, and we must treat all our people with the dignity and respect they deserve. Going forward, the Department of Defense must and will continue to improve how we do both. Our military's future strength depends on it.

The Office of the Under Secretary of Defense for Personnel and Readiness commissioned RAND to assess the implications of open trans service on military readiness and the defense budget. Several such studies were ordered throughout the decades of consideration and reconsideration around gay service, DADT, and women's combat exclusion, but this was the first of its kind regarding trans service. Published in 2016, the report again confirmed the research publicized by the Palm Center and other organizations. It went further, in fact, by demonstrating that the cost of *barring* trans people from service—processing and enacting separations for actively serving trans people and so forth—was unnecessarily burdensome for a military tasked with tightening budgets.[49] The study, in other words, made plain that excluding trans people from service was already costing the military money—more money, over time, than the changes required to implement full inclusion. As for the argument that transgender people are psychologically unfit for service by virtue of their gender identity/status, the report asserted the claim was so far out of step with current medical and psychological standards that it did not warrant serious consideration.

Obama's endorsement and Carter's announcement were watershed moments, but there were many more hearts and minds at the Pentagon in need of change. Sue Fulton set her sights on Mark Milley, the chief of staff for the Army, in May 2015. Without him, trans inclusion was dead in the water. For six months, the savvy strategist took every opportunity to get to know this linchpin figure and put trans inclusion on his radar, striking up conversations at a West Point reunion, a luncheon at the vice president's residence, and the Pentagon Christmas party. The legwork paid off when she secured a meeting between Milley and four transgender servicemembers and veterans:

> He gave us an hour for the meeting, just over lunch. They come in, and he starts off—pretty much, he listens to them, but he's like, "Here's the eleven reasons why we can't do this." But he listens to the soldiers, and one of them had actually won her combat infantry badge in Operation Anaconda in Afghanistan under his command. And they're both from Boston and they're talking Red Sox—this is like, he's really hearing everybody. The secretary of the Army has to leave. He stays. The G1 [deputy chief of staff for personnel] has to leave. He comes back, but the chief stays. The chief stayed there for two and a half hours and five minutes of a "one-hour" meeting.

During that meeting, Milley was moved by the story of Army captain Jenn Peace. As documented in *TransMilitary*, Peace's testimony about being misgendered and forced to use men's bathrooms proved pivotal in the chief's understanding of the issue. Alex Wagner, who helped organize the first Pentagon Pride event and worked with Fanning, recalled the story in this way:

> [Captain Peace told Milley,] "To use the bathroom, I have to run across to the exact opposite side of the base to use the port-a-potty that construction workers use." The chief of staff of the Army called up [Peace's] commander [after the meeting] and said—and I'm going to paraphrase, but this is pretty close—"Does Captain Peace look like a woman?" And [the commander] said "Yes," and then [Milley] said, "Then you better treat her like a woman; you wouldn't make any of your other soldiers run to a port-a-potty to use the bathroom." Whether or not he understood what it means to be transgender, it's the idea that one of his soldiers was being forced to do something demeaning, right? The other thing was, he asked, "Who's your best intelligence officer?" And this commander said, "It's Captain Peace" and that was such, I think, such a revelatory experience for him to hear. Here's their best intelligence officer, who is being forced into these inhumane conditions just to live her life, and he felt the responsibility to correct that.

In Sue Fulton's recollection, Milley stated his intention to call Peace's commander at the end of their meeting. "Jenn's like, 'Sir, all due respect, this isn't about me. This is about all of the soldiers.' He's like, 'I know, I know, I know—but I'm calling your division commander because he should be treating you as female." Milley's support was won through the power of personal testimony, and it would prove essential to the SPARTA team's eventual success. Fulton said appreciatively:

> Milley [was] the roadblock; the Navy's on board, the Air Force is on board.... It's all about the Army now. And we turned him around that day. He still had issues—he still couldn't wrap his mind around the open showers, he just couldn't quite get there. But in terms of treating soldiers like soldiers ... this is the thing about all great Army leaders—military leaders—is they love their soldiers. They love their troops. And he expected to see four transgender people, [but] when they came in and were in front of him, he saw four soldiers. And once he saw them as soldiers, I knew we had it, because all this is about soldiers being treated with respect—the other stuff is just details.

Fulton and SPARTA had cleared every obstacle in their path but one: then chairman of the Joint Chiefs of Staff, General Joseph Dunford. "By May of '16, we had had five visits with different groups of servicemembers—five visits and, I believe, ten meetings. Right up until June, when we were trying to get a meeting with [Dunford]—that was my white whale, getting [that] meeting," Sue remembered. But in the end, a Dunford meeting was rendered superfluous: "Out of the blue, we got an invitation to meet with Secretary Carter. We met with him on a Friday, and the following week, he announced an end to the trans ban."

After the inclusion decision was made, it was time to establish the policy regulations that would guide transgender service. At the broadest level, the new regulations required two distinct processes: one for trans personnel who were already serving (retention) and another for admitting new trans recruits (accession). Open service for current trans servicemembers went into effect on June 30, 2016, the date of Carter's announcement. However, implementing new admissions regulations would take more time. Eric Fanning explained the medical criteria established for new recruits:

> You have to be "stable in your target gender," I think, were the words they used. They picked eighteen months, which surprised me—I thought they

> were going to try and hit for twenty-four—and then you're medically fit to go. That undercut one of the arguments [against trans inclusion] right away, that waves of people are going to join the military to get medical care for transition. What kind of person would want to go through that and be in boot camp at the same time? But you have to be "stable" [in your gender] to join. You have to have figured out with your doctor what it is you want and then have eighteen months.

The DOD set the accession implementation deadline of July 2017, a target that was pushed back to January 1, 2018, amid legal challenges from the Trump administration. And in February 2018, the DOD confirmed that the first open transgender recruit had signed a service contract, despite the uncertain future of the inclusion policy.

THE TWEET HEARD ROUND THE WORLD

The status of trans military inclusion was made uncertain with a single tweet, despite the DOD's successful policy implementation. On July 23, 2017, then president Donald Trump tweeted that the US government would no longer allow transgender service, setting off a scramble. *Was this true? Was a policy announcement valid if it came via Twitter? And what about if it directly contravened a formal decision from the Department of Defense?* Every stakeholder I interviewed remembered the day well, especially the mad dash to refute Trump's claims in the media.

At the time, Eric Fanning was taking some time between the end of his previous post as an Obama appointee and his later work as CEO of the Aerospace Industry Association:

> I didn't start this job until this year, I just did what I wanted to do [in the interim]. I'd give a speech, go teach something, or travel.... [When the tweet came out,] I'm in shorts, a T-shirt, haven't shaved, haven't showered. I see the tweet and I close the computer. I went and I showered, I shaved, I put on a suit, and then I reopened the computer. I was on TV all day, I'm like, "Here it goes." [*CC: Tell me more about that day and your emotional reaction to this news.*] I think you run the range. I remember just feeling deflated at first. That was my first reaction, I felt like I just sank into the sofa. That was my first reaction—and then angry, of course, but very quickly, energized and excited because of the reaction.

SPARTA was just as quick to action. After all their work convincing policy stakeholders to repeal the ban, they were well-poised to react when the president suggested it was back. Brynn Tannehill explained, "The good news is SPARTA is media-trained and ready; we looked good on camera and were smart." She continued, "The day it happened, I took the rest of the day off and did *PBS Newshour* and a couple others. Within an hour of it happening, I was mic'ed up and sitting in the newsroom." The rest of the SPARTA leadership was equally on point: "Within 45 minutes of the tweets dropping, the board had our five primary talking points already mapped out." Blake Dremann recalled he had just left his desk for a smoke break when Trump posted his bombshell. Dremann had his response ready within minutes:

> I walk outside and, of course, now my phone is blowing up. And the third phone call I get is from SPARTA saying, "They want you on CNN at 3:00." [I clear it with my boss, then] I run downstairs, talk to the public affairs officer and I'm like, "Hey, I'm getting ready to go on both CBS at noon and CNN at 2:00." . . . I left for the day, I'm in my car, I did two interviews from my car. . . . And I mean, I was doing interviews from the time I saw it on CNN at 9:00 in the morning until 10:00 that night. My phone did not stop ringing. And I was still doing interviews the following day and the following day. We were actually in the news for four and a half straight days, which is unusual in this news cycle.

Also at the ready was Amanda Simpson, overseas on an official trip:

> [When it happened,] I'm in Kazakhstan, I was literally on a flight from the capital Astana to the biggest city in the country, Almaty. Got off the plane, got into the airport, and . . . I turn on my phone, and it just kind of blows up because of the time difference. It's thirteen hours' difference from there. It was craziness. So that night—I'm guessing morning here, the next day, or however it worked out—I'm now doing interviews on my iPad in the hotel room at like, midnight for a couple different Canadian [TV] and other stations. It was interesting . . . but I'm doing all these foreign press interviews while I'm sitting in Kazakhstan. [The tweet] pissed me off, particularly because we had gone through so much to validate that the fundamental rationale for the [original] ban was invalid. . . . To finally hear, "Yes, you can come out, and you get to serve" and then to see that tweet. It's just horribly upsetting, not just for future servicemembers, but those who are outwardly serving. I think Eric [Fanning] has it right; it's not a new ban, it's a purge.

> Because you're taking servicemembers who have been honorably, and sometimes distinguishedly, serving for decades, and now you're saying, "Your services are no longer required."

Initial reactions from Congress and the DOD to Trump's fiat-by-tweet seemed promising. Fanning noted that, on the day of the tweet, "three or four dozen" Democratic members of Congress showed up to a press conference on the Hill in support of continued trans inclusion. Fanning recalled, "I was standing behind the lectern watching these members, all of whom wanted to speak, they wanted to be on the record." He was amazed at how quickly and decisively so many came around to supporting the policy; despite its being a "relatively new concept for most people" that "happened pretty quickly" to outsider eyes, he thought, "[Trump has] actually done the trans community—probably given them a little help here, because the first time many people thought about this thing, they're thinking about them in uniform." He continued, "That's cognitive dissonance for the 70-year-old in Michigan where I grew up, who's like, 'Wait, they're already serving? They volunteered to serve? Well, it's not fair to kick them out.'"

Because the tweet brought attention to the open service policy *after* it came into effect, many people were just thinking about the issue for the very first time. They were, Fanning suspected, "not thinking about the trans thing—they're thinking about the fact that these are patriots." Alex Wagner said the same of military leadership:

> It's a lot easier, when you're a senior general, to prevent someone from putting on a uniform than to say to that person, who you now have a responsibility to, "Take it off," right? It's a totally different thing once they're a part of your [military] family and community and then [you] kick them out for no reason.

Wagner thought a policy reversal like that impossible, at least in what he called the "normal world"—in other words, in a political context in which a president doesn't simply fire off a tweet and undo years of carefully researched policy making and implementation. "How these policies come about," Wagner explained, "is you need buy in, but of course, this administration didn't feel like it needed to even talk to any of the senior uniformed officers before it made its politically motivated decision, trying to socially engineer its own way."

Mark Milley, once so resistant to open service, took a public stand against the trans ban tweet, Sue Fulton mentioned:

> If you go and look at the video of Mark Milley after the Trump tweet, he's speaking at a luncheon and talks about "We are now and will always treat *all* our servicemembers with respect, period, bar none." And I can hear in that his steel resolve, [which] started with seeing those trans soldiers.

Many anxious observers trusted that Trump's tweet, in the face of DOD reticence, was nothing more than political grandstanding that would have little effect on open service. Blake Dremann was among several who mentioned their attempts to calm themselves down: "I figured that they couldn't retroactively—well, my first reaction was 'Okay, it's just a tweet. There's no policy, there's no directive to the actual DOD to make this happen.'"

Just weeks later, in August 2017, the National Council of Labor Relations and GLAAD filed a lawsuit against the Trump administration (*Doe v. Trump*), setting off what would become a protracted legal battle over the legitimacy of Trump's pronouncement. On August 25, 2017, Trump issued a memo titled *Military Service by Transgender Individuals*, ordering Secretary of Defense James Mattis to set up a plan for implementing his exclusionary order with a deadline of February 21, 2018. Meanwhile, three similar suits were hot on *Doe v. Trump*'s heels: *Stone v. Trump*, *Karnoski v. Trump*, and *Stockman v. Trump*. Together, all four cases successfully sought injunctions against implementation.

In December, the DOD convened a panel of experts to review the policy transition. At first, that panel included a number of the senior Pentagon leaders who had been involved in removing the medical regulations. According to *With Honor & Integrity: Transgender Troops in Their Own Words*, this seemed like a promising start to the SPARTA team:

> "With the exception of a few individuals, the reception given to the service members was warm," recalls Lieutenant Colonel Bree Fram, one of the members called to speak. Each member recounted their story of open service and answered a question or two, before being thanked for their service. Fram, as the senior-most member present spoke last and closed stating,

> "The only thing we desire is to be treated like the soldiers, sailors, airmen, Marines (and Coast Guardsmen) that we are. We don't want special status; we don't want to be a different class of citizens. We want to serve."[50]

Things changed dramatically when the panel's director was replaced by the new Trump-appointed undersecretary of defense, Robert Wilkie: "Thereafter, the panel focused on writing a report that contained talking points straight from the ultra-conservative Heritage Foundation and deeply anti-trans author Ryan Anderson."[51] The committee's report would ultimately form the basis for the revival of the trans ban.

The subsequent Mattis plan severely limited but not *technically* ban transgender service by using gender dysphoria as a diagnostic criterion in medical assessments. Because courts have consistently upheld the principle that the military may restrict employment on the basis of medical "conditions" in ways that would be illegal in civilian employment, the Mattis plan disingenuously used trans healthcare needs as the mechanism by which they could be turned away.[52] It was a cruel way to exploit the heightened risk of depression, anxiety, and suicidal ideation that result from living as trans in a violently transphobic world, an inversion in which the mental health conditions symptomatic of abuse and repression are instead used as evidence that trans people are unsuitable for service, maybe even a danger to others.[53]

Under the new regulations, servicemembers who were diagnosed with gender dysphoria after the Carter plan but prior to the Mattis plan were allowed to continue to serve in their gender, but all others were either disqualified from service or made to serve in their birth-assigned sex. As for new entrants, the Mattis plan allowed for accession of recruits "with a history of gender dysphoria" but only if they had detransitioned, had been living in their birth-assigned sex for thirty-six months prior to enlistment, and agreed to serve *only* under their birth-assigned sex.[54] The memo reasserts a "clear line" between male and female troops, defined by birth-assigned sex. For new trans servicemembers, serving under these conditions would include deadnaming; revoked access to gender-affirming healthcare; and sex-segregated uniforms, grooming standards, housing, berthing, and showers that do not correspond to their gender. That line is necessary, per Mattis, because it "promotes good order and discipline, steady leadership, unit cohesion, and ultimately, military effectiveness and lethality because it ensures fairness, equity, and safety." That "fairness, equity, and safety" is defined by strict sex segregation and the "protection" of people assigned female at birth from the most punishing of physical standards, which they are assumed to be incapable of meeting. In essence, Mattis's memo states this book's thesis in plain language: misogyny, transphobia, and the stalwart maintenance of the sex/gender binary remain the core values of the military institution, even as gay friendliness is integrated into its ethos.

For a little over a year, the injunctions issued in the *Doe*, *Stone*, *Karnoski*, and *Stockman* cases held, preventing the implementation of the Mattis plan. In April 2018, Trump requested these injunctions be dissolved but was denied by the DC Circuit Court of Appeals by late summer. Trump then filed a cert before judgment asking the Supreme Court to hear the *Doe*, *Karnoski*, and *Stockman* cases; on January 22, 2019, the Supreme Court issued a temporary stay on the injunctions in two of the cases. They did not consent to hear those cases during the current term, thereby allowing all four cases to continue winding their way through the lower courts.

In the meantime, bills to overturn the ban were introduced in the House and Senate, and transgender servicemembers testified before the House Armed Services committee.[55] These efforts were rendered moot after the injunctions were lifted, and the DOD enacted the Trump trans ban regulations on April 12, 2019. The four cases—*Doe*, *Stone*, *Karnoski*, and *Stockman*—remained ongoing, joined in March 2020 by *Doe v. Esper*, a lawsuit filed by GLAAD and the NCLR on behalf of a transgender naval officer facing involuntary discharge.

Throughout the 2020 presidential campaign and after Trump's defeat, trans inclusion advocates directed their arguments toward incoming President Biden. In turn, he declared removing the trans ban a "day one priority." Indeed, Biden signed an executive order rolling back the Mattis plan five days after his inauguration, on January 25, 2021; the DOD announced the return to trans-inclusive retention and accession standards in March 2021. This time, the celebrations were far more muted than in 2013, the events that followed Trump's tweet having shown that, without further legislative action, the capricious whims of a more conservative future administration could dissolve trans military inclusion with a few keystrokes. As of this writing, SPARTA's organizers are lobbying Congress, aiming at legislative action that could end the political tug-of-war over open trans service for good.

THE AMBIVALENT EFFECTS OF TRANSNORMATIVITY

The specific constellation of interactive gender expectations that trans people must navigate is what I have called "doing transgender" in previous work.[56] While all people "do gender," transgender people are held to different sets of expectations about how they should properly enact and express their gender compared to cisgender people.[57] Sociologist Austin Johnson calls this "transnormativity," the "specific ideological accountability structure to which transgender people's presentations and experiences of gender are held accountable."[58] This structure is informed and supported by the medicalization of transgender, treated as a condition in need of remedy by medical, psychological, and legal authorities. Over the course of the twentieth century, the pathologization of transgender as a moral failure or mental illness was slowly (painfully slowly) replaced with a more affirming medical model. The current model treats transgender as a benign form of human variation that *can*, but does not always, require medical interventions to help trans people modify their bodies to suit their gendered needs. Without discounting the ways that trans medicine offers some trans people more livable and satisfying lives, critics of trans medicalization object to the gatekeeping it can engender.[59] To the extent that one's transgender status is only considered legible and legitimate if deemed so by the right experts, trans medicalization eclipses the universe of ways that trans people might otherwise do transgender. It has had a conservatizing effect on transgender politics and social movement strategies, corralling them with boundaries that look similar to the restrictive structures of homonormativity. The good transgender citizen should be passable, productive, and patriotic.[60]

The relationship between homonormativity and transnormativity is complex. This stigma-mitigating work of homonormativity displaces the gendered deviance of the homosexual onto the transsexual/transgender subject, thereby relying on transphobia and trans exclusion to assert itself.

It was in fact transgender activists who first articulated the homonormative critique, initially as a way of referencing the prioritization of "homo" over trans needs and voices within LGBT organizing.[61] Homonormativity's "straight acting" aspirations implicitly endorse the "realness"—and rightness—of men's inherent masculinity and women's femininity, thereby reinforcing a cisnormative set of gender expectations based on sex assigned at birth.

Homonormativity also encourages the deprioritization of the concerns that most directly affect the most vulnerable trans people—poverty and criminalization—and positions trans people as threats to LGB progress.[62] As but one example, gay rights power players in the protracted fight to pass the Employment Nondiscrimination Act (ENDA) resisted transgender-specific protections at every step.[63] Representative Barney Frank, the politician who sponsored ENDA, cut trans protections from the bill multiple times and continues to criticize trans-inclusive nondiscrimination legislation, saying: "I would say ridiculous trans activists are outraged [by their exclusion], who would prefer there be no rights for employment than this. That is an example of their political stupidity."[64]

Perhaps because homonormative social movement strategy has held most transgender people at arm's length, some trans activists have leaned into a similar political model. Dean Spade writes:

> In the 1980s and 1990s, and even somewhat in the 2000s, the gay and lesbian organizations that were forwarding the inclusion strategies, which operate on a politics of respectability that says "we are good citizens like you" and tend to represent people whose lives align with the racialized and antipoor norms of US morality, explicitly excluded trans people. After years of trans advocacy, as trans politics mainstreams, we are seeing a growing articulation of a trans inclusion politics that mirrors the gay and lesbian inclusion framework, and an ongoing debate about whether that is the right path.[65]

In many ways, then, transnormative politics look similar to homonormative ones, especially pertaining to military inclusion. The centrality of medicalization, however, introduces a crucial difference between homonormativity and transnormativity in terms of their history, goals, and outcomes. Homonormativity's success required the de-somatization of LGB status to establish the discursive conditions under which homosexuality is unexceptional and therefore unobjectionable. By contrast, transnormativity reinforces transgender as *quintessentially* somatized; the body is held up as the primary site of transition, so that transgender people are deemed incomplete without medical intervention. These opposing uses of the body help explain the differences in the reception I documented regarding policy inclusions for LGB and transgender service. To achieve its de-somatization, homonormativity required a divestment from gay liberation's embrace of gender nonnormativity. The move to gay rights reinforced the gender binary by implicitly endorsing masculinity as a property of maleness/manhood and femininity of femaleness/womanhood. Because of the relational and hierarchical relationship between masculinities and femininities in this binary system, homonormativity is inherently femmephobic, perpetuating the abject status of femininity. This has a disciplining effect on trans people, who trouble the presumed naturalness of the connections between sex, gender, and gender performance. As a result, homonormative politics are also inevitably cisnormative, even when they purport to be trans inclusive. No matter how transnormative politics mirror homonormativity by embracing respectability, assimilation, and militarism, trans people remain a potential threat to the homonormative bargain's continued success.

For cisgender lesbian, gay, and bisexual people, cooperation with the expectations enforced through queer social control—desexualized, depoliticized, and gender normal—has carved out some room for them in the deeply gendered organization of the military. It facilitates their incorporation into the intimate spaces of the military's same-sex living arrangements and into misogynistic military culture: remove the barriers to open service and just drag and drop LGBs from the closet to the convoy without missing a beat. Meanwhile, trans service introduces a more significant element of gender trouble—the gendered institutional logics sidestepped on the path to LGB service. *What should determine the classification of a trans servicemember as male or female? What about trans people who are neither male nor female? Which trans bodies belong in what uniforms, PT standards, showers, barracks? Can trans men be folded in as "one of the guys," or should they be made to run the gauntlet that grants some women "honorary male" status? Is it still OK to cross-dress for traditions like crossing the line, or will trans inclusion kill off such sacred rituals in the name of political correctness? Will trans service undo the gendered sorting of personnel, and would that mean demoting the privileges afforded to men and masculinities?* LGB servicemembers can be brought in line with the heterosexual matrix, but in this historical moment, trans servicemembers cannot.

The policy details of open trans service proactively attempt to remedy most of these "problems." Transgender accession standards require medical certifications and waiting periods between treatment for gender dysphoria or medical transitions and military entry. Trans applicants are even required to present legal documents that certify their gender: updated birth certificates, identification documents, or a court order establishing their legal right to live in their gender. These restrictions all but ensure obedience with transnormativity. First, they require a medically supervised transition and the accreditation of their gender by medico-legal authorities. Second, they establish the expectation that one's (trans)gender will be both stable and legible by cisnormative standards of gender expression. Together, these points ensure the gatekeeping of more unruly forms of transness that might be more threatening to the gendered organization of the military. And third, the restrictions reestablish the inevitability of the male/female binary by requiring the closely monitored movement of trans people from one to the other. Even under trans inclusion policy, nonbinary people must still serve in their birth-assigned sex, regardless of their gender.

Anti-LGBT organizers may have been caught unprepared the first time the trans ban was rescinded, but today the backlash against transgender rights is visible, organized, and growing. The seemingly endless march of anti-trans legislation across the nation is itself an engine of transnormativity, scaring trans people into compliance with the dictates of the "acceptable trans subject" in order to escape persecution, violence, and restrictions on their freedom of movement.[66] For example, anti-terrorist measures such as the Real ID Act pose a threat to transgender US citizens by making it more difficult to amend identification documents to fit their gender (the very documents required as evidence should they wish to join the military). To maintain freedom of movement, trans people must submit to securitization, which positions domestic, white, non-Muslim trans people as good citizens, safe travelers, and willing patriots in contrast to the gender deviants elsewhere who might well be terrorists in disguise.[67] Nurtured by homonormativity and neoliberal feminism, securitization induces trans people into compliance with what trans studies scholar Toby Beauchamp calls the surveillance state.[68]

In their meditation on the trans necropolitics that grant some communities life through "the ghosting of poor trans people, trans people of color, and trans people in the Global South," gender and sexuality scholars C. Riley Snorton and Jin Haritaworn are wary of positioning trans people as "first and foremost victimized."[69] And as Laurel Westbrook has also pointed out, the essentializing of trans life as inevitably defined by violence and victimization inadvertently creates more barriers to a livable trans life.[70] Accordingly, I am wary about treating transgender people as merely the victims of gay rights and feminist political repertoires. Yet it is crucial to acknowledge that the choices that have secured open LGB service and women's participation in combat are inseparable from how open trans service is received. To identify those connectivities does not foreclose concomitant critiques of transnormativity's own "complicities and convergences with biomedical, neoliberal, racist, imperialism projects."[71] For this, the insights of trans of color critique are essential. Such a critique, per historian Jules Gill-Peterson, "insists on naming, following Susan Stryker, the 'spectacular whiteness' of transsexuality as a colonial form of knowledge whose claims to jurisdiction over trans life must be contested."[72] The effort, Gill-Peterson argues, necessitates a "decolonial framework to think of transgender and sexuality as imperial formations of knowledge that circulate transnationally, but unevenly, across the Global North and the Global South."[73] This trans of color critique realigns trans politics with anti-imperialist and antiracist movements.

And of course, such realignments exist in queer and feminist scholarship as well. Queer, trans, and women of color critiques together illustrate how gender and sexuality are used to produce global racial formations that justify the subjugation of and violence against subaltern populations.[74] In this context, "what makes sense for trans politics is to be aligned with anti-war and anti-military movements worldwide." As Dean Spade reiterates:

> We have nothing to gain for being the new poster children for a US military branded as inclusive because it lets women serve in combat and has openly

LGBT service members. This is shoddy window dressing for the realities of US militarism, which is bad for the world and certainly bad for populations, like women and LGBT people, who are targets of sexual and gender violence.[75]

CONCLUSION

The conditions of trans service require adherence to transnormative logics that make it as palatable as possible for cis servicemembers. Yet as the next chapter shows, servicemembers' acceptance of trans service still lags behind their acceptance of LGB service. In particular, transphobia and femmephobia manifest in the projection of cisgender anxieties about trans inclusion (within and beyond the military) onto trans women. The swift comings and goings of open trans military service have created an unstable policy context at a time when civilian policies regarding trans employment, housing, and bathroom access are similarly unsettled. Fiona Dawson, *TransMilitary* filmmaker, remarked to me in 2017 that this chaos results in stunning inconsistencies. At the time of our interview, she said, trans people "can have a pee in Kandahar, but you can't use the toilet in Target." She continued, "You can sacrifice your life in a war zone, but you can still get fired in at least twenty-nine states."

The policy context is an effect of locating transness in the "borderlands," to borrow from Gloria Anzaldúa, between gender and sexuality politics.[76] Although transgender discrimination is about gender, it is also discursively coupled with sexuality-based discrimination through the ubiquitous formulation of "LGBT." Existing in this space in between/within gender and sexuality discourses, trans status is subject to clashing logics of inclusion and exclusion. Analyzing this liminality through the ambivalence of policy reception will clarify a number of adverse consequences that accrue when we divide gender politics from sexual ones. However, life in the borderlands is not all bad. It enables the development of what Chela Sandoval has termed a differential consciousness, which allows for the "weaving between and among" various modes of opposition to hegemonic norms, including "the pursuits of equal rights, revolution, separatism, and reappraisal of the value of the oppressed."[77] In the next chapter, I posit that a trans epistemology grounded in differential consciousness will provide the "trapdoor" we need: a way out of the mirrored, distorted funhouse of militarism that divides coalitional potential through gender and sexuality politics and a way into a more robust critique of the miseries of global racial capitalism.[78]

7 "You Can't Have Three Bathrooms at a Forward Operating Position"

GENDER PANIC IN THE TRANSGENDERING ORGANIZATION

Chase, a 33-year-old Latinx queer trans man, joined the Air Force in 2006, straight out of high school. After he came out as queer at age 17, his father was abusive; the military seemed like the best way out of a bad situation. "Joining the military was something I never thought about growing up," he explained, "but it was more of something I felt I had to do" to escape. While he was struggling to keep his head down, finish high school, and find a way out, he "happened to see a few recruiters at school." When the recruiter brought up DADT, Chase brushed it off—he was "already used to trying to hide."

"I wasn't thinking about [DADT] when entering. I was just so focused on getting away, that I was like, 'Well, if I have to, I'm going to do what I have to do to leave and to get something started with my life.'" That approach worked for a while. Chase loved the structure of boot camp and did well in technical training school. However, a seemingly inconsequential conversation about spousal benefits—he was unmarried at the time—brought it all crashing down:

> I got this feeling in my stomach. My stomach just dropped. . . . It really hit me that I had just left a homophobic home into a homophobic institution,

> where not only can I not talk about the person I love, but I could lose my career if I do. It just hit me so hard. Literally my stomach was turning, and I was like, "Oh my gosh, what did I just do?" And then I thought, "Well, I have nowhere to go, so what [else] can I really do [but endure]?"

Although the repeal was announced toward the end of his first contract, Chase had already decided to leave because of that feeling of disillusionment. After his discharge, though, "I missed the structure, I missed putting on my uniform. I missed that camaraderie—it's so silly, but I even missed building tents." After the DADT repeal went into effect without incident, Chase thought, "Well, now I can just show up as my authentic self." This time, he entered the Reserves, where he thought he could find a "good balance" between his desires to serve and to follow other civilian pursuits.

During that time, Chase came into his identity as a trans man. The formal end of the trans ban was still a year away when he told the members of his Reserve unit about his gender. Chase was elated that he was met with support. Soon, though, he discovered that even though he was out and accepted as transgender, the institution still treated him as female:

> I was out, I was the first trans person out in my unit. I was out, so I said, "Oh my gosh, I'm going to wear a tie, the male blues uniform, I'm going to wear it." And they were like, "But your gender marker hasn't changed." . . . Also, my hair wasn't in regs because on my deployment, I had grown my hair out and it was in a ponytail. So, it was [with]in female regs, but it wasn't in male regs. They were like, "You're not in [male] regs and your gender marker hasn't changed." Then I said, "Okay, well, fine. I'll wear the female blues uniform with the pants." And they were like, "But you can't wear pants to the ball. If females aren't going to wear pants to the ball, you have to wear that ugly skirt." I [had been] so excited . . . and I had just got promoted to tech sergeant, I'd just got my new ribbon. I was like, "Oh my gosh, I'm excited, I'm going to have my partner by my side." And they were like, "Nope, you can't do it like this," because this and that, and, "Nope you can't do this [either]," because of this and that. I was really heartbroken, because I was looking forward to going to the ball. I ended up going, and I had a great time—I just had to wear civilian clothes.

Chase was caught between the dichotomous standards of male and female regs and between the consideration and implementation of trans-inclusive policy change. He took an early leave on his contract and planned to come back after open trans service was fully implemented. Chase figured it would be fairly pro forma: "Great, trans folks could serve openly, let me get this together, I'll talk to the commander and I'll just go back in." Instead, Trump's tweet and the subsequent reintroduction of the ban thwarted his plans.

Chase was aware of the misogyny paradox and the discourses of patriotic paternalism identified in part 2 as well as how they informed the antipathy to women's combat participation.[1] With open LGB service, he said, people are able to shrug it off: "Oh well, they are gay. That doesn't bother me because we're still here, just doing our job." Women, however, seem to remain bothersome. The normalization of sexual harassment and assault of women within the institution—tools of social control—lead to excluding women "for their own good." Chase explained:

> This sums up the military's mentality. . . . "We're protecting her. We're looking after her." But you're not saying anything about these men, your battle buddies who are capable of raping somebody, of harassing somebody. . . . We need to be telling men, "Don't rape." We need to be telling people, "Respect people, leave them alone." We need to be teaching people about consent.

Women in combat earn their place by virtue of their "bad ass" abilities, said Chase, and their presence should in fact "increase ability and morale." But instead of dismantling the rape culture facilitated by the misogyny paradox, women's exclusion from the front lines is the solution prescribed by many.

The in-betweenness of Chase's personal service experience is in some ways emblematic of transgender service itself, floating somewhere between the logics that garnered support for the repeal and those that informed the antagonism toward women in combat. That tension was omnipresent throughout the interviews: *Is the removal of barriers to trans service like the end of DADT, or is it like the end of barriers to women's combat service?* The discursive grouping of "LGBT" symbolically links transgender rights to gay rights; accordingly, open trans service seems a natural complement to open LGB service. On the other hand, because transgender is about gender, not sexuality, it makes some sense that it would be actively resisted alongside combat integration. In all these ways, trans servicemembers have experienced a long period of literal and symbolic liminality: between male and female regulations, between sexuality and gender ideologies, between inclusion and exclusion (and back again).

In this chapter, I show how trans service is narrated by servicemembers. Respondents employ the same sorts of discourses of tolerance, diversity, and professionalism as they did with the repeal of DADT, as well as the same sorts of biology-as-destiny framings applied to women in combat. Their accounts document the sense of trans inclusion as a threat to the gendered organization of the military. In my previous work, I have shown how "doing transgender" is distinct from the process sociologists call "doing gender" because the latter, as both a theory and a process, is implicitly cisgender at its foundations.[2] Just as doing transgender potentially disrupts the flow of gendering interactions, transgendering the organization disrupts institutional gendering practices. Thus, in the following pages, I analyze the "transgendering" of the gendered organization using the quintessential case: the US military. The *transgendering organization* is doing transgender, but at the institutional rather than interactive level. As a transgendering organization, the military is both engaged in transgendering work (altering its sex-segregated policies, facilities, and practices to incorporate transness) and, on a metalevel, is itself transgendering, in the etymological sense: moving "across, beyond, through, and on the other side of" its own "assigned" sex and gender as a male, masculine, and cis institution. As the transgendering organization calls into question the spatial, visual, and regulatory processes that maintain and naturalize sex/gender difference in a highly sorted space, trans incorporation becomes a source of gender panic. Before going further, it must be acknowledged that as a word, *transgendering* bears an uncomfortable resemblance to the use of *transgenders* and *transgendered* to refer to trans people, which is generally to be avoided for the ways it objectifies and disempowers. That said, it is analytically important to show how, just as institutions are gendered, they can also be *trans*gendered—and in the case of the military, to show how they engage in transgender*ing* work via the ongoing, active accomplishment of transitioning its fundamental sex/gender logics. There is a meaningful and necessary political distinction to be made between calling *people* "transgendered" or "transgendering" and using such a term to describe an *organization* engaged in the process of making or doing transgender on an institutional level. For these reasons, and after much consideration, I have made a conscious choice to maintain the wording "the transgendering organization" for this concept, despite its potential for initial misrecognition.

I close this chapter with an analysis of a few "magnified moments" that stood out in interviews with trans servicemembers.[3] Like Chase's moment, these illustrate the consequences of transgender's liminal institutional position. Alongside its harms, liminality can help some trans servicemembers resist gendering organizational processes and critique the primacy of visibility in LGBT social movement strategy. These forms of "trans knowing," though they emerge from participation in an institution that perpetuates forms of queer and trans violence across the globe, function as crucial interventions in the growing dissonance between gender and sexuality politics.

THE SAME DIGNITY AND RESPECT

Greg Brown, who worked on both the DADT repeal and changes to medical regulations for trans service, noted a difference between the policies in terms of readiness impact: "I was not then nor am I now convinced that [trans inclusion] has the same impact as [repealing] Don't Ask, Don't Tell, or that this is just the logical next step" after open LGB service. "Everything we did in repealing Don't Ask, Don't Tell passed the military readiness test," but for open transgender service:

> If you do the cost/benefit analysis, I believe you *can* make a case that the military readiness [concern] is [valid]. For Don't Ask, Don't Tell, you could not make a case that it wasn't in the military's best interest. [With] this, there are facts that you could say aren't necessarily pro-readiness.

However, Brown said, because the regulations that prohibited trans service were based in "1950s science, 1950s medicine, 1950s thinking, and 1950s prejudices," they had no business in twenty-first-century policy. Ultimately, he believed both policy changes were about supporting "great Americans who have been and are serving their country," and in that respect, they had equal footing as issues of fairness.

Crystal's (33, white cis straight woman, Air Force) comparison of the policies led her to predict differences in terms of reception: "I think [transgender people are] going to have more challenges than just me, as a [cis] straight person, or someone who has identified as gay or lesbian but they're keeping their gender." She continued, "If you're completely changing your gender, I think people who are already in the service are going to have a harder time identifying with them." Like Brown, though, when she spoke of her personal attitude, she invoked fairness and tolerance frames similar to the argument for LGB inclusion: "I personally would treat anybody, no matter what, with the same dignity and respect I'm going to treat everybody else."

Fellow Air Force servicemember Alyssa (34, cis straight woman, race not given) drew parallels with DADT and the combat exclusion rule, commenting that trans inclusion seemed, to her, the same as "allowing women, the same [as] allowing gays to serve openly, which is that you should be basing it on the capability of the person." In pragmatic terms, she added, "If we want the most capable people, we have to have the widest possible pool of people to choose from." In Alyssa's emphasis on capability and on broadening the pool of potential servicemembers, we can see echoes of the professionalism frame. Others said similarly:

> Thomas (21, white cis gay man, Army ROTC): I completely believe that anybody who wants to serve, no matter how they identify, with their sexuality or gender or whatever, they should be allowed to serve. . . . It's up to the military as an institution to create an environment that makes people feel safe and makes people feel like they can do their job. That doesn't mean that you get to exclude people because it makes your job easier.

> Joseph (24, Latino cis straight man, Marines veteran): To me, I feel like it's like anything else; as long as you can do your job, that's all I care about. I think that's a perspective that I tried to take while I was in the military: do your job, do it well. . . . How someone identifies and who they are and what life they live, I don't think that's anyone's concern. As long as what they're doing is not putting their health in danger, or putting the lives of their fellow Marines in danger, I don't care what you're doing.

> Celeste (35, Latina cis lesbian woman, Navy): We actually had a couple of midshipmen get held up from graduation because of that, because they were transitioning or what-have-you. . . . Again, I kind of go back to: I don't really care who is helping me out of the fire, right? Just that there's a hand there.

Open trans service proponents leveraged diversity appeals like those that accompanied DADT repeal support, too. Crystal, for example, said of transgender inclusion:

> [Trans people] will provide the same—like we opened the doors for openly gay or lesbians. I think they're going to provide a skillset that we might not already have. I feel anytime you open the gates and don't just limit it to a certain gender or a certain orientation, you're automatically going to get different perspectives and different skills. It's going to make the overall organization better, in my opinion.

This is the foundational rationale for diversity: that adding those who have been historically excluded will bring different perspectives and skills that ultimately benefit the institution. Cristina (26, biracial cis lesbian woman, Navy) agreed and hoped her colleagues would be on board: "What I wish I was hearing from my peers," she said, was "'Finally, we're valuing diversity in our organization. Not only are you highly competent, but your perspective as a woman or who's non-white, or who's not cisgender, all of these things would be a great contribution to the job.'" Unfortunately—for Cristina and for trans servicemembers—this was largely not how many people narrated gender policy change.

"YOU CAN'T BE PANSY-ASSING THESE PEOPLE"

As with the question of women in combat, transgender service inspired readiness concerns that hinged on fears of an invasion of "political correctness." Nancy (59, white cis straight woman, Army veteran) explained, "Most people don't understand it if you've not been in the military. They think you can accommodate. You can't always accommodate everyone."

> I just think the military is designed to be a fighting machine. In society, you may be able to have three different kinds of bathrooms for whatever you need all the different bathrooms for nowadays. . . . There's all the different accommodations that you need for all the different aspects of society that we have nowadays. In the military, you don't have time to worry about that stuff. You're there to protect our country. It's more important that you have a forward fighting position that's functional than . . . I don't know how to say

> this. You can't have three bathrooms at a forward operating position. You can't be—military word—pansy-assing these people. You have to do that job, and that's all you have to worry about doing. You can't worry about people's feelings or people's families or people's sexuality or any of those things. You just have to do the job. That's different than in normal society.

To Nancy, there's no time to think about or nurture diversity, especially if it requires institutional accommodation or change. On the DADT repeal, Nancy had said, "Personally, to me it doesn't matter, as long as the person does their job. What they do in their private life, I couldn't care less." But when it came to combat integration and trans service, she resisted. Unlike the plug-and-play incorporation of LGBs, trans service and women's combat service would require time- and resource-consuming modifications to the gendered organization of the military. To her, the trade-off wasn't worth it.

Jackie's (22, white cis straight woman, Marines) description of the "problem" of trans service was nearly identical to the accusations often leveled against women in combat. Jackie was concerned about people "baby stepping around transgender people" because "they don't want to get called [out for] being discriminating against them." As she offered anecdotes and hypotheticals, Jackie repeatedly misgendered trans people:

> It is such a sensitive and new topic right now that that could happen. People don't know how to act or what to say that will get them in trouble. If they make a bad joke, or—I know a girl [*sic*] that's transitioning to be a guy in one of the units. I know my friend is over her [*sic, throughout*] and he was saying she gets special treatment, they can't make her do anything and they have to treat her actually different than how they treat everybody else, because the higher ups are really afraid that she'll call discrimination no matter. Even if she's getting treated the same as everybody else, it'll be like, "Oh, it's because I'm transgender," and then their whole command is getting kicked out.

With all those incorrect pronouns, one might wonder whether Jackie's fear about her friend getting in trouble for transphobia was displaced anxiety that she might face similar accusations. Further, as with stories I heard about women in combat needing or getting "special treatment," Jackie's apocryphal story of the trans man doing whatever he wants and getting away with it is steeped in worry about what increased inclusivity for some takes *away* from those who are already included.

Joseph, who did not share that fear, nonetheless predicted that trans women would be accused of trying to receive special treatment in the Marines:

> "Hey this is what you signed up for; if you don't like it, leave." . . . I think for a trans woman, the fact that she is a trans woman already sets up this "alpha versus beta" mentality of saying, "Oh, you couldn't even be a man and now you want to work with men. Why would you want to do that?" But at the same time, "You couldn't be and couldn't keep up with the standards of a man, so now you're going to ask us to treat you like a woman."

Cisgender women in the institution are suspect by virtue of their status as "not-men"; transmisogyny positions trans women as worse—as "failed men" ("couldn't keep up with the standards of a man, so now you're going to ask us to treat you like a woman," a further use of gendered subjugation). To some, the idea that a person assigned male at birth would reject the gender (and gender privilege) associated with that assignment but also demand access to the masculinist institution of the military is the ultimate affront.

A third parallel to the narratives I heard about combat integration arose in concerns about trans people's safety, especially from sexual violence, but these were not typically used as arguments against trans inclusion as they had been for the end of combat exclusion. Though he supported the policy change, Joseph worried that trans men would be subject to sexual violence "to put people in their place," as did Elise (23, white cis lesbian woman, Army ROTC), who said, "I would fear [cisgender] men who would eventually find out [would say] 'Oh, you used to be a woman? What?' That's scary to think about, they would probably beat the shit out of that person."

Justine (33, white cis lesbian woman, Air Force) was especially concerned about trans servicemembers' safety during deployment:

> It's one thing to talk about rules, regulations, military bearing, military code [when you are] stateside or on a base. I think in a deployed environment, you know, sometimes those things drop off a little bit because you're being shot at. . . . I know that a lot of our sexual assault has been either in a deployed environment or something like that.

Kyle (51, white cis straight man, Navy veteran) agreed, saying, "My biggest concern is someone's going to get hurt. Someone's going to get beat up, if not killed, by some hater out there. I don't want to see that happen." He continued, "I want someone to be already to the point where they now feel okay in their skin that they're willing to come out and say [they are trans], but they have to be able to feel safe and be okay outside their skin, too."

Himself a trans vet, Hank (30, biracial trans straight man, Air Force vet) confessed to having "mixed emotions" about trans inclusion. "It's great, it's amazing," he began. "But trans individuals are being killed at a high rate right now *out* of service; I can only imagine what's going to happen with 'friendly fire,' as it's called." Additionally, "The sexual assault rate is already extremely high in the military" and "the suicide rate is already extremely high in the military. And the LGBT suicide on top of that? That's already extremely high for civilians *and* for military." Overall, servicemembers narrated their responses to trans people's service in ways that positioned the issue closer to debates around women in combat than open LGB service (notably, the possibility of sexual violence on the basis of sexual identity wasn't raised in a single interview).

TRANSGENDERING THE GENDERED ORGANIZATION

As outlined in part 2, when cisgender women serve in combat, they disrupt the gendered organization by challenging divisions between men's work and women's work. Trans people don't just disrupt; their presence calls into the question the very necessity of classifying servicemembers by sex. If one can move between male and female classification, do those classifications hold any meaning at all? No one I interviewed raised this question directly, though their evident anxiety over fitting trans servicemembers into the gendered organization of the military suggests that this question is, consciously or not, at the heart of resistance to trans inclusion. This led to distinctions between the LGB and the T of "LGBT inclusion." Cassie (22, white cis lesbian woman, Army ROTC) explained:

> I think the hardest thing about the acronym "LGBT" is that we're all different from straight people, but we're also all different from each other.

> I believe that some folks are born—they don't identify with the gender that they're given. I think they should be able to work professionally, I've met [trans] people who are very professional. But the hardest thing for them in the military is going to be that things are gendered. If you're a female by birth but you identify as a male, you fall under the female standards and the male standards. I think that's going to be hard for the Army to decide what to do, which is . . . no fault of the transgender people.

Brian (40, white cis straight man, Navy) struggled to make sense of why he understood trans inclusion through a different lens than open LGB service. "You can be an openly gay man or woman without being closeted or being excessively discreet, while still conforming to the military appearance and culture," he said. Compared to trans service:

> I'll admit that I see the challenges of it. . . . I'm trying to think of how I want to phrase this. If you've got a gay man or a gay woman, they're still presenting as a man or a woman. This is me being an old guy, you understand. "I've got it. Gay or straight, I don't really care, it's a man or it's a woman so this person uses the men's room and this person uses the women's room. This person stays in the men's barracks, and this person stays in the women's barracks." Now [with trans inclusion], you don't have the more practical level. Which uniform does this person wear? Does this person have to get their hair cut or do they not have to get their hair cut?

One of Brian's concerns was taken off the table two months later, when the Navy announced its decision to phase out male/female uniforms in favor of a single standard for all. That decision angered Maryann (31, white cis straight woman, Navy), who attributed it directly to trans inclusion, though the Navy stated it was about promoting inclusion for (cisgender) women. Maryann charged that trans inclusion was "causing a lot more trouble than the Don't Ask, Don't Tell [repeal]" and said with evident frustration, "A lot of us females are getting pretty upset about that because you're making us wear uniforms that we don't look that good in." To her, the trans question was pressuring the Navy to go "gender neutral, gender neutral," which disadvantaged cisgender women. On the whole, the transgendering organization, she said, "caus[es] a lot of problems because of this whole gender identity thing, keeping everybody the same."

Just about everyone who shared their thoughts on trans inclusion was preoccupied with these kinds of classification dilemmas, regardless of whether they objected to trans service. Concerns of this sort fell largely into two categories: fitness standards and housing/bathrooms. The anxieties about trans incursion into these domains of military life resist the transgendering organization and are symptomatic of the gender panic triggered by transgendering work.

"From a Totally Objective Standpoint, I Don't Think That's Fair"

As it did in discussions about (presumed cisgender) women in combat, physical training (PT) made frequent appearances in conversations about trans inclusion. These concerns presupposed the immutability of sex and embodied sex difference. Cara, for example, reasoned, "If you're saying you're female but you're actually male [*sic*], that could give you an extremely unfair advantage because your body is naturally built so much differently and you are naturally stronger than [cisgender] females." She continued, "So many things are male or female, you have to be one or the other." Certainly she believed that trans servicemembers could display a strong "work ethic," "leadership skills," and "integrity," but she would "just be worried about [trans women] having an advantage" over her.

Cassie also wondered if trans men would be evaluated by the male or female standard: "If it's a female becoming a male [*sic*] but they want to hold that female [*sic*] to the female standards, then it's not technically fair if he is taking male hormones." Jesse (22, white cis straight man, Army ROTC), who disapproved of women in combat because "their bodies just aren't built for it," wondered aloud, "Would [a trans man] be graded on the PT test as a man or a woman?"

> Therein lies the dilemma, because if someone is born a woman [*sic*] but identifies as male, on a PT test they're going to be graded to a much higher standard than their biological body might be able to handle. . . . But in order to either alleviate that, they need to just totally kick their bodies into gear, to a level that's way above what's expected of most women.

As for trans women, Jesse said:

> I don't think it's fair to say, "I'm born a man [*sic*] but I identify as a woman." So now, on the PT test for example, I can get a ridiculously high score and be considered for a promotion way ahead of other people. Where a man

> [*sic*] can say, "I wanted to be graded to the female standard," that's totally unfair. But biologically, you have the body to be able to hit those different standards and numbers. So, from a totally objective standpoint, I don't think that's fair.

According to Jesse's beliefs about sex and physical ability, trans men cannot overcome the hindrance of having been "born a woman"; being held to the same expectations as other men is more than their "biological bodies" can handle, at least without an inordinate amount of work. Conversely, from a "totally objective standpoint," trans women "biologically have the body" to outscore cis women, which means they can unfairly outpace cis women on the promotion track. This argument has been in heavy rotation through the last several years of trans backlash: see, for example, the many bills and ordinances (both those proposed and those successfully passed) that bar trans women and girls from competitive sports because they have a "natural" unfair advantage. The myth of trans women's physical advantage has been roundly and robustly debunked by medical and scientific authorities, but its "truthiness" seems only to grow with time.[4]

Maryann claimed to have evidence that trans inclusion would allow people to exploit the different male and female PT standards to their advantage. She said that a friend "who worked with basically the policy-makers for the Navy" told her that "there was a man who was going to fail his body fat measurements, so he said that he identified as a female and therefore he should be able to follow the female standards and not get kicked out." Though this story has the air of an urban legend, its veracity is not the point: the story Maryann shared epitomized the fears unearthed by the transgendering of the military. *Without impermeable boundaries between male and female classifications, will the military's entire organization and ideological structure fall into ruin?*

Taken together, these comments about physical fitness standards also demonstrate the persistent biologization of sex and gender, compared to the declining belief in embodied differences of sexuality. Recall that the same biologizing logic was used to justify trans exclusion under the Mattis plan. The memo argued that trans inclusion will "unfairly discriminate" against cisgender men, who would be held to higher PT standards than trans women. This also purportedly disadvantages cisgender women, who "may be required to compete against such transgender females in training and athletic competition [and] would be potentially disadvantaged." In a patronizing tone, it continues that "this concern may seem trivial to those unfamiliar with military culture," but such competition is "indispensable to the training and preparation of warriors."

In reality, cisnormativity and transmisogyny delineate who is threatened and who is a threat in precisely the opposite order. Calls to protect cis people, particularly cis women, from trans people, particularly trans women, are false alarms. Trans women, especially trans women of color, are vastly overrepresented among targets of gendered violence and sexual assault. At the same time, the overwhelming number of those who enact this violence are white, cis, straight identified men. Such violence is not only *displaced* onto trans women; it is actively *nurtured* by this ongoing dehumanization and disregard of trans people's real lives.

"Are You Really Struggling with Your Gender Identity, or Are You Just Trying to Hang with a Bunch of Women?"

The Mattis plan, in another argument against trans inclusion, suggested it would "violate the privacy" of cis people to include trans people in sex-segregated facilities, a claim that reverberated through the interviews I conducted for this book. For example, Maryann's concerns about manipulation of PT standards extended to housing:

> How are you going to deal with a man [*sic, throughout*] who identifies as a female? Is he [*sic, throughout*] supposed to go to the female berthing? Or a woman who identifies as a male, is she [sic, throughout] supposed to go to the male berthing, or do you separate it out? . . . I would have a problem with a male coming into my berthing because are you *really* coming in because you identify as a female or are you saying that you identify as a female and you're just trying to be with the women? That's where my thought process goes. Are you really struggling with your gender identity or are you just trying to hang with a bunch of women?

The idea that trans women are "really" men is a classic trope of transmisogyny that has been used extensively in efforts to thwart trans rights (see for example bathroom bill propaganda).[5] Trans exclusionary radical feminists (TERFs) have played a key role in perpetuating this trope since the 1970s, arguing that trans women are in fact men who want to colonize women's culture, spaces, and bodies and violate women, both symbolically and literally.

Cisgender women's discomfort with living with trans women was omnipresent in these discussions. Expanding his earlier thoughts, Brian posed a hypothetical I would hear over and over:

> Let's say there's a transgender male-to-female [servicemember], and he's [*sic*] in the process of becoming transgendered. Now you assign a physiological male [*sic*] to live in the women's barracks, what about the [cis] women that live there that don't want to live [with that servicemember]? You see what I mean?

Although I did not, in fact, see the problem in Brian's example, Lily (white cis straight woman, Army, age not given) certainly did. Lily, who earlier expressed fear of showering with or being flirted with by lesbian and bisexual women, was equally concerned about the "low guy on the totem pole" who might be forced to bunk with a transgender roommate but feel unable to go to a superior about their transphobia: "Who do you tell, 'I'm uncomfortable with this, I can't be roommates with this person?' That's an awful position to put someone in." Notably, the person Lily imagines in the unenviable position is the cis servicemember, rather than the trans servicemember assigned to close quarters with a transphobic bunkmate.

Although the roommate hypothetical Lily proposed was nonspecific, her subsequent comments made it clear that she was primarily concerned about the inclusion of trans women. When I asked her to elaborate, she said, "I'll go right back to the shower scene," referring to her earlier hypotheticals about being made to shower with cisgender lesbian or bisexual servicemembers. "If there's somebody who says, 'I identify as a woman,' but you don't have the same biological features as [cisgender women], am I going to be comfortable to shower with that person? No. That's a big no, absolutely not." She concluded, "Obviously I can't speak for everybody, but I would be uncomfortable with somebody who has different body parts from me standing next to me in the shower."

Lorna (28, white cis lesbian, Army) evoked a similar scenario: "If a male [*sic*] is transitioning to a female and they still had a penis instead of a vagina, and you're taking a shower, I mean, I think I would probably be a little weirded out." While she allowed that separate showering facilities might be one solution, she felt that "you can't necessarily give special privileges in the field because someone's transgender." April (40, cis straight woman, Air Force) agreed:

> There are some places where it's very challenging to make accommodations—locker rooms, in certain deployed conditions, where if someone hasn't fully transitioned, it can be really uncomfortable to look fully female [*sic*] and be in a men's bathroom, because you haven't gone through the transition. Or the other way around, can you *imagine* a group of [cis] women in a women's bathroom seeing a trans female that hasn't fully transitioned?

April was concerned about how trans men might make men's bathrooms "uncomfortable" spaces, but she reserved her sense of horror for the possibility that cis women might be exposed to trans women's bodies. This too mirrors TERF logic, in which women's spaces are the exclusive property of "real women," "women socialized as women," "biological women"—in other words, cisgender women only. Trans women, especially trans women who have not had vaginoplasties, are unimaginable.

Sociologists Kristen Schilt and Laurel Westbrook argue that the bathroom makes for such a potent battleground over trans rights because it allows anti-trans activists to conflate sexually predators and trans women, who are both always imagined as male:

> This exclusive focus on "males" suggests that it is genitals—not gender identity and expression—that are driving what we term "gender panics"—moments where people react to a challenge to the gender binary by frantically asserting its naturalness. Because most people are assumed by others to be heterosexual, sex-segregated bathrooms are imagined by many people to be "sexuality-free" zones. Opponents' focus on bathrooms centers on fears of sexual impropriety that could be introduced by allowing the "wrong bodies"—or, to be more precise, penises—into spaces deemed as "for women only." Gender panics, thus, could easily be relabeled "penis panics."[6]

Again: sexual violence against women (cis *and* trans) is a very real social problem. Yet these discourses simultaneously and disingenuously frame cisgender women as inherent victims, uphold transmisogyny, and assert the belief that trans women aren't real women. Whether in bathrooms or barracks, trans women's existence challenges the logics of gender segregation.

April's inability to imagine a trans woman who isn't "fully transitioned" in a women's bathroom, and her assumption that her cisgender woman interviewer would naturally share her disbelief, demonstrates the continued cultural illegibility of trans women's bodies.[7] Marie (29, white cis straight woman, Air Force) used genital surgery as a dividing line between trans women who were legitimate women and those who were not: "I understand how that might make some people uncomfortable; male training instructors aren't allowed in the female dorm rooms after hours, so if it's a pre-op versus a post-op, I can see that being a little bit of a logistical nightmare." Marie's comments, you'll notice, imply that trans women are actually men by comparing them to "male training instructors." And for both April and Marie, trans women's bodies as they occur without surgical intervention are deemed monstrous: the stuff of nightmares, logistical and otherwise.

Sean (20, white cis straight man, Army ROTC) adhered to similar logic conflating gender and genitals:

> For me, it's just the fact that if you're born and sticking with this identifiable genitalia, that's what you are. That's what I think, like—that's what you are. You want to say you're not, but you physically are. That's almost—that's a kind of wall I would hit with that.

Shower-shy Lily offered this (still transphobic, highly specific, and fully conditional) hypothetical regarding what kind of trans women might be acceptable in the gendered spaces of the military:

> If someone came into the unit, and they had a sex change years before, and I had no idea, and I always looked at them like, "Chick looks like a dude, or talks like a dude, I can't quite figure them out," but they looked like me, I could accept that easier for some reason. More than you walking in the shower with some extra dangly parts, you know. That sort of thing. I don't know why, I guess it's just a mental hurdle, you look like me, I could kind of accept it, but *if you don't look like me, that makes me uncomfortable* [emphasis added].

The genital fixation in these narratives reflects four common trans misrecognitions, each of which, alone and in concert, exacerbates transmisogyny and transphobia and makes trans lives less livable. First, they show the effect of transnormativity: trans women (and trans people more generally) are regarded by cisgender people as gender imposters, illegitimate unless their genitalia line up with the sexed expectations of their gender. This perpetuates inequalities for many trans people who cannot or do not want to access surgery to define their sex/gender. Second, interpreting sex by genitalia perpetuates transphobic tropes, particularly that of transgender women as "men in dresses." Third, the line between "pre-" and "post-op" transition is *much* less well defined than they imagine; gender-affirming healthcare includes a broad range of surgical, hormonal, cosmetic, and psychotherapeutic services (or the absence of them!). There is no one way to be transgender. In fact, many would argue that the use of "pre-" and "post-" designations is itself transnormative, presuming that transgender necessitates embodied change if it is to be real or complete. As with the homonormative gender expectations placed on LGB servicemembers, transnormativity makes the slimmest possible amount of room for trans people; only those whose bodies and gender presentations fit normative expectations (and come with the imprimatur of medical personnel and government agencies) need apply. Fourth and finally, centering the question of showers and barracks on cisgender women is cisnormative. It reproduces the marginalization of trans people by making access a question not of trans women's privacy and safety, but of cis women's.

Moreover, all of this discursive work is done in the service of recuperating the gendered organization of the military despite its transgendering. Thinking about trans people's military service suddenly throws into relief the gendered decisions that are otherwise naturalized as obvious, inevitable, and inoffensive. When it becomes clear that adjudicating maleness/femaleness requires *decisions* and not just self-evident truths, the entire sex/gender/sexuality system is rendered suspect. The ensuing gender panic compels individuals and institutions to seek out new, harder boundaries around gender. As explained in chapter 6, for the institution, these boundaries are drawn through medical, psychological, and legal certification processes. For individual servicemembers, however, it's all about the genitals. Whether that includes only those you are born with or also those you can surgically construct, it is genital "congruence" that makes you a man or a woman.

Even then, trans people who have changed their bodies in ways deemed acceptable and normative by cis people remain suspect. Regardless of surgical status, trans women are presumed to have (or be trying to gain) physical advantage in competition with cisgender women. Trans men may not have an assumed standards advantage over their cis peers, but that doesn't let them off the hook: in the precarious context of a transgendering institution, servicemembers fret about trans men (who are not "really" men) "cheating" by using female PT standards. The gender essentialism and male domination unchanged by LGB open service penalizes cisgender women, but the harms are redoubled for trans servicemembers, especially trans women in service.

LIVING IN LIMINALITY

The interview pool of transgender servicemembers in this study was small compared to the cisgender LGB interview pool, yet their interviews were suffused with magnified moments that help illustrate the institutional liminality of transgender service. Sociologist Arlie Hochschild defines magnified moments as "episodes of heightened importance, either epiphanies, moments of intense glee or unusual insight, or moments in which things go intensely but meaningfully wrong. In either case, the moment stands out; it is metaphorically rich, unusually elaborate and often echoes."[8] For example, Chase's magnified moment was the Navy ball. In the moments I recount next, trans participants uncover additional, powerful insights into the gender borderlands they traverse.

SPARTA president and Navy commander Blake Dremann began his transition in 2011, under ironic circumstances. "I actually started to socially transition upon my return from Afghanistan in 2011. . . . I kind of came into my identity in Afghanistan a few months after I was selected to become the first female submariner. Talk about an identity crisis!" He continued:

> I was scared, I had just been selected for one of the Navy's most highly visible programs that they've had for women for a long time. I was very scared of embarrassing the Navy should I be discovered. I was lucky, in that

> they repealed Don't Ask, Don't Tell before I got to the submarine, because if they hadn't, I probably wouldn't have lasted six months on a boat. Not necessarily because I was gay, as much as it was they didn't want women on boats, right? So, it was a way to get somebody off [the submarine]. Gay sailors on submarines have existed since the beginning of submarines. It's not like being gay was the issue, but being female and gay or identifying as a lesbian would have been a problem.

Dremann was in a triple jeopardy of sorts: he was classified as female by the military, dated women, and was beginning a transition process in an institution hostile to all three. Covertly and carefully, he began taking testosterone while underway. "There were times when I might have been a day late or whatever on taking my shot because of just trying to find a time when I could get into the restroom to take it," he recalled. When I remarked that the process sounded stressful, Dremann added a complicating factor that made it even more so: subcutaneous shots, such as those he was taking, require oxygen to heal—but a submarine is a reduced oxygen environment. "If you think about the welts you get from a subcutaneous shot, multiply that by ten, and I got welts the size of oranges or grapefruits in my four shot sites!" Luckily, Dremann was able to cover: "It helped that I had a history of skin breakouts on the submarine, so that my doc didn't think it was funny when I came back for extra cortisone cream."

After this first submarine patrol was completed, Dremann went on several more, surreptitiously administering hormone shots each time. Only his roommate knew. Between patrols, he went on to get top surgery, still evading detection of his trans status upon return. He explained:

> I got my first top surgery signed off on . . . prior to [trans inclusive] policy change. In 2012, I got a referral to the doctor about doing a breast reduction due to a large chest. . . . I did my eight [required] weeks of physical therapy in 2012 and they made the referral to get breast reduction; however, in 2013, I spent nine out of the twelve months of that year either on the boat or underway. So, there was no time to go to the doctor and get that taken care of. At the beginning of 2013, I finally got re-entered for a referral and we were going into an extended yard period for about eight weeks before the boat got underway. . . . [S]o if I needed to be gone for a few weeks, then it wasn't going to be an impact on readiness. My captain agreed, and I had the surgery on March the 20th and was back at work—they gave me 17 days of convalescent leave—I was back two weeks later and out of the vest two

> weeks after that. Now, granted, it wasn't perfect; [the doctor] gave me what he called the "fat boy breast reduction" because the scarring was the same. I would say he probably *knew* but didn't *know*, right? Because when I went in there and he was like, "Yeah, if I do breast reduction surgery, you're not gonna have anything left." And I go, "Well, that's kind of what I want." . . . [*CC: Your captain who approved it, did they know why you were pursuing this?*] They understood it to be a reduction, and that was it. Now, he has told me since that he and his wife suspected, but their concern was that I was a good supply officer and if they fire me there's nobody to replace me, so you don't do that. . . . Nobody [knew] that I [was] transitioning at all except for some close friends and the church.

A couple years later, knowing that the trans inclusion policy could be around the corner, Dremann "took a chance." He told his supervisors about his name change and, two nerve-wracking days later, his supervisor called: "'Okay, we've discussed it amongst our division and if you're ok with it we'd like to call you Blake." Using the cover of referring to his name as a call sign, he was able to go by Blake without incident until Carter put transgender inclusion in the spotlight. "That's when people really started to ask questions," Dremann recalled. One of those people was the captain of his division, and Dremann told him the truth. He paraphrased the captain's affirming reply: "'You know what? You're a really good sailor, you're doing really good work, and I want to make sure that we do what's best for you and regardless of what happens with the policy, let's keep going until we're told otherwise.'"

A few weeks later, Dremann was promoted to lieutenant commander (and later, commander) and awarded the Vice Admiral Bachelor award. "There were a couple of big things in succession that lent credibility to my reputation [and helped] me to be able to stay in," he explained. First, Dremann was chosen as part of the team of trans servicemembers who met with Pentagon officials and gave media appearances, thus raising his profile as a trans servicemember considerably. Interestingly, at the time we spoke, few people in his unit knew this history. "I'm at a different command than where I started most of my activism," he explained, "Most of them have no idea." A two-star admiral at his new post, he said, "is the only one that's ever tried to make me bring it up, as in asking leading questions of 'Is there anything else I need to know about?'" Dremann continued,

"I just said, 'No sir, there's nothing else you need to know,' because I had no intention of being as visible as I am right now." By the time he became the leader of SPARTA, "We had already repealed the policy, we were working through getting the kinks out." Then Trump's trans ban tweet pushed him directly back into the spotlight.

Blake Dremann's story illustrates how, much like many cis LGB servicemembers, trans people were serving well before formal inclusive policy changes. It also demonstrates how trans people find creative pathways to gender-affirming care. Finally, it shows how in practice, DADT, gender segregation, and trans exclusion policies have overlapping and compounding effects, especially for those whose gender performances diverge from the expectations placed upon them by birth-assigned sex. In a 2008 survey of trans servicemembers and veterans, nearly 40 percent reported violations of the "don't ask" part of DADT from colleagues and supervisors inquiring about their sexual identity (this was twice as likely to happen to trans men as trans women).[9] The repeal of DADT made enough room for Dremann to avoid its deployment as a tactic of intimidation on his submarine; however, the gender trouble his presence made, both by virtue of being someone assigned female at birth (and therefore unwelcome) and as a transgender man (and therefore prohibited), put him in a precarious position and forced him to seek out incomplete and potentially dangerous solutions to receiving the healthcare he needed.

Hank, a 30-year-old biracial trans man and Air Force veteran, also felt the compounding effects of DADT and trans exclusion. When Hank joined in the mid-2000s, he was classified as female and experienced overlapping forms of discrimination and harassment by virtue of his race, gender, and sexuality (see chapter 5). After a rocky start, Hank found acceptance and respect within his squadron and spoke freely about his life with colleagues, including about his relationship with a woman. Under DADT, this could have led to his discharge, but no one reported him. In fact, most people, Hank said, knew him not as a lesbian, but as a man. They just didn't make it explicit:

> I think that it was always known to most people that I was essentially trans identified, even though at that time I never even really knew what that term was. We all knew that I was male, basically. That's kind of how I was

> addressed most of the time by people, by friends, like, "That's my brother." Always pretty much male terms. I just basically still had a female name and a female ID. That's pretty much all it was, essentially, yes.

The only time Hank's gender was an issue was when outsiders made it one:

> I was very male presenting. I had a fade [hairstyle]—I didn't have any hair; all my hair was gone. Every now and again it would cause some controversy, like, if I would go to search a female, they would be like, "Why is this guy searching?" Then we'd have to be like, "Well, *technically*, it's not a guy, so . . ." It caused some friction sometimes, but . . . once pretty much everyone on base knew who I was, once I was there long enough, we were good to go. It was cool.

Hank's gender and sexuality put him in a bind. Because of his technical status as female per the institution, dating women was a violation of DADT policy; because of his social status as a man, he could run afoul of the transgender ban. Somehow, he managed to walk this fine line. When DADT was repealed but open trans service remained prohibited, Hank said, "I felt like it was kind of like a slap in the face." He went on:

> They're like, "Okay, we're going to give you this little bit." It's like someone saying they're going to give you some money, but then reminding you that you owe them money. Like, "Here, I'm going to hand you this twenty dollars, but don't forget, you owe me ten dollars, can I get that ten dollars back?" . . . We get there a little bit, and now we're coming backward. [*CC: That must have been tough for you, like, well okay, now I can be open that I date women, but I can't be open about my gender identity.*] Yeah, it's kind of a Catch-22 situation. That's essentially what it was for a lot of people. A lot of people were, like myself, trans identified. . . . [N]ow you have to still carry this identity [i.e., birth-assigned sex] that does not really fit with who you are. It didn't make any sense.

Like Dremann, Hank found a way to be a man in an institution that didn't officially allow him to be. In both cases, the relative invisibility of transgender within the military milieu allowed them to be men without being officially designated as transgender. The spaces they created for themselves run contrary to our expectations about the value of visibility as a rights project. For Dremann, Carter's announcement spoke transgender into existence: it was the moment when people within his unit "really started to ask questions" about his gender. For Hank, it was the end of DADT that unraveled his unspoken manhood. As long as there had been prohibitions against asking and telling, Hank's gender and sexuality were just "there," accepted by his peers. But in the context of the repeal, talking about his relationship with a woman would render him a lesbian, rather than a man. Although the circumstances were not always ideal, it was the invisibility of transgender within the institution that enabled Dremann and Hank to be men in plain sight.

For the last magnified moment, I turn to Brynn Tannehill, a pivotal figure in the development of SPARTA and the activism that led to the DOD's trans-inclusive policy change. Tannehill struggled with the disjunction between her gender identity and her sex classification during the time of her service. "I've been dealing with gender dysphoria since I was 13 and just trying to push it into the background," she shared. "It started really coming to a head during my time in the Middle East and during my final sea tour." By 2010, she said, "I just can't juggle the inconsistency between my gender identity and untreated gender dysphoria. . . . At this point, I've got thirteen good years of service." Subsequently, she moved into the Individual Ready Reserves, where those who have trained and served as active duty agree to serve again should they be called up to replace or support active duty troops. Tannehill got another three years served through IRR, totaling sixteen "good" (or qualifying) years: four shy of the threshold to qualify for a full military retirement. She then applied for an extension, requesting four more years in the IRR, but she was denied. Tannehill was "kicked out at twenty years of service, only sixteen of them 'good', on June 1, 2017."

Trump's trans ban tweet happened less than two months later.

Tannehill remembers that she began "angling for any conceivable way" to pick up more time in the Reserves: "I tried to set myself up such that getting back into the Reserves would be—I would be the easiest possible test case [of trans accession]: somebody who's done with everything, who's got their clearance, has changed all their paperwork, has changed their medical records, has changed everything." Carter's open trans service plan established separate timelines for retention and accession (see chapter 6). When Tannehill came out as trans during her time in the IRR, she was retainable as trans, but as a Reserves applicant, she became subject to the accession policy, which would not be active for another six months. Tannehill was trapped: she had to wait for the trans accession policy to go into effect but also hurry to reenter before a ban could be restored. Using her tenure and connections, she worked back channels to find another way in before the axe fell.

At the time of our interview, Trump's trans ban was still being litigated, but the writing was on the wall: Brynn saw the window closing a bit more every day. Because she lost her civilian job in 2012 "as part of her transition," accessing her military pension was urgent:

> I've taken losses and sacrificed a lot. Lost $110,000 on my house, spent $60,000 out of my own pocket on medical expenses, lost a job, lost my income from the Reserves. I've come to accept that if I don't find a way to get my pension, I'm going to die at my desk at the age of 75, because I will never live to retire. We're wiped out.

Brynn Tannehill's story highlights the contradictions and no-win situations created by the wavering between trans exclusion and inclusion, the four separate policy regimes in four years. Dremann's and Hank's service as men with female classifications is one kind of trans liminality; Tannehill's was another. She did everything right in terms of following the trans service policy, but where the borderlands between the gendered and transgendering organization of the military offered Hank protections, they yanked them away from Tannehill when she reapplied. For Dremann, the military unwittingly facilitated his transition, but the seesaw of policy shifts made that transition more dangerous medically, professionally, and personally.

These magnified moments demonstrate the limitations of visibility politics. Visibility opens access to forms of rights within the neoliberal state, which requires the making of a stable and properly bounded population in need of protection. It is, as Gossett, Stanley, and Burton state in *Trap Door: Trans Cultural Production and the Politics of Visibility*, "offered to us as the primary path through which trans people might have access to livable lives."[10] Visibility through policy created a space within the military for genders that previously dared not speak their names. However, visibility also "can be and is used to restrict the possibilities of trans people flourishing in hostile worlds."[11]

The trans policy change promised that visibility would mean a better life for trans servicemembers. But that visibility drew Trump's ire, which brought a vicious anti-trans backlash. This created a no-man's-land for servicemembers like Brynn Tannehill, who came out during the window of open service only to be kicked out and refused reentry when that window closed. This is not to say that the activists dedicated to improving the lives of their trans constituents made the wrong strategic choice or are somehow to blame for the reinstatement of the trans ban under Trump. It is only to say that visibility offers both doors—"entrances to visibility, to resources, to recognition, and to understanding"—*and* traps: "accommodating trans bodies, histories, and culture only insofar as they can be forced to hew to hegemonic modalities."[12] The reinstatement of open trans service in 2021 is a new door, but the transnormative service requirements remain a trap.

CONCLUSION

There are material consequences to living in liminality. Some are devastating, and we cannot take this lightly. Accordingly, we must be cautious about overly romanticizing liminality as a critical hermeneutic. Nonetheless, it must also be acknowledged that in-betweenness is a space of possibility. From it, transgender epistemologies emerge, bringing with them new possibilities for transformation. Transgender phenomena, per Susan Stryker, "point the way to a different understanding of how bodies mean, how representation works, and what counts as legitimate knowledge."[13] Transgender epistemology "takes aim at the modernist epistemology that treats gender merely as a social, linguistic, or subjective representation of an objectively knowable material sex."[14] Instead, trans ways of knowing reveal that "'sex is a mash-up, a story we mix about *how* the body means, which parts matter most, and how they register in the our consciousness of field of vision."[15]

This epistemological insight makes visible both the conservatizing and radicalizing potential of transgendering organizations. As opposed to the symbolic stillness of the past-tense-gendered organization, already made by gender, the transgendering organization is an active, contested, even chaotic site (and source) of process, as the case of the military aptly demonstrates. The transgendering organization reconstructs and renegotiates the previously unassailable sex/gender foundation of the gendered organization. The possibility of denaturalizing sex and gender altogether is introduced, in this context, but its potential impact is neutralized by the forces of transnormativity demanded to soothe gender panic. (As an example: even under trans inclusion, you still cannot "be" nonbinary or gender fluid in the eyes of the institution; you must still submit to durable, binary sex categorizations regardless of your self-defined gender.) The epistemological transformation of trans knowing is thwarted, to the extent that it is used *solely* to move people from one side of a dualism—male/female, man/woman, masculine/feminine, cis/trans—to the other. Its other, fuller possibilities are just beneath the surface, lying in wait. I believe it is our moral responsibility to clear the way for those possibilities to surface.

In that spirit, I have used part 3 of this book to interrogate the political conditions that opened the door to trans service faster than many could have imagined, then slammed it shut almost as soon as anyone stepped through. The trap of institutional closure unfairly limited opportunities to serve openly to a select few, who would also be trapped by other forms of injustice and trauma. This is the paradox at the heart of this book: the consequences of visibility and inclusion are at once heartening and horrifying.

Cumulatively, this research suggests that gender nonconformity—in queer people, trans people, and women both cis and trans—is, to military policy and culture, a menace that must be contained. In different ways, each policy case is enervated by femmephobia. And, like the homo- and transphobia that also characterize the institution, femmephobia cannot be cured by inclusion. LGB inclusion hinges on the containment of gendered queerness. Trans inclusion requires the medical and legal legitimation of transness. And combat inclusion for women entails placating patriotic paternalism and submitting to gendered social control. None of these pathways truly address the fundamental inequalities sustained by the heterosexual matrix.

As long as the military exists and LGBTs and cis straight women participate in it, the work of improving the conditions of service and the transgendering organization remain important. My hope is that more attention will turn to the practice of a critical trans politics that "demands more than legal recognition and inclusion, seeking instead to transform current logics of state, civil society, security and social equality." These politics, argues Dean Spade, "refuse to take for granted national stories about social change that actually operate to maintain conditions of suffering and disparity." They are about "practice and process, rather than a point of arrival, resisting hierarchies of truth and reality and instead naming and refusing state violence."[16]

A critical trans politics is also a queer and a feminist politics, a recuperative place outside the normalizing, securitizing, imperialist impulses that have colonized the public imagination of women's and LGBT rights. And for many LGBTs and cis/straight women, it is a politics already in practice. Such a critique precedes, exists alongside, and I hope will succeed the limitations of homonormative, transnormative, and security feminist social movement practice. I hope to platform and advocate for that work with this book; to that end, I conclude with these words from Susan Stryker's "My Words to Victor Frankenstein above the Village of Chamounix":

> I want to lay claim to the dark power of my monstrous identity without using it as a weapon against others or being wounded by it myself. I will say this as bluntly as I know how: I am a transsexual, and therefore I am a monster. Monsters, like angels, functioned as messengers and heralds of the extraordinary. They served to announce impending revelation, saying, in effect, "Pay attention; something of profound importance is happening." Hearken unto me, fellow creatures. I who have dwelt in a form unmatched with my desire, I whose flesh has become an assemblage of incongruous anatomical parts, I who achieve the similitude of a natural body only through an unnatural process, I offer you this warning: The Nature you bedevil me with is a lie. Do not trust it to protect you from what I represent, for it is a fabrication that cloaks the groundlessness of the privilege you seek to maintain for yourself at my expense. You are as constructed as me; the same anarchic Womb has birthed us both. I call upon you to investigate your nature as I have been compelled to confront mine. I challenge you to risk abjection and flourish as well as have I. Heed my words, and you may well discover the seams and sutures in yourself.[17]

PART 4 Conclusion

8 We Will Be Greeted as Gay Liberators?

Jude, a biracial queer trans man and Army vet, was one of the many transgender servicemembers separated under DADT.[1] In basic training, he said, a commanding officer took a dislike to him: "She just poked at me and poked at me and poked at me" until: "One night I was in the showers, and I was having a conversation with another recruit who was a woman, a lesbian, and [the commanding officer] walks in and we abruptly stopped our conversation. She took that as a sign that something was going on." In the paperwork on Jude's alleged "conduct unbecoming," he was "accused of fondling another woman's breasts." "Under Don't Ask, Don't Tell," he explained, "the accusation was enough, they don't have to have proof." Jude believed that his commanding officer disliked him for being "visibly queer" and exploited the shower encounter as a way of getting rid of him. Being separated was, at the time, doubly devastating. Not only had he "begun to thrive" in basic training, he had no viable plan B. When he entered the military, Jude was a high school dropout, homeless since the age of 14 due to parental rejection of his gender/sexuality.

Left homeless, jobless, and directionless by DADT, Jude should have every reason to be overjoyed by the policy's demise. When we spoke fifteen years after his discharge, though, his feelings about the repeal and the end of the (first) trans ban were ambivalent. "When Don't Ask, Don't Tell was lifted," he said, "I had mixed feelings, because I don't like the idea that poor people need to join, specifically because it's one of the only routes we have. I don't like that." Jude knew firsthand that poverty was a powerfully coercive force, and that poor and working-class people were pulled into the institution just because they needed a job, a place to live, food, and clothing. It happened all the time. Where but the military was a poor high school dropout going to find a secure career path?

Jude was also skeptical about the steep qualifications for transgender accession, especially the requirement of eighteen months, supervised and certified by a doctor, in one's "target gender":

> The entire narrative of what's going on with trans visibility . . . that's what the military would be basically doing, making sure that normative bodies are the only ones allowed in. I think that's really dangerous, because that's painting a very small picture of what it means to be trans. It's also creating this dichotomy between what other people view as, "Oh, then you are only trans if you do this." That's very divisive. It's a very divisive way of looking at things. It doesn't take into account the fact that, financially, most people can't afford—some people can't even afford testosterone if they wanted, because it may be too expensive.

He continued, "Of course, there are people who are serving, who should be able to serve openly." Jude paused, seemingly weighing the consequences of being quoted on this subject.

> I know some people are going to think that, "Oh, here's this educated, elitist asshole who thinks we should take away the military, when it is one of the last places to become financially stable." I understand where low-income people would push their children to go that route, because it is stability. I just don't like the way the system is set up to where that is the *only* option. We should stop demonizing blue-collar work and pay people what they're worth. . . . If we paid people what they were worth and gave them economic opportunities without being a war machine, that's what I would prefer. I've seen what the military does to people. I've had friends who have gone off to Afghanistan and come back—not only are they not mentally okay, but a lot of them don't know how to be anything other than that. I've had friends who spent their four years, left, became civilians and in a year or two, went right back because they don't know how to be a "normal" person. They actually

say, "I'm better at being a killing machine." That is not a human being. I would never condone that for anyone.

When I asked, "If you were to counsel an 18-year-old queer or trans kid who said, 'I want to join,' what would you say to them?" Jude replied:

> Well, first, I would try and convince them not to join. If I can't, I would tell them . . . . . get the job you need, but remember it's a job. That you don't have to buy into the institution. My uncle used to say this to me, he said, "You know, it's like putting on a costume, look at the military as if you're putting on a costume and you're playing your part." If you look at it as a tool for what you want and not lose yourself in that process, that's what I would want for a queer or trans person.

Jude's perspective runs contrary to the optimistic expectation that the military will be greeted as gay liberators, to paraphrase Vice President Dick Cheney's infamous prediction of the US military's reception by the Iraqi people. But the reality is that liberation—LGBT or otherwise—will not be won through militarism.

In this book, I have argued that despite what good they may do for some, the military's gender and sexuality policy changes are ultimately strategies of maintaining American empire, facilitated by the narrowing imaginations evident in changing gender and sexuality social movement strategies. In particular, the epoch of homonormativity gave rise to the "homopatriot," thereby linking LGBT rights to nationalism, securitization, and American exceptionalism.[2] As Dean Spade has remarked, "The most violent and harmful institutions in our society, which faced a legitimacy crisis in the wake of the domestic and global antiwar, anticolonial, feminist, and antiracist movements of the 1960s and 1970s, got a makeover as they were cast as sites of liberation and inclusion for gay and lesbian people."[3] This makeover is the outcome of the homonormative bargain. In attributing this shift to gay rights discourse, I do not mean to deny the ways that liberal feminism and transnormativity are implicated in the military's kinder, gentler recasting. However, my data suggest that the homonormative bargain has been, by far, the most successful of these social movement trade-offs, and that it has used gender conservatism to underwrite it. The choice to foreground the interests of (often white, middle-class) gender-conforming gays and lesbians (and to a lesser extent, bisexuals) in sexual politics left everyone else behind to fend for themselves. The radical and coalitional liberation politics of the late 1960s and 1970s were dissolved, creating silos of identity politics competing against each other for scarce resources.

The suite of military policy changes I have explored in this book appear to have redressed sexual and gender inequities, but looking into the ways they were received has revealed something more fractured. In the significant gulf between the reception of sexuality-based policies (like the DADT repeal) and gender-based policies (women's combat integration and open transgender service), we can see, for instance, that homosexuality per se no longer poses as big a threat to the masculinist values of the military. The homonormative bargain severed the ties between homosexuality and effeminacy, repositioned cis LGBs as fundamentally capable of "normality," and insisted that they are virtually indistinguishable from their straight counterparts.[4] As homosexualities are mainstreamed, even institutions as traditionally homophobic as the US military feel the effects.

Even still, the success of LGB incorporation hinges on cooperation with queer social control practices. A closer examination of repeal opinions demonstrates the extent to which the conditional inclusion of LGBs depends on their extreme discretion, gender normativity, and complicity with the masculinist and cis-sexist culture of the military. Appeals to LGB professionalism, almost exclusively coded as heterosexual and gender normative, mask discomfort with inclusion by curtailing any signs of visible queerness or same-sex sexuality on the job (which, in the military, is not uncommonly a 24/7 job).[5] For most straight cadets, servicemembers, and veterans, the acceptance of gender-nonconforming LGBs—especially effeminate men—remains beyond the pale.

The widespread approval for the repeal of DADT did not extend to interviewees' attitudes toward women's participation in combat. Like gender-nonconforming gay and bisexual men, women servicemembers are inherently gender transgressive by virtue of their participation in this deeply masculine institution.[6] The ideological system of patriotic paternalism frames women—including women who serve on the front lines—as victims in need of the military's masculine protection. Asserting vague and inaccurate claims about the science of sex, women are figured as constitutionally incapable of the mental and physical toughness combat requires. At the same time, men are imagined as so irrepressibly (hetero) sexual that they cannot be trusted to focus on their jobs when sexual opportunity knocks. National security is endangered when women, objectified as just such an opportunity (and/or as potential victims in need of protection when they overestimate their abilities) enter the field of combat. Liberal feminism offers a compelling critique of the paternalistic, but not of the patriotic, part of this equation, thereby perpetuating militarism in feminist politics as well.

Finally, transgender service introduces an even more substantial threat to the institution than the incorporation of (presumed cisgender) women. Treated as a harbinger of a chaotic, structural undoing, trans inclusion threatens to dismantle the binary sex classification system that governs so many bureaucratic domains: uniforms, housing, bathrooms, PT standards, and, until recently, combat eligibility. And so it too triggers gender panic. The narratives of cis participants are full of concerns about the process of reinterpreting or reconsidering sex/gender classifications to incorporate transgender members, a process I refer to as transgendering the gendered organization. Although framed as merely pragmatic, in their recitation these concerns reveal the depths of the institution's cisnormativity, transphobia, and transmisogyny. Transgender's ideological positioning in the liminal space between sexuality and gender ideologies results in divergent interpretations of trans belonging in the military. As members of the LGBT acronym, they are capable professionals and diversity value-adds; as a form of gender trouble, they introduce distraction, danger, and doubt. If the transgendering organization of the military presses too far, then the ideological apparatus of sex/gender difference could be upended. That would be devastating to militarism itself, which is predicated on gender essentialism and male authority. Both the institution and its members attempt to contain this threat through regulations and expectations that keep the institutional impacts of trans service as minimal as possible.

Among other things, these differences in policy reception uncloak the subtle cisnormativity that pervades discussions of the repeal and the end of combat exclusion: LGBs and women are definitionally, though inaccurately, "not-trans" in the meaning-making around the military's changing policy context. If LGBs were conceptualized as potentially simultaneously transgender, appeals to tolerance and "benign" diversity would be clouded.

Meanwhile, if women in combat are recognized as both cisgender and transgender, it would muddy the waters of biologized narratives of women's (in) capabilities. The "good" kind of difference that LGB servicemembers are expected to bring in is predicated on their cisgender status. The "bad" kind of difference that women and trans others introduce into combat is rendered through cissexist definitions of gender and embodiment.

These policies' potential for disruption to the previously all-male bastions of the military—the storied foxholes and front lines—threatens the foundations of the institution's mythology. And thus, the preservation work on behalf of the masculinist institution and cis men's superiority persists, regardless of policy shifts, regardless of any evidence to the contrary. The accrual of privilege to white cis straight men (and with it, to the white cis straight imperialist American project) requires the subordination of all others. In response, a "queer class" of servicemembers—defined collectively by its subordination—has, inch by inch, asserted its right to self-determination. These servicemembers hold the potential to queer the social relations that uphold racist, sexist, homophobic, transphobic relations of power. And yet as long as that potential remains entangled with US imperialism, it is no transformational threat at all.

Cynthia Enloe, the preeminent scholar of gender and US militarism, has noted that "the most optimistic calculation is to figure that when a country's military admits a once excluded or despised group, that institution is transformed and made more compatible with democratic culture."[7] "In this perhaps too-sanguine scenario," Enloe continues, "the outsider group campaigning to enter the military doesn't become militarized; rather the newly diversified military becomes democratized." This book is certainly a killjoy to the sanguinity of that hope. However, to quote "feminist killjoy" Sara Ahmed, "To kill joy . . . is to open a life, to make room for life, to make room for possibility, for chance. My aim in this book is to make room."[8]

IMPLICATIONS FOR POLICY AND PRACTICE

Military Policy

One of the more distinct challenges of this project has been the rapidly unfolding and reversing policy changes during data collection.[9] When

I began this research, the DADT repeal was the only game in town. A quarter of the way in, gender integration of combat went live. Halfway in, trans inclusion passed, then three-quarters of the way in, it was revoked. Only days after I finished writing this manuscript, Biden restored it. At every step, the analytical terrain fell away just as soon as I got my bearings. For now, battles over open LGBT service and women's combat participation seem behind us, but if the outlandish political maneuvers of the past few years have taught us anything, it is that a right won is not a right secured.[10]

In my ideal world, the right to serve would be immaterial to LGBT and feminist organizing, because in that world, such organizing would be fundamentally antiwar and antimilitarism. That said, as long as cis straight women, queer people, and trans people continue to desire to serve, I want to preserve their right to do so. Far greater investments in support services specifically for LGBT servicemembers and vets could ameliorate some of the harms and forms of trauma that emerge at the intersections of militarism, homophobia, and transphobia. And whether or not they serve in the armed forces, women, queer, and trans people absolutely deserve stronger nondiscrimination protections, more robust sexual harassment and assault prevention and protection, less gender gatekeeping, and far more room for queerer expressions of self.

Expanding Alternative Economic and Educational Opportunities

A core platform of the argument for LGBT inclusion was the military's role as a "de facto jobs program" for people with limited economic opportunities, which includes many queer and trans people.[11] Certainly the military provided vital resources for participants in this study, like Jude, who fled homelessness by entering the military (only to be discharged under DADT while still in basic training). But I also think about Jude's proposed counsel to a hypothetical young queer or trans person thinking about serving: don't do it. In their critique of LGBT inclusion, Eli Massey and Yasmin Nair argue that although the military is indeed a "source of a stable job, free healthcare, and funding for college," there is no nobility, no justice in asking people to "sign up for the possibility of losing life and limb in order to be guaranteed such basic entitlements."[12] Whether flag-waving patriot or ardent military abolitionist, each of us must reckon with the profound, perverse injustice of coercing vulnerable people to risk their lives in exchange for subsistence. If the US military is the AVF it purports to be, participation must be a choice made free of economic deprivation and desperation. Why have a de facto jobs (or healthcare or education) program when a real one is possible?

Defense budget conservation, such as nuclear disarmament (or even selective decommissioning), could save trillions of dollars over the coming decade—easily enough to fund such programs.[13] Just eliminating budget waste and inefficiencies alone could shave $1.2 trillion off the military's price tag over the next ten years.[14] These changes would free up resources that could be used to provide living wages, universal basic income, universal healthcare, student loan forgiveness, college tuition caps, and more robust resources for community college and vocational training. These are the kinds of policy changes that will give young people like Jude once was meaningful options that do not require a (literal and figurative) blood sacrifice.

The problem with using military policy to enable opportunities for some is that "singling out the issue of inclusion without examining the institution itself produces morally incoherent stances."[15] Is it a moral victory to secure equal opportunity to participate in disaster capitalism, death, and debility? No doubt there are readers who will scoff at my continued return to the military objective of "lethality" throughout this book. Some will call me naïve and misinformed. But if I could ask for one concession from such opponents, it is their serious and sustained attention to lethality's moral weight and the "death worlds" it sustains.[16] The repeated, quotidian use of lethality as a measurement of military effectiveness desensitizes us to its meaning. Lethality is a technology of governance that gives the military the right to determine whose lives are expendable and whose are not. The calculated decisions to murder people, even "noncombatants," in the name of political control is *exactly* what patriots abhor in acts of terrorism. Terror is a two-way street. The more we dull our senses to the consequences of lethality as a paramount institutional metric, the more we are all implicated in its body count.

In *Frames of War*, Judith Butler argues that the grievability of life lost at the hands of our own government is obscured; we cannot reckon with those deaths if we have not first seen them as living.[17] The same is true of other "casualties," those left alive but having experienced debility or other forms of death: spiritual, emotional, mental.[18] When the Abu Ghraib torture photos surfaced, the possibility that those lives would be made grievable sent the Bush administration scrambling for a cover-up. When they couldn't be unseen, they were excused away. Defense Secretary Donald Rumsfield bemoaned "the heartbreak of acknowledging the evil in our midst," neglecting to acknowledge that he personally signed the torture memos that authorized such evil. President George Bush condemned this "disgraceful conduct by a few American troops who dishonored our country and disregarded our values," though he, too, signed off on the "enhanced interrogation techniques" that made torture standard operating practice. And so the war on terror marches on.

In fact, as I researched the scandal for this book, I realized how little of it I actually knew, how little time I had spent in contemplation of the images and details. As I settled into that contemplation—of the leaked photographs, the torture memos, the media coverage, the photos we didn't see because they were so damning they were buried deeper and deeper and deeper—I gained an invaluable education in what militaries do in "our" name. Today, I firmly believe a critical education in peace, war, and conflict, one that entails sustained contemplation of this sort, is a civic duty. Education as a strategy of resistance has its limits. But if war and torture are what US democracy requires, it should be every American's responsibility to reckon with those terms.

LGBT Social Movement Priorities

The homonormative bargain is another uncomfortable place to dig deeply. There we find the upsetting truth that the social movement for sexual sovereignty divested from liberation to purchase the most paltry, violently earned, and heavily conditional rights. Homonationalism does violence to queer and trans servicemembers who are used as cannon fodder *and* to the racialized queer Other on the receiving end of the cannon. Signing on to the discourse of US sexual exceptionalism displaces queerness onto the feminized "radical Islamic terrorist" whose defenses must be penetrated by the dominant, masculinized figure of rainbow patriotism. This "militarization of gay identity" justifies the continued incursion and murder in the Middle East in the name of extending the liberal values of the exceptionalist United States.[19] In 2019 alone, the US military accepted responsibility for 132 civilian deaths in Afghanistan, Iraq, Syria, and Somalia—a number that is surely a dramatic undercount.[20]

Still, it is a difficult time to critique inclusion. As fascist politicians continue to chip away at what were once taken-for-granted LGB, trans, and women's rights, it feels strange—even dangerous—to lay out any criticisms of this goal. Maddeningly, their political rhetoric has slyly co-opted queer critique to its own anti-queer ends—for example, decrying "identity politics" as a way to silence crucial, urgent discussions about racism. And yet it remains imperative that we critically interrogate the consequences and costs of inclusion. As Dean Spade writes:

> In studying the histories of antiwar and anti-imperialist Black liberation, indigenous resistance, and feminist resistance, I have observed how frequently visionary activists were at odds with other people in their own movements who were fighting for military inclusion or other assimilationist or institution-supporting reforms. None of those debates end just because the inclusion reform in question happens. The rise of the #BlackLivesMatter movement, with its critique of "respectability politics," is a powerful example of how Black liberation activists are still pushing back on the limits of a narrow "equality" framework. The rise of the #Not1More deportation movement, with its critique of the Dream Act and comprehensive immigration reform—both of which strengthen border enforcement and divide migrants into categories of "deserving" and "undeserving" of immigration relief—also speaks to these ongoing movement divides regarding what justice is and should be. As these contemporary examples show, it matters whether we shape our struggles to fit the norms of violent institutions that make many in our communities disposable, or whether we fight for justice for the most vulnerable people in our communities and in the world. It matters because it will determine what we get as we fight and because our politics is always in formation.[21]

To move forward as a more compassionate, more radical, more expansive LGBT justice movement, we cannot skip past the movement's present. Few people tolerate ambivalence well, and the uneven consequences of prioritizing inclusion over liberation force us into a great deal of handwringing. The homonormative bargain brought immense relief for some and suffering for others. Many more people could claim to have experienced both. I believe we have a queer obligation to engage with this messiness. As I have written elsewhere, an "epistemology of contradiction" and the practice of "ambivalent observance" are essential tools of queer research methods.[22] The point of queer research is not to correct or suppress ambivalence and contradiction—either in the data or in one's orientation to the data—but to submit to both, even revel in them. Queer evades categorization or resolution; queerness is perpetually "not yet here." Rather, says queer theorist José Muñoz, it approaches "like a crushing wave of potentiality," and "willingly, we let ourselves feel queerness' pull, knowing it as something else that we can feel, that we *must* feel. . . . [We must step] out of place and time to something fuller, vaster, more sensual, and brighter."[23] To that end, I conclude with a plea: let's, all of us together, give in to our most radical, limitless, liberatory imaginations of what could be rather than settle for the miserly concessions of the homonormative bargain. The radical reconfiguration of LGBT social movement practice will not come from papering over the unintended consequences of past efforts but in embracing the queerness of both reality and possibility.

For many queer critics, the ethical question at hand is not whether LGBTs should be *able* to serve in the military, but whether LGBTs should be *willing* to serve under repressive global conditions, to vie for "inclusion in the atrocious."[24] What if, instead of asking under what conditions we might gain permission to join a conservatizing institution, we instead set out to find out what more liberatory projects could build? To quote activist Mattilda Bernstein Sycamore:

> For me, the possibility of a trans or queer politic lies in using identity as a starting point for challenging the violence of the world around us, and building something else, creating more possibilities for everyone. I'm interested in a movement that fights for universal access to basic needs, as a starting point—housing, health care, food, the right to stay in this country or leave if you want to, a sex life that matters. I'm interested in gender, sexual, social and political self-determination. The possibility of a trans or queer identity lies in annihilating all hierarchies and creating something else in the ruins, something bolder and more caring, communal and daring.[25]

DREAMING BIGGER

That possibility of unlocking a radically different future with the key of trans and queer potentiality has thrummed within me as a personal, political, and pedagogical motivation since I began my sociological career two decades ago. Accordingly, I make a practice of concluding every semester of teaching with class sessions on queer utopia.[26] After fifteen weeks of laying out, with unflagging cynicism, the inequality that lurks at every turn, I spend our last sessions together asking what the opposite might look like. Typically, the mildest proposals—*universal healthcare! A mandated living wage!*—are regarded with incredulity. In what world are such pie-in-the-sky proposals even worth entertaining, they ask? Eager cohorts of students in each class push themselves, yet ultimately struggle to envision the possibilities beyond consumer activism, media representation, or asking for state recognition. It is as though, having been scolded for raising our eyebrows at the "abundance" of civil rights we've already been "granted," we have internalized our own queer social control. *How dare we imagine more?*

That is, until now. The year 2020 will be remembered as a moment when the starkness of US inequality was unveiled to all but the most sheltered few. Privileges could not protect many from the fullness of global agony or the chokehold of state-sanctioned domestic terror. But just as hegemony begets resistance, the literal and symbolic weight of oppression fomented an urgent clamor for change. Despite blatant gerrymandering and voter suppression, millions of people targeted for disenfranchisement stood in day-long lines to unseat Trump and his administration. It was the highest turnout in 120 years, a testament to the endurance of the political will of the marginalized (and to the long, difficult fights that lie ahead).[27] Changes in political representation are not the answer, but here they are at least evidence of the power of mass mobilization against inequality. Much more promisingly, calls for prison abolition, public health infrastructure and the rallying cry #DefundThePolice also made the mainstream in a big way. The places in my curriculum where students used to scoff are suddenly the places they want to dwell, to reach deeply into. They are ready to imagine better.

No, a single year cannot bring about irreversible course correction, as have now already seen. Social change is pendulous, never losing momentum as it swings between change and backlash. And if the two years that have since followed are any indication, we are still deep, if not deeper, into the swing of backlash. But I suspect—I *hope*—that in their very boldness and imprudence over the last few years, the forces of domination have made a crucial error of exposure. If I may hypocritically borrow a militaristic metaphor to protest militarism: right now, this very moment, is an opportunity to wrest victory from the jaws of defeat. And that goes for whatever moment you happen to be reading in, because misery laid bare will always present an invitation to redress, to incite a creative, critical mass to imagine and greet the future as its true queer liberators.

Methodological Appendix A

It's a tricky thing to try to assess the outcomes of social change as it happens. In the present research, the task was made more difficult by the rapidity and reversals of the particular set of changes I set out to study. When I began researching, the ink was still fresh on the repeal of the Don't Ask, Don't Tell policy. It stood alone in the field of military policy shifts related to gender and sexuality. In 2013, the Combat Exclusion policy was lifted, though it would be three more years before its implementation. This meant that during the first round of interviews I conducted in 2015, Army Ranger School had just accepted its first women applicants, and the integration of infantry and ground combat was just around the corner. During my second round of data collection, in the summer of 2016, Secretary of Defense Ash Carter unexpectedly announced the end of medical disqualifications of transgender service members. I began writing this book in 2017 as an account of the end of gender- and sexuality-based exclusions from US military service, then Trump abruptly tossed out the years of preparation, revision, and implementation efforts around the transgender retention and accession standards. I began a third round of interviews in the summer of 2018, speaking with policy stakeholders shortly after the release of the Mattis plan, when it was under court-ordered injunctions. Then I conducted another round of interviews in 2020, after it went into effect. Now, as I revise and edit and tweak my manuscript in 2022, the Biden administration has thus far kept its promise to restore open trans service. Where things will go next, I don't dare guess.

In practical terms, all this has made publishing especially difficult. For example, I submitted a journal manuscript on the significance of LGB inclusion arriving absent trans inclusion in June 2016: two weeks before Carter's trans inclusion bombshell. In addition to the usual lengthy rounds of revision attending any academic publication, now I had to completely reframe the piece, refresh the policy history, and rewrite the analysis to bring my article into the new policy context. Just about a year later, on the morning of July 26, that article went live on the journal's website—and within *hours*, Trump's tweet damned it to obsolescence. It was much the same with this book. One week after I submitted the full manuscript, Biden reinstated trans inclusion. And this was after I had already rewritten the conclusion a number of times: after Trump lost the election, as he refused to concede the election, as he fomented an insurrection two weeks before Biden's inauguration, as he was impeached by the House of Representatives. I would have to be foolish, at this point, to assume no great history-making changes will happen between my penning these words and you plucking the book off a shelf to peruse. For example, Biden's 2021 retreat from Afghanistan will likely change the overall terrain of the war on terror (though I doubt from my current vantage point that it signals an impending end to it).

In terms of theoretical challenges, this chaos has made it especially tricky to analyze and assert the meaning of policy changes so sweeping, new, and precarious all at once. How can I assess a fledgling policy regime that changes everything about gender and sexuality restrictions in the military while remaining manifestly unsettled? Using an abductive methodological approach, I ultimately chose to focus on how members of the military also struggle to make sense of the evolving conditions of service.[1] Contextualizing their narrated meaning-making processes when the conditions that inform them are in such dramatic flux has been the most formidable challenge of my research career.

The churn of policy change has also complicated the process of making meaningful comparisons within the dataset. Interviewees were responding to entirely different policy conditions if they spoke with me in 2015 versus 2016, 2018, or 2020. For these and other methodological reasons, I chose to use the individual policy conversations as the primary points of comparison. In the analysis stage, I found that although the conditions changed radically between each wave of interviews, the tensions underlying the reception of these policy changes remained constant. The personnel I interviewed in spring 2015 were grappling with the same thorny questions as those I would interview in fall 2020. This coherence cemented my decision to organize the book not by chronology, but by policy. That is not to say that other comparative approaches would have no utility. At each significant juncture in a research process, methodological choices spin off alternative universes of data with different potential outcomes: each node in a decision tree of methods sends a project in new directions. In the end, some of the alternative universes created from choices made or dismissed may bear little resemblance to that in which your "final" work resides. The most important thing about responding to changing methodological conditions is matching the research question to the data universe you land in. Those other worlds are not *irrelevant* to the field of study; they simply become less crucial to answering the question at hand.

Finally, as always, I was challenged in this work by the persistent, nagging, unanswerable question: When is research *done*? That answer remains elusive, but at some point we must all declare the current research done, no matter how unstable, how full of surprises, reversals, and reveals the object of focus continues to be. I attend to the more formal question of reaching theoretical saturation in the following, but in this research, the question of "done" was also temporal. Choosing when to stop and make meaningful conclusions in this quixotic, rapid-fire timeline was agonizing (hardly different from the quintessential ethnographer's dilemma about leaving the field, mine is not an entirely novel methodological concern). There have been many points along the research process where, had I stopped, this book would have felt incomplete and perhaps even obsolete. Nonetheless, in the end, pragmatic concerns—my career, my life, my rapidly aging data, a global pandemic—brought about a natural conclusion to the project. No matter the circumstances, all research must come to an end, and time will always march on beyond it, creating new social conditions for new generations of scholars to analyze.

IN-DEPTH INTERVIEWING

I chose in-depth interviewing as the research method for this project after carefully considering other avenues, including archival research, content analysis, focus groups, survey research, and ethnography. I was particularly drawn to ethnography as a complementary method. Spending time on military bases or attending social events with servicemembers could have added rich detail, confirmed or disconfirmed parts of my argument, or led me in new directions entirely. Indeed, I pursued ethnographic opportunities throughout the data collection process. Very early on, I considered gaining access through my younger brother, who was at that time serving in the Navy, but he was discharged shortly thereafter. Later, the tenure clock and still later, the responsibilities of my administrative role as director of BU's Women's, Gender, and Sexuality Studies Program encroached on my ethnographic capacity. Still, I spent years looking for opportunities to attend gatherings of LGBT and women servicemembers, veterans, or policy makers, but the timing never worked out. The annual conferences and professional organizations that sprang up around each policy change effort would cool off in the lull after each policy's announcement. The trans ban whiplash had everyone on edge. In 2020, I sought and secured permission to attend a conference of transgender veterans, only to be thwarted by the COVID-19 pandemic.

My ethnographic ambitions were not realized in this project, and yet I believe I nonetheless ended up centering the most appropriate and essential technique for my research questions: interviewing. The object of my inquiry was the symbolic boundaries that institutional actors drew around the policy changes. I was interested in evaluating how cadets, servicemembers, and veterans assessed the legitimacy and significance of these specific policy changes, and that was best accomplished by eliciting those narratives directly.

Next came decisions about whose narration should be included. I was curious how career stage might affect beliefs about this emerging "new normal," so I chose to interview incoming officers, current servicemembers, and veterans. Each set of participants had distinct vantage points and different kinds of investments in these changes; ultimately, though, they drew on very similar discourses. Where I intended to capture variation by career cohort, instead I found the salience of variation by policy.[2] The same was true as I compared other cohorts, by military branch, age, and to some extent, gender. Participants presumed differences on these axes—commonly noting that Marines would surely be more resistant than airmen, that younger people would be more receptive to progressive change, or that women would be more welcoming of combat inclusion than men—and they made sense of their own perspectives through comparison. But when I looked for evidence of significant distinctions across these axes, I did not find them in these data. A representative survey large enough to test the statistical significance of differences by branch, specialization, occupation, branch, career stage, age, gender, or race could very well produce meaningful results. For the purposes of my research question, however, identifying similarities across units of observation was equally relevant.

Most of the interviews with ROTC cadets (fifteen of sixteen) and policy stakeholders (five of eight) were conducted in person; all interviews with servicemembers and veterans were over the phone or Zoom. Conducting interviews over the phone introduces unique challenges compared to in-person or Zoom interviews. Eye contact and body language are powerful tools for eliciting rich answers from interviewees. As a general rule, active listening, which involves the management of facial expression, body language, and other nonverbal cues, facilitates better interview data. Phone interviews impede these cues. Those conducted by cell phone can further reduce the quality of conversation by way of sound delays, echoes, and other connectivity issues. (The same is true of Zoom interviews, but at least visual cues prevent some miscommunications.) In phone interviewing, active listening is generally reduced to verbal cues ("mmm," "mmm hmm," "huh," "ah ha," "umph," etc.), and though these can still build rapport and facilitate communication, they also risk disrupting the narrative in a way nonverbal signals may not. Pauses are tougher to decipher in a voice-only interview, when it is difficult to know whether the respondent has paused momentarily or finished answering, and it becomes more difficult to accurately interpret tone when you cannot observe facial expressions or hand gestures.

Despite these perils, phone and Zoom interviews allowed me to seek out an interview pool broader by branch, geography, and participant. I spoke to servicemembers stationed across the globe and deployed overseas—all but impossible had I restricted responses to in-person conversations. I also think phone/Zoom interviews can be more attractive to participants with limited time, increasing the likelihood that they will agree to an interview. Picking up the phone from the office, home, or car is a more appealing and efficient prospect for many. (In fact, many of those I've interviewed in the last two decades have asked why we couldn't just hop on a call instead of meeting up in person. I expect, after adjusting to Zoom amid the COVID-19 pandemic, this request will become more frequent for future researchers.)

Interviewees were recruited through a combination of convenience, snowball, and purposive sampling. Initial recruits were solicited through personal networks, then I snowballed the sample by asking participants to recruit or recommend additional participants. I advertised on relevant email lists, internet boards, and social media groups, conducting more snowball sampling from there. For the stakeholder interviews, I was fortunate to access one key stakeholder through my personal networks, who began the snowball sampling by referring me to others who then did the same. I consciously set broad criteria for study inclusion to maximize variation, seeking out cadets, servicemembers, and veterans of any sexual identity, gender, age, race, branch, and rank. Sample variation by career stage, sexual identity, gender, age, and rank emerged more or less organically through the convenience and snowball sampling strategies. Among servicemembers and vets, I was able to secure participation from equal numbers of respondents from the Air Force, Army, and Navy, but fewer from the Marines and none from the Coast Guard. (The newest branch of the military, Space Force, did not exist when I began my research.)

In the second half of data collection, I purposively sought out more Marines and "coasties" but was unsuccessful. The Coast Guard is somewhat set apart from the other branches because it falls under the jurisdiction of the Department of Homeland Security rather than the Department of Defense.[3] In fact, it is only classified as a branch of the military because its assets can be transferred to the Navy during wartime. At roughly 42,000 strong, the Coast Guard is significantly smaller than the other four branches (the Army stands over one million, the Navy and Air Force have about half a million members each, and the Marines number about 300,000). On account of its outlier size and relationship to DOD policies, I deemed it unnecessary to pursue further Coast Guard recruitment. More concerning was the insufficient representation of people of color within the sample at this stage. I transitioned to targeted recruiting for servicemembers and vets of color, Black and Latine in particular, adding six more interviews (see the introduction for more detail).

I followed the principle of theoretical saturation, seeking the point at which no distinctive new insights would be yielded from additional data collection, to determine the appropriate number of interviews to address the central research question.[4] Ten of the sixty-one total interviews were conducted by a research assistant (Heather Mooney, Boston University) in the summer of 2017 using similar recruitment methods. We each coded these interviews separately, then collaborated to merge our codes; she also wrote and shared interview memos that included descriptive detail and in situ analytical reflections. Interviews lasted between forty minutes and three hours; most lasted about an hour and a half. Interviewees were asked to give a brief overview of their service (why they entered, how long they served, and in what capacity), describe a typical day in the life of their career stages, reflect on the gender and sexuality policy changes, and share the highs and lows of their service experience (see appendix C for the interview guide). These interviews were semistructured, guided by a list of basic questions, though the order of the questions and the ultimate direction of the conversations varied depending on flow, relevance to participants' experience, and time constraints. Unless they were so off topic as to significantly derail the conversation, we probed most digressions and asked impromptu questions as relevant. Unanticipated associations or topics raised by participants are often significant and can even be more important sites of data than those directly solicited. As patterns of new topics began to emerge through the interview collection process, the interview guide was modified accordingly, in keeping with the abductive orientation of this research process.

Aside from the ten interviews conducted by the project's research assistant and coded jointly, I coded the dataset independently using Nvivo software. Generally speaking, data analysis was an iterative process that occurred alongside or in between waves of data collection. That analysis was aided by the abductive methodological recommendations articulated by Timmermans and Tavory: revisiting the phenomenon (repetition of analysis at multiple points in the research process and at different stages of policy change), defamiliarization (distancing from various taken-for-granted assumptions or interpretations to find themes and connections that might otherwise be missed), and alternative casing (considering the data through different theoretical lenses, comparison strategies, and alternative interpretations).[5]

My coding strategy is most similar to what Deterding and Waters call a "flexible coding" approach.[6] In the broadest strokes, I start with index coding, an inventory of the data taken by reading all transcripts as a whole and sorting large chunks of the data into categories (e.g., "jokes and teasing," "sexual harassment," "hormones"). This is the opposite of the traditional grounded theory approach, which generally starts with line-by-line coding that describes the action of each line of text.[7] At the indexing stage, I develop superordinate categories that I later refine and split into basic and then subordinate categories in subsequent reiterations, creating code trees. Data relevant to different superordinate, basic, or subordinate categories are cross-referenced; any given excerpt might be indexed in multiple categories. Throughout the indexing process, I write analytic memos to document emergent connections, concepts, definitions, and hypotheses as they arise. I conduct several indexing passes to identify any significant categories I may have missed; these passes fall into two roughly distinct categories: organic and defamiliarized. Organic passes organize the data a priori through as unfettered and dispassionate a review as possible; the goal is strong objectivity that involves researcher reflexivity and acknowledgment that no researcher can proceed without *any* preconceptions or native orientations.[8] Defamiliarizing passes are a concerted effort to approach the data with inclinations different from the researchers' intuitions. As I try to see the data through someone else's eyes, I might, for example, imagine the code index a scholar in another subdiscipline or an entirely different field of study might develop. This allows for the data to take on new salience and for useful alternate categories to emerge.

After indexing comes analytic coding, which decontextualizes quotes and excerpts from their transcripts of origin and organizes them into increasingly fine-grained clusters that demonstrate patterns. Analytic coding is oriented toward specific research questions or data themes; for example, while indexing ROTC interviews, *place* was an emergent theme in their explanations of the relative gay friendliness of military settings. For a 2017 article, I engaged in analytic data coding to reveal how, why, in what patterns, and under what conditions cadets attribute inclusivity to geographic location (e.g., rural vs. urban, US north vs. US south comparisons).[9] Later, I conducted more iterations of analytic coding related to each chapter of this book and for its overarching argument. Each round involved multiple steps, including alternative casing, varying configurations of code families, modeling various typologies, and comparing code frequency or salience across subgroups. In the example of my 2017 article, the process included running comparisons to assess whether straight and LGB cadets narrated geography and LGBT attitudes differently and whether a participant's own place of origin impacted their explanation of that relationship.

For the book, analytic coding first provided systematic confirmation of my observation that there were contradictory patterns in meaning making surrounding the DADT repeal compared to processes around combat integration and trans inclusion. I used subsequent rounds to test potential hypotheses about that incongruity and, later, to build my final argument using supporting (and discrepant) evidence. In one of my last major coding iterations, I recoded data into ideological orientations (e.g., "trans service is too costly" or "women's bodies are not fit to serve"), which allowed me to identify the logics of inclusion or exclusion in play. The number and the organization of codes evolved over time and adapted to different purposes (articles, presentations, the book).

The final code structure included twelve superordinate codes (what Nvivo calls nodes) and seventy-nine subordinate codes/nodes. This coding hierarchy was less stratified than previous ones, which involved three levels of abstraction but included fewer total codes. This is not because the final code structure was the evolution of partial or less-refined coding "drafts" that could not stand up on their own, but because it was the right structure and level of granularity for this book's analysis. If I publish from this dataset again, I will likely recode and revise the index yet again.

The coding process described here is a recursive one; not only do I reconsider the data at multiple points and for different purposes, I move between indexing and analytic coding as needed. And even a single round of coding involves reiteration; for example, a salient code may occur to me in the twentieth transcript and demand recoding the previous nineteen to index that newly emergent theme. The repeated widening and narrowing of the analytical aperture and the infinite potential strategies of organization make coding a messy, nonlinear practice, but it is necessary to develop construct validity and ultimately, theoretical validity: an abstract explanation of the observed phenomenon that uses concepts developed from and firmly grounded in the data.

BALANCING QUEER CRITICISM AND FEMINIST ETHICS OF CARE

From its first stirrings to its culmination, this research has come with a distressing conflict between my political and intellectual orientation and my empathy for research subjects. My perspective is embedded in queer antiwar and anti-imperialist critique; I am deeply opposed to the nationalist zeal and exceptionalism that sustains US interventionist practices of wealth extraction and dominance by violence (symbolic, literal, and fatal). Throughout this research, I have asked myself: How do I simultaneously critique an institution with which I am at odds while balancing my scholarly inclination to identify with (some might say overidentify with) its participants? Interviewees' accounts of their experiences of inclusion were frequently passionate, persuasive, and emotionally affecting; I often stumbled over myself when, after I walked away or hung up the phone, I processed the emotional highs and lows elicited in the conversations. Even now, as I listen to the interviews, I keenly *feel* the triumph of organizing the first Pride event at the Pentagon, the dread of taking surreptitious hormone shots on a submarine full of cisgender men, the thrill of breaking glass ceilings. And then whiplash would set in as those feelings crashed into the brick wall of what these exhilarating moments respond to: complicity with and enactment of various forms of domination that sustain xenophobia, racism, exploitation, and violence.

That resounding ambivalence has been a source of emotional exhaustion and delayed the completion of this project. It also sabotaged efforts to engage in public sociology or advocacy work along the way. I have written, rewritten, and abandoned a half dozen op-eds on the trans ban, because I couldn't decide what ethical position to take. My instinct is to argue on behalf of the transgender soldiers whose careers and lives were put at risk, whose ambitions were thwarted (for instance, Riley Dosh, the first openly trans graduate of West Point, who found herself unable to commission as an officer and was discharged upon graduation).[10] But every time I tried to lay out an argument, I ran into my own politics. I would write a draft and read it through the eyes of my research participants, then again through the eyes of a queer abolitionist. What did it mean to advocate for the right to be included in this institution that maintains violence, apartheid, and tyranny the world over? Eventually, I would close my laptop, abandon the drafts, and walk away. I hope that, in the fullness of this book-length argument, I have been able to make a coherent argument about incoherent policies as both a critic and an advocate of inclusion. Regardless, the source of that tension bears further reflection.

For many years, I have ruminated on what I see as a nearly irreconcilable tension between feminist and queer theory. I was trained in a feminist methodology grounded in the commitment to theorize and understand the social world through the everyday experiences, or standpoint, of those marginalized within it. Feminist research ethics borrow from Carol Gilligan's "ethics of care," an orientation to action that emphasizes relationality, mutuality, and rapport.[11] In feminist methodology, this often translates into principles of reciprocity, collaboration, and empathy with research participants. Research practices guided by an ethics of care can include paying careful attention to the power dynamics between the research and the researched, consulting or collaborating with research participants in analysis and publication, and "giving back" to researched individuals and communities (through participation incentives, workshops or clinics, amplifying their voices, and advocating for resources).

Although queer analysis shares overlapping concerns—challenging injustice, theorizing from margin to center, and foregrounding power as a primary analytic—it also carries a fundamental cynicism about the liberatory possibilities of research. (To be fair, feminist methods are far from naïve in this regard; see, for example, Judith Stacey's "Can There Be a Feminist Ethnography?")[12] A queer conceptualization of power sees it as something that not only is exerted upon us but also moves through us, is *constitutive of us.* In such a context, changes in research ethics offer no escape hatch. We can never stand outside of power, no matter how exhaustive our attempts. Queer theory has a particularly antagonistic relationship to social science because of its attempts to discipline the social world into observable and reliable patterns, categories, and relations. Queer theory's humanistic origins in literature and philosophy largely obviated the need for such methodological questions, though a literature on queer methods has emerged in recent years.[13] Feminist social science is fundamentally about problems in need of solutions; queer theory is, with scant exception, antinormative and pessimistic, and thereby suspicious of both solution and resolution.[14]

It is this push/pull that churns just below the surface of my specific concerns about this project: on one side is an urge to seek redress to inequalities through research, and on the other, an urge to resist both redress *and* research because they flatten the complexities of social experience and can be repurposed as blunt instruments of governmentality. My own "escape hatches" emerged in the form of two possible vehicles for meaningful rapprochement: transnational feminist interventions and queer praxis, both of which I have integrated into my analysis. Transnational feminism redresses the flaws in feminist conceptualizations of sex, gender, and sexuality that result from exclusive focus on the Global North as the site of its production.[15] The forces of European empire *have* altered racial, gender, and sexual formations across the globe, but those formations are particular to temporal, spatial, and institutional contexts.[16] The Global North does not simply act upon the rest of the globe in a process of one-way diffusion; in reality, a dialectal relationship produces a global network of "webbed connectivities" that link sex/gender/sexuality regimes across time and place.[17] Among other contributions, transnational feminist theory enables us to "think sideways," as Vrushali Patil puts it, tracing connectivities across sites, including those seemingly disparate and unrelated.[18] Applying a transnational feminist analytic to this research raised new considerations. How do research ethics of care shift when we expand the notion of research participants to include those whose lives—and deaths—our direct participants touch? How does bestowing inclusion upon LGBT servicemembers perpetuate a pinkwashing that papers over subaltern violence with diversity "happy talk"?[19]

I also see promise for reconciliation in the arena of queer praxis, particularly in the concept of mutual aid.[20] Mutual aid is a form of political participation that operates outside the confines of the state and state agents. No matter the fatalism a queer theoretical orientation might induce, it is morally indefensible to see the crises of climate change, mass incarceration, border enforcement, poverty, and police brutality and not be called to action. Mutual aid as queer praxis disregards the paltry offerings of reformism; asking for incremental change can never be sufficient for addressing present need—in fact, it only bolsters state power over the marginalized. For example, police reforms like mandatory body cams disguise the inherent subjectivity of policing practices, are selectively enforced, are manipulated to make police brutality look defensible, have a negligible deterrent effect, and can increase criminalizing surveillant gazes when mined not for police misconduct but for potential countervailing civilian misconduct. Mutual aid, on the other hand, responds to obvious and local problems by establishing new social relations that don't rely on government oversight. This can include providing food, housing, and ride shares; creating bail funds and prisoner reentry resources; assembling rapid response networks to obstruct deportations and arrest; and staffing childcare and eldercare collectives. Such projects resist the carceral or capitalist "solutions" that produce new problems of inequality by directly addressing needs without questioning those in need.

Thinking about research methods as queer praxis induces new ways of knowing and distributing knowledge. Can research be a form of queer praxis even though social science is a technology of subordination? How might "giving back" to a research community look different if it operated from a place of mutual aid rather than researcher benevolence? As with all things queer, raising the inherent contradictions in my relationship to this research is less about finding a way to cancel them out or find some sort of half-hearted resolution than about exploring the process that links these contradictions above, below, around, through, and doubling back again. To quote Eve Sedgwick, queer is the "open mesh of possibilities, gaps, overlaps, dissonances and resonances, lapses and excesses of meaning when the constituent elements of anyone's gender, of anyone's sexuality"—or in this case, anyone's research—"can't be made to signify monolithically."[21] Peering through this mesh, this kaleidoscopic lens, finding creative new ways to see and experience the world, might encourage a scholarly reorientation toward liberation, however distant it may appear.

Methodological Appendix B

Table 1 Descriptive Statistics of Servicemember Sample

Participant Characteristics	*N*	%
Age		
18–24	17	29.8
25–29	7	12.3
30–39	14	24.6
40–49	8	14.0
50 and over	8	14.0
Race/Ethnicity		
White	43	75.4
Black	4	7.0
Biracial	2	3.5
Asian	3	5.3
Latine/x/o/a	3	5.3
Gender		
Cisgender	50	87.7
Transgender	7	12.3
Man	32	56.1
Woman	25	43.9
Sexual Identity		
Lesbian	9	15.8
Gay	4	7.0
Bisexual	1	1.8
Queer	6	10.5
Straight	37	64.9
Branch		
Air Force	12	21.1
Army	12	21.1
Marines	3	5.3
Navy	14	24.6
Army ROTC	16	28.1
Years of Service		
< 5 years	26	45.6
5–10 years	10	17.5
11 years or more	21	36.8

Note: Three participants did not provide their age, and two did not report race/ethnicity.

Methodological Appendix C

INTERVIEW GUIDE

I. Current (or most recent) military experiences

1. Are you currently serving? If so, what kind of work/responsibilities do you have? If not, when did you finish your service, and why?
2. Are you interested in having a family/do you have a family? How do you balance service and your personal or family life?
3. Tell me about your friendships and relationships in the military. Are/were they gender mixed? Did you have any outside hobbies or interests? Tell me about those. What kinds of things would you do to blow off steam?
4. What about fraternization rules? How do you manage friendships/relationships in the military given these codes?
5. What about relationships with supervisors? Subordinates? Who do you consider your role models on the job?
6. Did you ever participate in any hazing rituals or traditions as part of your service? What were those like? Do you think that women and openly LGBT people entering formerly all-male and ostensibly heterosexual areas of the military will change/has changed these rituals? Do you miss them or wish you'd experienced them?
7. Have you received training in sexual assault/sexual harassment? What was it like? Have you ever encountered issues of sexual harassment or assault yourself? How did you deal with it?
8. How do you feel about recent changes that allow women into previously all-male programs and positions, such as Ranger School or certain infantry positions? Do

you think opening combat to women has changed the military in any significant way?

9. Were you in the military at the time of the DADT repeal? What do you remember about that time? What did your supervisors tell you about the repeal? What was the feeling about it among your coworkers? (If not, do you know any stories from other soldiers, friends, or family members about what it was like before the repeal?)
10. How do you feel about the repeal? Do you think it has changed the military in any significant way?
11. Were you/do you know anyone who is/was open about being LGBT? How would you characterize your/their service experience?
12. In recent years, the DOD policy changed to allow transgender individuals to serve, which has since been temporarily suspended at the behest of Trump. How do you feel about the DOD's policy and Trump's reversal? Are there particular problems and/or benefits you foresee with full, open trans service?

II. Future plans

1. What are your plans for the rest of your service (or post-service)?
2. What do you like best about a career in the military? What do you like least?
3. What's the one misconception about the military you hear the most and you'd like to clear up for people?

Notes

INTRODUCTION

1. Reddy (2011).

2. See George H. W. Bush Presidential Museum (1991) for the transcript of this speech in full.

3. Puar (2007).

4. For pragmatic purposes, I sometimes refer to LGB, women, and trans servicemembers as distinct groups to indicate the lines that participants drew between each of the relevant policies and the questions around inclusion that they evoke. I do not mean to imply that these are mutually exclusive (or unrelated) categories.

5. See Street, Vogt, and Dutra (2009) for a discussion of cisgender women's presence on the front lines in Iraq and Afghanistan during the past two decades.

6. Although somewhat unwieldy, I use the term *servicemembers* throughout to refer collectively to the armed forces instead of *soldier*, commonly mistaken as synonymous with servicemember by civilians. Soldier refers only to members of the Army and not the Air Force (*airmen*), Coast Guard (*coasties*), Navy (*sailors*), or the Marines (*Marines*).

7. See Hennen (2008) on the effeminacy effect.

8. Abu-Lughod (2015); Alexander (2006); Khalid (2011); Lobasz (2008); Puar (2007).

9. Grewal (2017).

10. See Acker (1990) on the theory of gendered organizations.

11. Krafft-Ebing (1886).

12. Canaday (2009).

13. See Valentine (2007) for this history and an analysis of its relationship to changes in gender/sexuality paradigms.

14. Butler (1990). See Patil (2018) for a discussion of how the heterosexual matrix both is an imperial formation *and* is shaped by the various sites of its influence, which in turn affects both Western and non-Western sex/gender/sexuality formations.

15. Westbrook and Schilt (2014, 34).

16. Patil (2018).

17. Somerville (2000).

18. See Garner and Selod (2015); and Zopf (2018).

19. Puar (2007).

20. Khalili (2011).

21. Ferguson (2018).

22. Ferguson (2018).

23. For more on social movement tactical repertoires, see Taylor and Van Dyke (2008).

24. Duggan (2002). See also Gilreath (2011) for how homonormativity set the stage for the DADT repeal.

25. Yoshino (1998).

26. Hennen (2008, 48).

27. The popular "origin story" of homosexuality still relied on the body, but the shift from gender confusion to genetic predisposition had moved the source to DNA and away from the visible body.

28. Kandiyoti (1988).

29. Enloe (2000).

30. For more on gendered 9/11 discourse, see Drew (2004); Puar and Rai (2002); and Feitz and Nagel (2008).

31. See Nagel (1998); and Mikdashi and Puar (2016) for more on sexualized militarism, including the sexualization of the "enemy" as perverse or pathetic vis-à-vis the sexually normalized patriot.

32. Puar and Rai (2002).

33. Montegary (2015).

34. Puar (2007).

35. Allsep (2013); Connell (1993] 2005, 77).

36. Bayard de Volo and Hall (2015); Banner (2012); Burke (2004); Ward (2015).

37. Brown (2008, 95).

38. See Schulman (2011) for more on the practice of pinkwashing.

39. Walters (2014).

40. Spivak (1985).

41. cooke (2002, 486).

42. See Chandra Talpade Mohanty's (1988) classic transnational feminist critique, "Under Western Eyes."

43. Grewal (2017).

44. Beauchamp (2019, 2).

45. Beauchamp (2009, 356).

46. See Johnson (2016) on transnormativity.

47. See Spade (2011).

48. Quoted in Hajjar (2014, 121).

49. Lamont and Swidler (2014).

50. Although I recruited seven new participants, one person was ultimately too busy to participate and dropped out of the study prior to our interview.

51. These numbers include policy stakeholders who had served or were serving in the military at the time of our interview, for a total of fifty-seven interviews with military personnel. See appendix A for a more detailed breakdown of the gender and sexual identities of research participants.

52. All stakeholder interviewees' names are used with permission; all other participants' names are pseudonyms.

53. Brown (2012, 1066).

54. Brown (2012, 1067).

55. Spade and Belkin (2021, 296).

56. Epstein (1994).

57. For more on the promise of queer sociological methods for deciphering "the mess" of social relations, see Meadow, Schilt, and Compton (2018).

58. Westbrook (2020).

59. Butler (2004, 31, 29).

60. For more on necropolitics, see Mbembe (2019).

CHAPTER 1. A HISTORY OF THE GAY BAN

1. With the exception of policy stakeholders who agreed to be identified by name, all names are pseudonyms to protect the confidentiality of research participants. In each chapter, the first mention of a participant includes age, race, gender, and military branch; thereafter, I use the pseudonym only.

2. Canaday (2009).

3. Puri (2016).

4. See McRuer (2010) on sexuality and compulsory able-bodiedness. See Montegary (2015) for the continued history of this anxiety in the DADT era.

5. Terry (1999).

6. Montegary (2015).

7. Alexander (2006).

8. Canaday (2009).

9. Banner (2012); Evans (2001); Shilts (1994).

10. Jane Ward (2020) documents the "heterosexual repair industry" devoted to this work in *The Tragedy of Heterosexuality.*

11. Quoted in Canaday (2009, 70).

12. Quoted in Canaday (2009, 79).

13. Bérubé (1990).

14. This was reinforced in the language of sodomy statues ("conduct unbecoming of an officer and a *gentleman*"); see Banner (2012).

15. Evans (2001).

16. Banner (2012).

17. Canaday (2009, 177–78).

18. Canaday (2009, 178).

19. Banner (2012); Damiano (1998).

20. Canaday (2009).

21. Johnson (2004).

22. Office of the Secretary of Defense (1962).

23. Korb (1994); Rostker et al. (1993).

24. US Dep't of Def. Dir. 1332.14, Enlisted Administrative Separations (January 15, 1981).

25. This phrasing is a spin on Stein's famous line, "A rose is a rose is a rose" in her 1922 poem, "Sacred Emily." The line is commonly interpreted as a statement of the law of identity—or put in other words, "It is what it is."

26. Korb and Rothman (2013).

27. See C-SPAN (1993) for a transcript of the full press conference.

28. Halley (1999).

29. Halley (1999, 2). See also Banner (2012).

30. Montegary (2015).

31. Department of Defense (2010).

32. Banner (2012).

33. Benecke (2011).

34. Dang and Frazer (2005).

35. Neff and Edgell (2013).

36. 658 F.3d 1162 (9th Cir. 2004), 429 F. Supp. 2d 385 (D. Mass. 2006), and 527 F.3d 806 (9th Cir. 2008), respectively.

37. See Frank (2013).

38. Belkin and Bateman (2003); Trivette (2010).

39. Rostker et al. (1993).

40. Neff and Edgell (2013); Parco and Levy (2013).

41. See Belkin (2011) for a comprehensive review of repeal strategy.

42. Belkin (2011); Frank (2013); Neff and Edgell (2013).

43. Belkin (2011).
44. See Belkin et al. (2012).
45. Fulton (2013); Neff and Edgell (2013).
46. Belkin (2011, 191).
47. Belkin (2011); Trivette (2010).
48. See, for example, Moradi (2009).
49. Montegary (2015, 899).
50. Grewal (2017).
51. Reddy (2011).
52. See also Puar (2007).
53. Puar (2007).
54. Moussawi (2020).
55. Coates (2019).
56. Puar (2007).
57. See *New York Times* (1989) for the full transcript of this speech.
58. National and sexual exceptionalism is not the sole purview of the United States; I specify the United States here to contextualize sexual exceptionalism in DADT repeal discourse.
59. Puar and Rai (2002).
60. Montegary (2015, 893).
61. Puar (2007, 9).
62. Gilreath (2011).
63. Puar (2017b).
64. Spade and Willse (2014).
65. Gilreath (2011); Puar (2007); Spade and Willse (2014).
66. See C-SPAN (1993).
67. See Belkin et al. (2013) for more on Amos's comments on the repeal.
68. For more, see Enloe (2000).
69. Duggan (2003, 50).
70. Spade and Willse (2014, 7).
71. Title 10 of the US Code legislates the armed forces; the Repeal Act that did end DADT did not include nondiscrimination protections, though they were later added in 2015.
72. Belkin et al. (2009).
73. Belkin (2011); Parco and Levy (2013).
74. For example, Crandall (2012).
75. For example, Rich, Schutten, and Rogers (2012).
76. For example, Johnson et al. (2013).
77. For example, Wilder and Wilder (2012).
78. For example, Goldbach and Castro (2016).
79. Belkin et al. (2012); Ender et al. (2013).

80. Spade and Belkin (2021, 288).
81. Massey and Nair (2018).
82. Gossett, Stanley, and Burton (2017).

CHAPTER 2. STRIKING THE HOMONORMATIVE BARGAIN

1. McPeak (2010).
2. For more on securitization, see Grewal (2017).
3. Ahmed (2012).
4. Rich (1980).
5. Wittig (1992, 40).
6. Puar (2007, xii).
7. Ward (2008, 2).
8. The anonymous research participants are identified by race, gender, sexual identity, and branch the first time they are introduced in each chapter. Unless explicitly identified as a veteran or an ROTC cadet, participants can be assumed to be current servicemembers.
9. Sedgwick (1990).
10. Trivette (2010).
11. Connell (2014).
12. See Rich, Schutten, and Rogers (2012).
13. See Canaday (2009) for the history and management of these anxieties in the military.
14. Quoted in Shawver (1995, 158).
15. For more on diversity work in institutions, see Ahmed (2012).
16. Seidman (2004).
17. See Williams and Connell (2010).
18. Connell (2014).
19. See Ferguson (2004, 2018); Gossett, Stanley, and Burton (2017); Muñoz (2009).
20. Walters (2014); Brown (2008).
21. Brown (2008).
22. For critiques of diversity and multiculturalism discourse and its relationship to militarism, see Grewal (2017); Montegary (2015).
23. Ahmed (2012).
24. And indeed, this claim has been made frequently of late by liberal college and university administrators in support of campus events featuring Ben Shapiro, Milo Yiannopoulos, and others.
25. See Ray (2018) for a discussion of conservative appeals for diversity of thought in higher education.
26. Burke (2004).
27. Rich, Schutten, and Rogers (2012).

28. Connell (2014).

29. Somerville (2005); *Loving v. Virginia* was the 1967 Supreme Court case that declared unconstitutional laws against interracial marriage ("miscegenation"). The Supreme Court overturned DOMA in *United States v. Windsor* in 2013. Both decisions hinged on violations of the due process clause. See also Reddy (2008) for a critical reading of the use of *Loving* to overturn DOMA.

30. Montegary (2015, 901).

31. See Zopf (2018) for a discussion of how race, ethnicity, national origin, religion, and discourse on terrorism combine to racialize Arabs and Middle Easterners as brown.

32. Mbembe (2019).

33. Interestingly enough, "the turban is not a hat" has been a slogan for religious headwear accommodations. Whether intentional or not, Christopher's use of hat as synonymous with turban thwarts liberal Sikh advocacy group efforts "driven by a desire to inhabit a proper Sikh American heteromasculinity, one at significant remove from the perverse sexualities ascribed to terrorist bodies" (Puar 2007, 167).

34. Grewal (2017, 13).

35. Lange (2018).

36. Haritaworn, Kuntsman, and Posocco (2014).

CHAPTER 3. OPEN LGB SERVICE AND QUEER SOCIAL CONTROL

1. Bérubé (1990, 72).
2. Bérubé (1990, 87).
3. Burke (2004); Ward (2015).
4. See Williams, Guiffre, and Dellinger (2009).
5. See Hoskin (2020) for an analysis of how femmephobia structures (lesbian, gay, bisexual, transgender, queer) LGBTQ+ experience.
6. Bailey (2021, 1).
7. Nash and Browne (2020).
8. Connell (2014).
9. Goffman (1959).
10. For more on the queer control complex, see Robinson (2020).
11. Trivette (2010).
12. See Ward (2015).
13. Belkin (2001).
14. Belkin (2001); Bérubé (1990); Zeeland (1995).
15. Zeeland (1995).
16. Ward (2015).

17. Ward (2015); Zeeland (1995).
18. See, for example Burke (2004); Serlin (2003); Ward (2015); Zeeland (1995).
19. Serlin (2003).
20. Burke (2004); Bronner (2007).
21. Serlin (2003, 152).
22. For example, see Serlin's (2003) analysis of The Amputettes.
23. Ward (2015).
24. Butler (1997).
25. Banner (2012); Damiano (1998).
26. Shawver (1995).
27. See Turley (2010).
28. For statistics on LGBT experiences of sexual harassment and assault post-repeal, see Gurung et al. (2018); and Morral et al. (2015).
29. See chapter 1 for an explanation of gender trouble and the regulatory regimes like the military that try to contain it (Butler 1990).
30. Carian and Johnson (2022).
31. Bourdieu (1984).
32. Halperin (2014).
33. Yoshino (2006, 22–23).
34. Banner (2012).
35. Banner (2012).
36. Banner (2012); Damiano (1998); Herbert (1998); Rich, Schutten, and Rogers (2012).
37. Banner (2012, 111).
38. Benecke and Dodge (1990); Britton and Williams (1995); Damiano (1998); Herbert (1998).
39. Herbert (1998). In the past several years, the armed forces have begun to move toward a more gender-neutral uniform standard; see part 2 for more discussion.
40. Dang and Frazer (2005).
41. See the introduction as well as Schilt and Westbrook (2009) for more on the sociology of gender panic.
42. See the introduction for further contextualization of hegemonic masculinity (Connell 1993).
43. Somerville (2000).
44. Collins (2000).
45. See Asch, Miller, and Malchiodi (2012); Foynes, Shipherd, and Harrington (2013).
46. For example, Banner (2012).
47. Department of Defense (2010, 131).
48. See also Banner (2012).
49. West and Zimmerman (1987).

50. Pascoe (2011).

51. Pascoe (2011, 91).

52. See chapter 2 for more on the use of tolerance as a rationale for open service.

53. See chapter 2 and Cohen (1997) for more on this use of queerness, which differs from its use as a sexual identity signifier.

54. See Han (2021) for an analysis of Orientalism in discourses about Asian men's race, gender, sexuality, and embodiment.

55. Bayard de Volo and Hall (2015, 865–66).

56. Pascoe (2013).

57. For more on the social construction of the "normal gay," see Seidman (2002).

58. Coronges et al. (2013).

CHAPTER 4. THE IMPOSSIBILITY OF WOMEN WARRIORS

1. Alvarez (2009); Holmstedt (2008).

2. Alvarez (2009).

3. Banner (2012); Benecke and Dodge (1990); Damiano (1998); Herbert (1998).

4. Allsep (2013); Feitz and Nagel (2008); Herbert (1998); Millar (2015).

5. Grewal (2017).

6. Razavi (2021).

7. Gibson (1994).

8. Allsep (2013).

9. Pauw (1981); Massey (1994).

10. For a discussion of gender trouble and its significance in the context of the military refer to the introduction.

11. Benecke and Dodge (1990, 219).

12. Scrivener (1999).

13. Scrivener (1999, 365).

14. Canaday (2009, 196).

15. Canaday (2009, 213).

16. Canaday (2009, 210).

17. The 2 percent quota was not abolished until the Vietnam War, when the military was once again in need of recruits and such gender quotas became inconvenient. See Szitanyi (2020) for more.

18. Szitanyi (2020).

19. Connell (1993).

20. Bailey (2009); Szitanyi (2020).

21. Rimalt (2003); Szitanyi (2020).

22. Herbert (1998).

23. Quoted in Kamarck (2016).

24. Kamarck (2016, 4, 6).

25. Turchik and Wilson (2010).
26. Quoted in Herbert (1998, 30).
27. Peterson (1999).
28. Bayard de Volo and Hall (2015); Burke (2004).
29. Bayard de Volo and Hall (2015, 876).
30. Brownson (2014); King (2015); Ward (2015).
31. Quoted in Banner (2012, 62).
32. Herbert (1998).
33. Brownson (2014, 765).
34. Brownson (2014, 785).
35. King (2015).
36. Millar (2015). See also Butler (2016) on the concept of "grievability" in the frames of war.
37. MacKenzie (2015); Street, Vogt and Dutra (2009).
38. Holmstedt (2008); MacKenzie (2015).
39. Alvarez (2009).
40. Alvarez (2009).
41. Kamarck (2016).
42. Mattocks et al. (2012).
43. For example, Crandall (2012).
44. Razavi (2021).
45. Trobaugh (2018).
46. Maginnis (2013, 227).
47. Abramson (2013).
48. Parker (2015).
49. See Schaefer et al. (2015) for one such analysis.
50. Kamarck (2016); Rosen, Knudson, and Fancher (2003).
51. Abramson (2013).
52. Brownson (2014, 776).
53. Brownson (2014, 776).
54. Clark (2021).
55. Peach (1994); Rollins (2011).
56. See Gutmann (2000); King (2015); Manninger (2008); Browne (2007); Mitchell (1997).
57. See Gutmann (2000) as an example and MacKenzie (2015) for analysis of "natural order" rhetoric.
58. Fine (2017); Enloe (2000).
59. See, for example, the outrage and inquiry over the first women to pass Ranger School.
60. *Military Times* (2013).
61. Szitanyi (2020); Crandall (2012); Howard and Prividera (2004).
62. For a definition of benevolent sexism, see Glick and Fiske (1996).

63. Holland (2006); Howard and Prividera (2004); Kumar (2007); Lobasz (2008).
64. Holland (2006); Howard and Prividera (2004).
65. Quoted in Howard and Prividera (2004, 94).
66. Holland (2006).
67. Bragg (2004, 37).
68. Quoted in Howard and Prividera (2004, 93).
69. Quoted in Lobasz (2008, 313).
70. Quoted in Howard and Prividera (2004, 95).
71. Hyland (2003).
72. Holland (2006); Lobasz (2008).
73. Holland (2006, 40).
74. Kumar (2007, 302).
75. See also Collins (2000) on the "controlling image" of the Welfare Queen, a rhetorical device used to demonize the sexuality of women of color, Black women in particular.
76. Lobasz (2008, 316–17).
77. Lobasz (2008).
78. Gronnvoll (2007, 376).
79. Lobasz (2008, 325).
80. Gronnvoll (2007); Lobasz (2008).
81. Lobasz (2008, 326).
82. Holland (2006, 44).
83. Holland (2006, 43).
84. Quoted in Kaufman-Osborn (2005, 601).
85. Quoted in Gronnvoll (2007, 383).
86. Quoted in Gronnvoll (2007, 384).
87. Quoted in Lobasz (2008, 328).
88. Ehrenreich (2004).
89. Grewal (2017, 120).
90. Ravazi (2021, 362).
91. Puar and Rai (2002, 127).
92. Spivak (1985).
93. For an example of this argument, see MacKenzie (2015).
94. Mesok (2016, 46).
95. See #NatSecGirlSquad (n.d.)
96. Mesok (2016, 56).
97. Ravazi (2021).
98. Mesok (2016, 68).
99. Quoted in Rosenberg and Phillips (2015).
100. Women have successfully passed all of these courses except the Air Force's special forces training program; two women are enrolled in the program at the time of this writing.

CHAPTER 5. PATRIOTIC PATERNALISM OF COMBAT EXCLUSION

1. Asch, Miller, and Malchiodi (2012) find that women in occupations partially closed by restrictions on their participation in ground combat earn less than those in fully open occupations, suggesting that the end of combat exclusion may improve the earnings of this group of women.

2. Asch, Miller, and Malchiodi (2012). This research also shows that men of color experience lower rates of promotion compared to white men, but not lower levels of retention, which offsets their wage penalty.

3. Quoted in Lamothe (2015).

4. SOFREP (2015).

5. See previous chapters for a definition of necropolitics and analysis of how they shaped LGB inclusion.

6. Ferguson (2018).

7. Bonnes (2017).

8. Crawley, Foley, and Shehan (2008); Hively and El-Alayli (2014); Young (1980).

9. Farber (2017).

10. Brownson (2014).

11. See Fine (2017) for a review of scientific studies on testosterone's effects.

12. Rubin (1975, 182).

13. Dinnerstein ([1976] 1999).

14. McCaughey (2008).

15. Parker (2015).

16. Mattocks et al. (2012); Street, Vogt, and Dutra (2009); Turchik and Wilson (2010).

17. Kaufman-Osborn (2005, 601).

18. Parker (2015).

19. Estes (2012).

20. Puar (2007). For more on homonationalism, see chapter 2.

21. Bonnes (2017).

22. Bailey (2021); see 49–50 for more on how colorism is implicated in the social experience of misogynoir.

CHAPTER 6. THE TRANS BAN TUG OF WAR

1. Pesquiera was not interviewed for this book; his experience is recreated here from journalistic accounts (see Allen 2019; GMA 2019; Hernandez 2019; Leffler 2019).

2. See Hernandez (2019).

3. Accession essentially refers to joining the military, as opposed to retention; both Carter's and Mattis's plans maintained separate policies governing accession and retention.

4. Servicemembers who entered and were diagnosed with or treated for gender dysphoria prior to April 12, 2019, were allowed to continue and to receive the relevant healthcare.

5. Hernandez (2019).

6. Allen (2019).

7. Quoted in Allen (2019).

8. GMA (2019).

9. Elders et al. (2015).

10. Blosnich et al. (2013); Bryant and Schilt (2008); Harrison-Quintana and Herman (2013).

11. James et al. (2016).

12. Connell (2017); Ender, Rohall, and Matthews (2016).

13. Elders et al. (2015); Kerrigan (2012); Parco, Levy, and Spears (2015); Yerke and Mitchell (2013).

14. Crosbie and Posard (2016); Elders et al. (2015); Mazur (2014); Schaefer et al. (2015).

15. For example, Belkin (2015); Elders and Steinman (2014); Mazur (2014).

16. See Harrison-Quintana and Herman (2013); and Parco, Levy, and Spears (2015) on serving in silence. See Schaefer et al. (2015) on military fitness. See Kerrigan (2012); Okros and Scott (2014); and Yerke and Mitchell (2013) for case studies of transgender service in other national contexts.

17. See Embser-Herbert and Fram (2021) for an (illuminating) exception.

18. See Johnson (2016) on the concept of transnormativity.

19. Shuster (2021).

20. Schilt and Westbrook (2015).

21. Meyerowitz (2002).

22. Kalin (2021).

23. Skidmore (2011); Meyerowitz (2002); Gill-Peterson (2018).

24. Gill-Peterson (2018).

25. Skidmore (2011).

26. Skidmore (2011, 284).

27. Embser-Herbert and Fram (2021). The question of whether these servicemembers were women who strategically presented themselves as men to be eligible to serve or if they were transsexual/transgender men is a complicated one, which I bracket here for the sake of expediency. See Gill-Peterson (2018); Meyerowitz (2002); and Stryker (2008) for more on the difficulties of pronouncing as definitively cisgender or transgender such historical figures.

28. Canaday (2009).

29. "TS Discharged from Naval Reserve" (1978, 6).

30. "TS Discharged from Naval Reserve" (1978, 7).

31. In addition to DODI 6130.03 and 1332.14, the criteria of "conduct unbecoming" and "prejudicial to good order" that warrant sanction by the Uniform Code of Military Justice (UCMJ) have been used to discharge possibly transgender servicemembers for "cross-dressing" (see, e.g., *US v. Davis*, 1988 and *US v. Guerrero*, 1991). Ironically, cross-dressing is a tradition in the military, including "King Neptune" or "crossing the line" ceremonies; in this context, cross-dressing is not seen as conduct unbecoming but rather as important to maintaining morale.

32. Elders et al. (2015, 211).

33. Kerrigan (2012).

34. See Hepler (2010).

35. Spade and Belkin (2021).

36. Juro (2014).

37. See Sparts (n.d.).

38. Belkin (2016).

39. See Belkin and Mazur (2015); Elders and Steinman (2014); Okros and Scott (2014).

40. Belkin (2015); Elders and Steinman (2014); Mazur (2014).

41. Belkin (2015).

42. Brown and Jones (2016); Bryant and Schilt (2008); Shipherd et al. (2012).

43. Bryant and Schilt (2008); Harrison-Quintana and Herman (2013); Hill et al. (2016); Shipherd et al. (2012).

44. Yerke and Mitchell (2013).

45. Belkin and Spade (2021).

46. Loss of lethality also shows up as a primary rationale for the return to a trans ban; see Mattis (2018). See parts 1 and 2 for more discussion of the necropolitical implications of this preoccupation.

47. See Department of Defense (2015a) for the full transcript.

48. See Department of Defense (2015b) for the press release.

49. Schafer et al. (2016).

50. Embser-Herbert and Fram (2021, 29).

51. Embser-Herbert and Fram (2021, 29).

52. See Kerrigan (2012) for more detail on the relevant case law regarding transgender medical restrictions prior to the Carter plan.

53. Bryant and Schilt (2008); Harrison-Quintana and Herman (2013); Hill et al. (2016); Shipherd et al. (2010).

54. See Mattis (2018).

55. See Embser-Herbert and Fram (2021) for an extended description of these hearings and their media coverage.

56. Connell (2010).

57. West and Zimmerman (1987).

58. Johnson (2016).

59. Gill-Peterson (2018); shuster (2021); Spade (2011).

60. *Passibility* refers to trans people's abilities to "pass" as cisgender (or people of color as white, as it is used in the context of race). It has been rightly critiqued for privileging a cisgender standard of trans "success" (Bornstein 1995) and for reinforcing discrimination against those who can't or won't participate in passing (Beauchamp 2019).

61. Stryker (2008).

62. Spade and Belkin (2021).

63. Since 2015, the Equality Act has succeeded ENDA as the preferred vehicle for LGBT nondiscrimination legislation. The Equality Act is inclusive of gender identity and expression and expands the scope to include not just employment but also public accommodations, housing, education, federally funded programs, credit, and jury service.

64. Chibarro (2011).

65. Spade and Belkin (2021, 284).

66. Beauchamp (2009).

67. Beauchamp (2009).

68. Beauchamp (2019).

69. Snorton and Haritaworn (2013, 67).

70. Westbrook (2020).

71. Snorton and Haritaworn (2013, 67).

72. Gill-Peterson (2018, 28).

73. Gill-Peterson (2018, 26). See also Patil (2018).

74. For example, Grewal (2017); Gosset, Stanley, and Burton (2017); Reddy (2011); Ferguson (2004); Patil (2018); Puar (2007); Snorton (2017).

75. Spade quoted in Geidner (2013).

76. Anzaldúa (1987).

77. Sandoval (1991, 12).

78. Gossett, Stanley, and Burton (2017).

CHAPTER 7. THE TRANSGENDERING ORGANIZATION

1. For more on the misogyny paradox, see Ward (2020).

2. See Connell (2010).

3. See Hochschild (1994) on the concept of "magnified moments."

4. *Truthiness* references the ability of a political assertion to carry the weight of a fact, even absence of any evidence.

5. Schilt and Westbrook (2015).

6. Schilt and Westbrook (2015, 34).

7. This interview was one of ten conducted by a graduate research assistant (Heather Mooney, Boston University). See Stryker and Whittle (2006).

8. Hochschild (1994, 4).

9. Bryant and Schilt (2008).
10. Gossett, Stanley, and Burton (2017, xv).
11. Gossett, Stanley, and Burton (2017, xvi).
12. Gossett, Stanley, and Burton (2017, xxvii).
13. Stryker (2006, 8).
14. Stryker (2006, 8).
15. Stryker (2006, 9).
16. Spade (2011, 20).
17. Stryker (1994, 246–47).

CHAPTER 8. WE WILL BE GREETED AS GAY LIBERATORS?

1. Kerrigan (2012).
2. Montegary (2015).
3. Spade and Belkin (2021, 298).
4. Duggan (2002).
5. Connell (2014); Rumens and Kerfoot (2009).
6. Allsep (2013); Banner (2012); Britton and Williams (1995); Herbert (1998).
7. Enloe (2000, 16).
8. Ahmed (2010, 20). See appendix A for more.
9. See appendix A for more.
10. See, as just a few examples, challenges to housing nondiscrimination, abortion access, sexual harassment protections, and voter enfranchisement law.
11. Farrow (2011, 9).
12. Massey and Nair (2018).
13. Negin (2020).
14. See Hartung and Freeman (2020) for a report detailing such a budget adjustment.
15. Massey and Nair (2018).
16. See Haritaworn, Kuntsman, and Posocco (2014) on the construction of necropolitical death worlds.
17. Butler (2016).
18. See Puar (2017a).
19. Conrad and Sycamore (2011, 8).
20. See Gibbons-Neff (2020).
21. Spade and Belkin (2021, 292).
22. Connell (2018). The concepts of ambivalent observance and epistemology of contradiction were coined, respectively, by Jodi O'Brien (2009, 471) and Jessica Fields (2013, 6).
23. Muñoz (2009, 189).
24. Gilreath (2011); Massey and Nair (2018).

25. Sycamore (2013).

26. See Muñoz (2009) for more on the concept of queer utopia.

27. I say this not to position Biden as the solution to inequalities—far from it, in fact—but to acknowledge the hard work and courage of those who made this possible.

METHODOLOGICAL APPENDIX A

1. Timmermans and Tavory (2012) characterize the abductive methodological approach as the creative inferential development of hypotheses based on surprising evidence. In this case, the dissonance between opinions on the DADT repeal compared to opinions on cisgender women's combat service and trans inclusion produced a revised research question/interview guide and guided coding and analysis.

2. In an abductive or grounded theory approach, analysis follows from data.

3. Prior to its transfer to Homeland Security in 2003, it operated under the Departments of Treasury (1790–1966) and Transportation (1967–2003); it has never been operated directly by the Department of Defense.

4. Glaser and Strauss (1967); see also Hennink, Kaiser, and Marconi (2017) for a detailed discussion of thresholds for code saturation versus meaning saturation.

5. Timmermans and Tavory (2012).

6. Deterding and Waters (2018).

7. See, for example, Charmaz's (2006) coding instruction in *Constructing Grounded Theory*.

8. See Harding (1992).

9. Connell (2017).

10. Dosh (2019).

11. See Gilligan (1982).

12. Stacey (1988).

13. Queer methods bring analytic attention to queer experience, aesthetics, and sensibilities and pay particular attention to transgression and contradiction as especially fruitful analytics; for more see Meadow, Schilt, and Compton (2018) or Ghaziani and Brim (2019).

14. For a notable and highly generative anomaly, see Muñoz (2009).

15. See Patil (2013, 2018).

16. See Patil (2018); Puri (2016).

17. Kim-Puri (2005).

18. Patil (2018).

19. Ahmed (2010); Bell and Hartmann (2007).

20. For a discussion of mutual aid and its relationship to queer praxis, see Spade (2020).

21. Sedgwick (1993, 8).

References

Abramson, Larry. 2013. "Women in Combat: Obstacles Remain as Exclusion Policy Ends." *Morning Edition*, National Public Radio, May 13.

Abu-Lughod, Lila. 2015. "Introduction: The Politics of Feminist Politics." *Comparative Studies of South Asia, Africa and the Middle East* 35 (3): 505–7.

Acker, Joan. 1990. "Hierarchies, Jobs, Bodies: A Theory of Gendered Organizations." *Gender & Society* 4 (2): 139–58.

Ahmed, Sara. 2010. *The Promise of Happiness*. Durham, NC: Duke University Press.

———. 2012. *On Being Included: Racism and Diversity in Institutional Life*. Durham, NC: Duke University Press.

———. 2016. *Living a Feminist Life*. Durham, NC: Duke University Press.

———. 2017. *Living a Feminist Life*. Durham, NC: Duke University Press.

Alexander, M. Jacqui. 2006. "Not Just (Any)Body Can Be a Patriot: 'Homeland' Security as Empire Building." In *Interrogating Imperialism*, edited by R. L. Riley and N. Inayatullah, 207–40 . New York: Palgrave Macmillan US.

Alford, Brandon, and Shawna J. Lee. 2016. "Toward Complete Inclusion: Lesbian, Gay, Bisexual, and Transgender Military Service Members after Repeal of Don't Ask, Don't Tell." *Social Work* 61 (3): 257–65.

Allen, Samantha. 2019. "Meet Map Pesqueira, the First Trans Person Prevented from Joining the Military by Trump's Ban." *Daily Beast*, April 19. www

.thedailybeast.com/meet-map-pesqueira-the-first-trans-person-prevented-from-joining-the-military-by-trumps-ban.

Allsep, L. Michael. 2013. "The Myth of the Warrior: Martial Masculinity and the End of Don't Ask, Don't Tell." *Journal of Homosexuality* 60 (2–3): 381–400.

Alvarez, Lizette. 2009. "G.I. Jane Breaks the Combat Barrier." *New York Times*, August 15. www.nytimes.com/2009/08/16/us/16women.html.

Anzaldúa, Gloria. 1987. *Borderlands/La Frontera: The New Mestiza*. San Francisco: Aunt Lute Books.

Asch, Beth J., Trey Miller, and Alessandro Malchiodi. 2012. *A New Look at Gender and Minority Differences in Officer Career Progression in the Military*. Rand Corporation Technical Reports. www.rand.org/pubs/technical_reports/TR1159.html.

Bailey, Beth L. 2009. *America's Army: Making the All-Volunteer Force*. Cambridge, MA: Harvard University Press.

Bailey, Moya. 2021. *Misogynoir Transformed: Black Women's Digital Resistance*. New York: NYU Press.

Banner, Francine. 2012. "It's Not All Flowers and Daisies: Masculinity, Heteronormativity and the Obscuring of Lesbian Identity in the Repeal of Don't Ask, Don't Tell." *Yale Journal of Law & Feminism* 24: 61–117.

Bayard de Volo, Lorraine, and Lynn K. Hall. 2015. "'I Wish All the Ladies Were Holes in the Road': The US Air Force Academy and the Gendered Continuum of Violence." *Signs: Journal of Women in Culture and Society* 40 (4): 865–89.

Beauchamp, Toby. 2009. "Artful Concealment and Strategic Visibility: Transgender Bodies and U.S. State Surveillance after 9/11." *Surveillance & Society* 6 (4): 356–66.

———. 2019. *Going Stealth: Transgender Politics and U.S. Surveillance Practices*. Durham, NC: Duke University Press.

Belkin, Aaron. 2001. "Breaking Rank: Military Homophobia and the Production of Queer Practices and Identities." *Georgetown Journal of Gender and the Law* 3: 83.

———. 2003. "Don't Ask, Don't Tell: Is the Gay Ban Based on Military Necessity?" *Parameters* 33 (2): 108–19.

———. 2011. *How We Won: Progressive Lessons from the Repeal of "Don't Ask, Don't Tell."* New York: Huffington Post Media Group.

———. 2015. *Caring for Our Transgender Troops*. Santa Barbara, CA: Palm Center.

Belkin, Aaron, and Geoffrey Bateman. 2003. *Don't Ask, Don't Tell: Debating the Gay Ban in the Military*. London: Lynne Rienner.

Belkin, Aaron, Morten G. Ender, Nathaniel Frank, Stacie R. Furia, George Lucas, Gary Packard, Steven M. Samuels, Tammy Schultz, and David R.

Segal. 2013. "Readiness and DADT Repeal: Has the New Policy of Open Service Undermined the Military?" *Armed Forces & Society* 39 (4): 587–601.

Belkin, Aaron, Nathaniel Frank, Stacie Furia, George R. Lucas, Gary Packard Jr., Tammy S. Schultz, Steven M. Samuels, and David R. Segal. 2012. *One Year Out: An Assessment of DADT Repeal's Impact on Military Readiness.* Santa Barbara, CA: Palm Center.

Belkin, Aaron, Nathaniel Frank, Gregory M. Herek, Elizabeth L. Hillman, Diane F. Mazur, and Bridget J. Wilson. 2009. *How to End "Don't Ask, Don't Tell": A Roadmap of Political, Legal, Regulatory, and Organizational Steps to Equal Treatment.* Santa Barbara, CA: Palm Center.

Belkin, Aaron, and Diane H. Mazur. 2015. *Presidential Leadership and Military Discrimination.* Santa Barbara, CA: Palm Center.

Bell, Joyce M., and Douglas Hartmann. 2007. "Diversity in Everyday Discourse: The Cultural Ambiguities and Consequences of 'Happy Talk.'" *American Sociological Review* 72 (6): 895–914.

Benecke, Michelle. 2011. "Turning Points: Challenges and Successes in Ending Don't Ask, Don't Tell." *William & Mary Journal of Women & the Law* 18: 35—86.

Benecke, Michelle M., and Kirstin S. Dodge. 1990. "Military Women in Nontraditional Job Fields: Casualties of the Armed Forces' War on Homosexuals Recent Developments." *Harvard Women's Law Journal* 13: 215–50.

Bérubé, Allan. 1990. *Coming Out Under Fire.* New York: Free Press.

Blosnich, John R., George R. Brown, Jillian C. Shipherd, Michael Kauth, Rebecca I. Piegari, and Robert M. Bossarte. 2013. "Prevalence of Gender Identity Disorder and Suicide Risk among Transgender Veterans Utilizing Veterans Health Administration Care." *American Journal of Public Health* 103 (10): 27–32.

Bonnes, Stephanie. 2017. "The Bureaucratic Harassment of U.S. Servicewomen." *Gender & Society* 31 (6): 804–29.

Bornstein, Kate. 1995. *Gender Outlaw: On Men, Women, and the Rest of Us.* New York: Vintage Books.

Bourdieu, Pierre. 1984. *Distinction: A Social Critique of the Judgement of Taste.* Cambridge, MA: Harvard University Press.

Bragg, Rick. 2004. *I Am a Soldier, Too: The Jessica Lynch Story.* New York: Vintage Books.

Britton, Dana M., and Christine L. Williams. 1995. "'Don't Ask, Don't Tell, Don't Pursue': Military Policy and the Construction of Heterosexual Masculinity." *Journal of Homosexuality* 30 (1): 1–21.

Bronner, Simon J. 2007. *Crossing the Line: Violence, Play, and Drama in Naval Equator Traditions.* Amsterdam: Amsterdam University Press.

Brown, Gavin. 2012. "Homonormativity: A Metropolitan Concept That Denigrates 'Ordinary' Gay Lives. *Journal of Homosexuality* 59 (7): 1065–72.

Brown, George R., and Kenneth T. Jones. 2016. "Mental Health and Medical Health Disparities in 5135 Transgender Veterans Receiving Healthcare in the Veterans Health Administration: A Case–Control Study." *LGBT Health* 3 (2): 122–31.

Brown, Wendy. 2008. *Regulating Aversion: Tolerance in the Age of Identity and Empire*. Princeton, NJ: Princeton University Press.

Browne, Kingsley. 2007. *Co-Ed Combat: The New Evidence That Women Shouldn't Fight the Nation's Wars*. 1st ed. New York: Sentinel HC.

Brownson, Connie. 2014. "The Battle for Equivalency: Female US Marines Discuss Sexuality, Physical Fitness, and Military Leadership." *Armed Forces & Society* 40 (4): 765–88.

Bryant, Karl, and Kristen Schilt. 2008. *Transgender People in the U.S. Military: Summary and Analysis, the 2008 Transgender American Veterans Association Survey*. Santa Barbara, CA: Palm Center.

Burke, Carol. 2004. *Camp All-American, Hanoi Jane, and the High-and-Tight: Gender, Folklore, and Changing Military Culture*. Boston: Beacon Press.

Butler, Judith. 1990. *Gender Trouble: Feminism and the Subversion of Identity*. New York: Routledge.

———. 1997. *Excitable Speech: A Politics of the Performative*. New York: Routledge.

———. 2004. *Undoing Gender*. London: Psychology Press.

———. 2016. *Frames of War: When Is Life Grievable?* Reprint ed. New York: Verso.

Canaday, Margot. 2009. *The Straight State: Sexuality and Citizenship in Twentieth-Century America*. Princeton, NJ: Princeton University Press.

Carian, Emily K., and Amy L. Johnson. 2022. "The Agency Myth: Persistence in Individual Explanations for Gender Inequality." *Social Problems* 69 (1): 123–42.

Charmaz, Kathy. 2006. *Constructing Grounded Theory: A Practical Guide through Qualitative Analysis*. Thousand Oaks, CA: Sage Publications.

Chibarro, Lou. 2011. "Barney, Speaking Frankly." *Washington Blade*, December 8.

Clark, Lindsay C. 2021. "Delivering Life, Delivering Death: Reaper Drones, Hysteria and Maternity." *Security Dialogue*, April 27: 1–18.

Coates, Oliver. 2019. "Collateral Damage: Warfare, Death, and Queer Theory in the Global South." *GLQ: A Journal of Lesbian and Gay Studies* 25 (1): 131–35.

Cohen, Cathy J. 1997. "Punks, Bulldaggers, and Welfare Queens: The Radical Potential of Queer Politics?" *GLQ: A Journal of Lesbian and Gay Studies* 3 (4): 437–65.

Collins, Patricia Hill. 2000. *Black Feminist Thought: Knowledge, Consciousness, and the Politics of Empowerment*. New York: Routledge.

Connell, Catherine. 2010. "Doing, Undoing, or Redoing Gender? Learning from the Workplace Experiences of Transpeople." *Gender & Society* 24 (1): 31–55.

——. 2014. *School's Out: Gay and Lesbian Teachers in the Classroom*. Oakland: University of California Press.
——. 2017. "'Different Than an Infantry Unit down in Georgia': Narratives of Queer Liberation in the Post-DADT Military." *Sexualities* 21 (5–6): 776–92.
——. 2018. "'Thank You for Coming Out Today': The Queer Discomforts of In-Depth Interviewing." In *Other, Please Specify: Queer Methods in Sociology*, edited byT. Meadow, K. Schilt, and D. Compton, 126–39. Oakland: University of California Press.
Connell, R. W. (1993) 2005. *Masculinities*. Cambridge, UK: Polity.
Conrad, Ryan, and Mattila Bernstein Sycamore. 2011. *Against Equality: Don't Ask to Fight Their Wars*. Lewiston, MA: Against Equality Press.
cooke, miriam. 2002. "Saving Brown Women." *Signs* 28 (1): 468–70.
Coronges, Kathryn A., Katherine A. Miller, Christina I. Tamayo, and Morten G. Ender. 2013. "A Network Evaluation of Attitudes toward Gays and Lesbians among U.S. Military Cadets." *Journal of Homosexuality* 60 (11): 1557–80.
Crandall, Carla. 2012. "Effects of Repealing Don't Ask, Don't Tell: Is the Combat Exclusion the Next Casualty in the March Toward Integration." *Georgetown Journal of Law & Public Policy* 10: 15–33.
Crawley, Sara L., Lara J. Foley, and Constance L. Shehan. 2008. *Gendering Bodies*. New York: Rowman & Littlefield.
Crosbie, Thomas, and Marek N. Posard. 2016. "Barriers to Serve: Social Policy and the Transgendered Military." *Journal of Sociology* 52 (3): 569–85.
C-SPAN. 1993. *Homosexuals in the Military*. Video, January 29. www.c-span.org/video/?37566-1/homosexuals-military.
Damiano, Christin M. 1998. "Lesbian Baiting in the Military: Institutionalized Sexual Harassment under Don't Ask, Don't Tell, Don't Pursue." *American University Journal of Gender, Social Policy & The Law* 7: 499–522.
Dang, Alain, and Somjen Frazer. 2005. *Black Same-Sex Households in the United States: A Report from the 2000 Census*. NGLT Policy Institute. www.lgbtracialequity.org/publications/2000blacksamesexhouseholds_ngltf.pdf.
Department of Defense. 2010. *Report of the Comprehensive Review of the Issues Associated with a Repeal of "Don't Ask, Don't Tell."* https://archive.defense.gov/home/features/2010/0610_dadt/DADTReport-SPI_FINAL_20101130%28secure-hires%29.pdf.
——. 2013. "DOD Announces Same-Sex Spouse Benefits." https://archive.defense.gov/releases/release.aspx?releaseid=16203.
——. 2015a. "Remarks by Secretary Carter at a Troop Event in Kandahar, Afghanistan." Transcript, February 22. www.defense.gov/Newsroom/Transcripts/Transcript/Article/607016/.
——. 2015b. "Working Group to Study Implications of Transgender Service." Press release, July 13. www.defense.gov/News/News-Stories/Article/Article/612640/.

Deterding, Nicole M., and Mary C. Waters. 2018. "Flexible Coding of In-Depth Interviews: A Twenty-First-Century Approach." *Sociological Methods & Research* 50 (2): 708–39.

Dinnerstein, Dorothy. (1976) 1999. *The Mermaid and the Minotaur: Sexual Arrangements and Human Malaise.* New York: Other Press.

Dosh, Riley. 2019. "I Was Discharged from the Military for Being Trans: I'm Losing Hope of Ever Serving Again." *Vox*, January 25. www.vox.com/first-person/2019/1/24/18195975/trump-trans-military-ban-supreme-court-decision.

Drew, Julie. 2004. "Identity Crisis: Gender, Public Discourse, and 9/11." *Women and Language* 27 (2): 71–77.

Duggan, L. 2002. "The New Homonormativity: The Sexual Politics of Neoliberalism." In *Materializing Democracy: Toward a Revitalized Cultural Politics*, ed. R Castronovo and D. Nelson, 175–94. Durham, NC: Duke University Press.

Ehrenreich, Barbara. 2004. "Feminism's Assumptions Upended." *Los Angeles Times*, May 16. www.latimes.com/archives/la-xpm-2004-may-16-op-ehrenreich16-story.html.

Elders, Joycelyn, and Alan M. Steinman. 2014. *Report of the Transgender Military Service Commission.* Santa Barbara, CA: Palm Center.

Elders, M. Joycelyn, George R. Brown, Eli Coleman, Thomas A. Kolditz, and Alan M. Steinman. 2015. "Medical Aspects of Transgender Military Service." *Armed Forces & Society* 41 (2): 199–220.

Embser-Herbert, Mael, and Bree Fram. 2021. *With Honor and Integrity: Transgender Troops in Their Own Words.* New York: NYU Press.

Ender, Morten G., Nathaniel Frank, Stacie R. Furia, George Lucas, Gary Packard, Steven M. Samuels, Tammy Schultz, and David Segal. 2013. "Readiness and DADT Repeal: Has the New Policy of Open Service Undermined the Military?" *Armed Forces and Society* 39 (4): 587–601.

Ender, Morten G., David E. Rohall, and Michael D. Matthews. 2016. "Cadet and Civilian Undergraduate Attitudes toward Transgender People: A Research Note." *Armed Forces & Society* 42 (2): 427–35.

Enloe, Cynthia. 2000. *Maneuvers: The International Politics of Militarizing Women's Lives.* Berkeley: University of California Press.

——. 2004. "Wielding Masculinity inside Abu Ghraib: Making Feminist Sense of an American Military Scandal." *Asian Journal of Women's Studies* 10 (3): 89–102.

Epstein, Steven. 1994. "A Queer Encounter: Sociology and the Study of Sexuality." *Sociological Theory* 12 (2): 188.

Estes, Adam Clark. 2012. "Eight Years after Abu Ghraib, Lynndie England's Not Doing So Well." *Atlantic*, March 19. www.theatlantic.com/national/archive/2012/03/eight-years-after-abu-ghraib-lynndie-englands-not-doing-so-well/330398/.

Evans, Rhonda. 2001. *U.S Military Policies Concerning Homosexuals: Development, Implementation and Outcomes*. Santa Barbara, CA: Palm Center.

Farber, Rebecca. 2017. "'Transing' Fitness and Remapping Transgender Male Masculinity in Online Message Boards." *Journal of Gender Studies* 26 (3): 254–68.

Farrow, Kenyon. 2011. "A Military Job Is Not Economic Justice: QEJ Statement on DADT." In *Against Equality: Queer Revolution, Not Mere Inclusion*, edited by R. Conrad, 9–11. Oakland, CA: AK Press.

Feitz, Lindsey, and Joane Nagel. 2008. "The Militarization of Gender and Sexuality in the Iraq War." In *Women in the Military and in Armed Conflict*, 201–25. Wiesbaden: Springer.

Ferguson, Roderick A. 2004. *Aberrations in Black: Toward a Queer of Color Critique*. Minneapolis: University of Minnesota Press.

———. 2018. *One-Dimensional Queer*. New York: John Wiley & Sons.

Fields, Jessica. 2013. "Feminist Ethnography: Critique, Conflict, and Ambivalent Observance." *Journal of Contemporary Ethnography* 42 (4): 492–500.

Fine, Cordelia. 2017. *Testosterone Rex: Myths of Sex, Science, and Society*. New York: W. W. Norton.

Foynes, Melissa Ming, Jillian C. Shipherd, and Ellen F. Harrington. 2013. "Race and Gender Discrimination in the Marines." *Cultural Diversity and Ethnic Minority Psychology* 19 (1): 111–19.

Frank, Nathaniel. 2013. "The President's Pleasant Surprise: How LGBT Advocates Ended Don't Ask, Don't Tell." *Journal of Homosexuality* 60 (2–3): 159–213.

Fulton, Brenda Sue. 2013. "OutServe: An Underground Network Stands Up." *Journal of Homosexuality* 60 (2–3): 219–31.

Garner, Steve, and Saher Selod. 2015. "The Racialization of Muslims: Empirical Studies of Islamophobia." *Critical Sociology* 41 (1): 9–19.

Geidner, Chris. 2013. "Meet the Trans Scholar Fighting against the Campaign for Out Trans Military Service." *Buzzfeed*, September 9. www.buzzfeednews.com/article/chrisgeidner/meet-the-trans-scholar-fighting-against-the-campaign-for-out.

George H. W. Bush Presidential Museum. 1991. "Address to the Nation Announcing Allied Military Action in the Persian Gulf," January 16. Public Papers. https://bush41library.tamu.edu/archives/public-papers/2625.

Ghaziani, Amin, and Matt Brim. 2019. *Queer Methods*. New York: NYU Press.

Gibbons-Neff, Thomas. 2020. "U.S. Military Killed 132 Civilians in Wars Last Year, Pentagon Says." *New York Times*, May 7.

Gibson, James William. 1994. *Warrior Dreams: Violence and Manhood in Post-Vietnam America*. New York: Hill and Wang.

Gilligan, Carol. 1982. *In a Different Voice: Psychological Theory and Women's Development*. Cambridge, MA: Harvard University Press.

Gill-Peterson, Jules. 2018. *Histories of the Transgender Child*. Minneapolis: University of Minnesota Press.

Gilreath, Shannon. 2011. "Why Gays Should Not Serve in the United States Armed Forces: A Gay Liberationist Statement of Principle." *William & Mary Journal of Women and the Law*. 18: 7–34.

Glaser, Barney G., and Anselm L. Strauss. 1967. *The Discovery of Grounded Theory: Strategies for Qualitative Research*. New York: Routledge.

Glick, Peter, and S. T. Fiske. 1996. "The Ambivalent Sexism Inventory: Differentiating Hostile and Benevolent Sexism." *Journal of Personality and Social Psychology* 70 (3): 491–512.

GMA. 2019. "Caitlyn Jenner Surprises Trans Student Who Lost ROTC Scholarship with a $25K Check." *Good Morning America*, June 27. www.goodmorningamerica.com/culture/story/caitlyn-jenner-surprises-trans-student-lost-rotc-scholarship-63976226.

Goffman, Erving. 1959. *The Presentation of Self in Everyday Life*. New York: Doubleday.

Goldbach, Jeremy T., and Carl Andrew Castro. 2016. "Lesbian, Gay, Bisexual, and Transgender (LGBT) Service Members: Life after Don't Ask, Don't Tell." *Current Psychiatry Reports* 18 (6): 1–7.

Gossett, Reina, Eric A. Stanley, and Johanna Burton, eds. 2017. *Trap Door: Trans Cultural Production and the Politics of Visibility*. Illus. ed. Cambridge, MA: MIT Press.

Grewal, Inderpal. 2017. *Saving the Security State: Exceptional Citizens in Twenty-First-Century America*. Durham, NC: Duke University Press.

Gronnvoll, Marita. 2007. *Media Representations of Gender and Torture Post-9/11*. New York: Routledge.

Gurung, Sitaji, Ana Ventuneac, H. Jonathon Rendina, Elizabeth Savarese, Christian Grov, and Jeffrey T. Parsons. 2018. "Prevalence of Military Sexual Trauma and Sexual Orientation Discrimination among Lesbian, Gay, Bisexual, and Transgender Military Personnel: A Descriptive Study." *Sexuality Research and Social Policy* 15 (1): 74–82.

Gutmann, Stephanie. 2000. *The Kinder, Gentler Military: Can America's Gender-Neutral Fighting Force Still Win Wars*. New York: Scribner.

Hajjar, Remi M. 2014. "Emergent Postmodern US Military Culture." *Armed Forces & Society* 40 (1): 118–45.

Halley, Janet E. 1999. *Don't: A Reader's Guide to the Military's Anti-Gay Policy*. Durham, NC: Duke University Press.

Halperin, David M. 2014. *How to Be Gay*. Cambridge, MA: Harvard University Press.

Han, C. Winter. 2021. *Racial Erotics: Gay Men of Color, Sexual Racism, and the Politics of Desire*. Seattle: University of Washington Press.

Harding, Sandra. 1992. "Rethinking Standpoint Epistemology: What Is 'Strong Objectivity'?" *Centennial Review* 36 (3): 437–70.

Haritaworn, Jin, Adi Kuntsman, and Silvia Posocco. 2014. *Queer Necropolitics.* New York: Routledge.

Harrison-Quintana, Jack, and Jody Herman. 2013. "Still Serving in Silence: Transgender Service Members and Veterans in the National Transgender Discrimination Survey." *LGBTQ Policy Journal at the Harvard Kennedy School* 3: 1–13.

Hartung, William D., and Ben Freeman. 2020. *Sustainable Defense: A Pentagon Spending Plan for 2021 and Beyond.* Center for International Policy. www.defenseone.com/ideas/2018/12/would-700-billion-budget-really-sink-pentagon/153291.

Hennen, Peter. 2008. *Faeries, Bears, and Leathermen: Men in Community Queering the Masculine.* Chicago: University of Chicago Press.

Hennink, Monique M., Bonnie N. Kaiser, and Vincent C. Marconi. 2017. "Code Saturation Versus Meaning Saturation: How Many Interviews Are Enough?" *Qualitative Health Research* 27 (4): 591–608.

Hepler, Lauren. 2010. "'Don't Ask, Don't Tell' Lobbying Surges as Repeal Fight Nears Climax." Open Secrets, December 3. www.opensecrets.org/news/2010/12/dont-ask-dont-tell-lobbying/.

Herbert, Melissa S. 1998. *Camouflage Isn't Only for Combat: Gender, Sexuality, and Women in the Military.* New York: NYU Press.

Hernandez, Emily. 2019. "UT Freshman Loses Military Scholarship Because He Is Transgender." *Daily Texan*, April 16. www.dailytexanonline.com/2019/04/16/ut-freshman-loses-military-scholarship-because-he-is-transgender.

Hill, Brandon J., Alida Bouris, Joshua Trey Barnett, and Dayna Walker. 2016. "Fit to Serve? Exploring Mental and Physical Health and Well-Being among Transgender Active-Duty Service Members and Veterans in the U.S. Military." *Transgender Health* 1 (1): 4–11.

Hively, Kimberly, and Amani El-Alayli. 2014. "'You Throw like a Girl': The Effect of Stereotype Threat on Women's Athletic Performance and Gender Stereotypes." *Psychology of Sport and Exercise* 15 (1): 48–55.

Hochschild, Arlie. 1994. "The Commercial Spirit of Intimate Life and the Abduction of Feminism: Signs from Women's Advice Books." *Theory, Culture & Society* 11 (2): 1–24.

Holland, Shannon L. 2006. "The Dangers of Playing Dress-up: Popular Representations of Jessica Lynch and the Controversy Regarding Women in Combat." *Quarterly Journal of Speech* 92 (1): 27–50.

Holmstedt, Kirsten. 2008. *Band of Sisters: American Women at War in Iraq.* Mechanicsburg, PA: Stackpole Books.

Hoskin, Rhea Ashley. 2020. "'Femininity? It's the Aesthetic of Subordination': Examining Femmephobia, the Gender Binary, and Experiences of Oppression among Sexual and Gender Minorities." *Archives of Sexual Behavior* 49: 2319–39.

Howard, John W., and Laura C. Prividera. 2004. "Rescuing Patriarchy or Saving 'Jessica Lynch': The Rhetorical Construction of the American Woman Soldier." *Women and Language* 27 (2): 89–97.

Hyland, Julie. 2003. "BBC Documentary Exposes Pentagon Lies: The Staged Rescue of Private Jessica Lynch." *World Socialist Web Site.*

James, Sandy E., Jody L. Herman, Susan Rankin, Mara Keisling, and Ma'ayan Anafi. 2016. *Report of the 2015 U.S. Transgender Survey.* Washington, DC: National Center for Transgender Equality.

Johnson, Austin H. 2016. "Transnormativity: A New Concept and Its Validation through Documentary Film about Transgender Men." *Sociological Inquiry* 86 (4): 465–91.

Johnson, David K. 2004. *The Lavender Scare: The Cold War Persecution of Gays and Lesbians in the Federal Government.* Chicago: University of Chicago Press.

Johnson, W. Brad, Judith E. Rosenstein, Robin A. Buhrke, and Douglas C. Haldeman. 2013. "After 'Don't Ask Don't Tell': Competent Care of Lesbian, Gay and Bisexual Military Personnel during the DoD Policy Transition." *Professional Psychology: Research and Practice* 46 (2): 107–15.

Juro, Rebecca. 2014. "Working While Trans." *Advocate*, July 17. www.advocate.com/print-issue/current-issue/2014/07/17/working-while-trans.

Kalin, Tom, dir. 2021. *Pride.* Episode 1. Aired May 14. Santa Monica, CA: Hulu.

Kamarck, Kristy N. 2016. *Women in Combat: Issues for Congress.* Washington, DC: Congressional Research Service.

Kandiyoti, Deniz. 1988. "Bargaining with Patriarchy." *Gender and Society* 2 (3): 274–90.

Kaufman-Osborn, Timothy. 2005. "Gender Trouble at Abu Ghraib?" *Politics & Gender* 1 (4): 597–619.

Kerrigan, Matthew F. 2012. "Transgender Discrimination in the Military: The New Don't Ask, Don't Tell." *Psychology, Public Policy, and Law* 18 (3): 500–518.

Khalid, Maryam. 2011. "Gender, Orientalism and Representations of the 'Other' in the War on Terror." *Global Change, Peace & Security* 23 (1): 15–29.

Khalili, Laleh. 2011. "Gendered Practices of Counterinsurgency." *Review of International Studies* 37 (4): 1471–91.

Kim-Puri, H. J. 2005. "Conceptualizing Gender-Sexuality-State-Nation: An Introduction." *Gender & Society* 19 (2): 137–59.

King, Anthony C. 2015. "Women Warriors: Female Accession to Ground Combat." *Armed Forces & Society* 41 (2): 379–87.

Korb, Lawrence. 1994. "Evolving Perspectives on the Military's Policy on Homosexuals: A Personal Note." In *Gays and Lesbians in the Military: Issues, Concerns, and Contrasts*, edited by W. J. Scott and S. C. Stanley, 219–29. New York : Aldine de Gruyter.

Korb, Lawrence J., and Alexander Rothman. 2013. "Formalizing the Ban: My Experience in the Reagan Administration." *Journal of Homosexuality* 60 (2–3): 273–81.

Krafft-Ebing, Richard von. 1886. *Psychopathia Sexualis: With Especial Reference to Contrary Sexual Instinct; A Medico-Legal Study*. Stuttgart: Ferdinand Enke.

Kumar, Deepa. 2007. "War Propaganda and the (AB)Uses of Women." *Feminist Media Studies* 4 (3): 297–313.

Lamont, Michèle, and Ann Swidler. 2014. "Methodological Pluralism and the Possibilities and Limits of Interviewing." *Qualitative Sociology* 37 (2): 153–71.

Lamothe, Dan. 2015. "Ranger School Officer Combats Rumors about How Women Passed in a Pointed Facebook Post." *Washington Post*, August 20 .www.washingtonpost.com/news/checkpoint/wp/2015/08/20/ranger-school-officer-combats-rumors-about-how-women-passed-in-pointed-facebook-post/.

Lange, Katie. 2018. *National Defense Strategy: Lethality*. US Department of Defense. October 8.www.defense.gov/News/Feature-Stories/story/Article/1656335/national-defense-strategy-lethality/.

Leffler, David. 2019. "Map Pesqueira: The Face of Trump's Transgender Military Ban." *Austin Monthly Magazine*, September. www.austinmonthly.com/map-pesqueira-the-face-of-trumps-transgender-military-ban/.

Lobasz, Jennifer K. 2008. "The Woman in Peril and the Ruined Woman: Representations of Female Soldiers in the Iraq War." *Journal of Women, Politics & Policy* 29 (3): 305–34.

MacKenzie, Megan. 2015. *Beyond the Band of Brothers: The US Military and the Myth That Women Can't Fight*. Cambridge: Cambridge University Press.

Maginnis, Robert L. 2013. *Deadly Consequences: How Cowards Are Pushing Women into Combat*. Washington, DC: Regnery Publishing.

Maninger, Stephan. 2008. "Women in Combat: Reconsidering the Case against the Deployment of Women in Combat-Support and Combat Units." In *Women in the Military and in Armed Conflict*, edited by H. Carreiras and G. Kummel. 9–27. Wiesbaden: Springer.

Massey, Eli, and Yasmin Nair. 2018. "Inclusion in the Atrocious." *Current Affairs*, March 22. www.currentaffairs.org/2018/03/inclusion-in-the-atrocious.

Massey, Mary Elizabeth. 1994. *Women in the Civil War*. Lincoln: University of Nebraska Press.

Mattis, James M. 2018. *Department of Defense Report and Recommendations on Military Service by Transgender Persons*. https://media.defense.gov/2018/Mar/23/2001894037/-1/-1/0/MILITARY-SERVICE-BY-TRANSGENDER-INDIVIDUALS.PDF.

Mattocks, Kristin M., Sally G. Haskell, Erin E. Krebs, Amy C. Justice, Elizabeth M. Yano, and Cynthia Brandt. 2012. "Women at War: Understanding How Women Veterans Cope with Combat and Military Sexual Trauma." *Social Science & Medicine* 74 (4): 537–45.

Mazur, Diane H. 2014. *Arbitrary and Capricious: Six Inconsistencies Distinguishing Military Medial Politics for Transgender and Non-transgender Personnel.* Santa Barbara, CA: Palm Center.

Mbembe, Achille. 2019. *Necropolitics.* Durham NC: Duke University Press.

McCaughey, Martha. 2008. *The Caveman Mystique: Pop-Darwinism and the Debates over Sex, Violence, and Science.* New York: Routledge.

McPeak, Merrill A. 2010. "Opinion: Don't Change 'Don't Ask, Don't Tell.'" *New York Times,* March 4.

McRuer, Robert. 2010. "Compulsory Able-Bodiedness and Queer/Disabled Existence." In *The Disability Studies Reader,* edited by L. J. Davis, 369–80. New York: Routledge.

Meadow, Tey, Kristen Schilt, and D'Lane Compton, eds. 2018. *Other, Please Specify: Queer Methods in Sociology.* Oakland: University of California Press.

Mesok, Elizabeth. 2016. "Sexual Violence and the US Military: Feminism, US Empire, and the Failure of Liberal Equality." *Feminist Studies* 42 (1): 41–69.

Meyerowitz, Joanne. 2002. *How Sex Changed: A History of Transsexuality in the United States.* Cambridge, MA: Harvard University Press.

Mikdashi, Maya, and Jasbir K. Puar. 2016. "Queer Theory and Permanent War." *GLQ: A Journal of Lesbian and Gay Studies* 22 (2): 215–22.

Military Times. 2013. "Tech. Sgts. Take Heat after Receiving Medals." March 28. www.militarytimes.com/2013/03/28/tech-sgts-take-heat-after-receiving-medals/#:~:text=%22My%20brother%20in%20the%20army,%22a%20female%20or%20minority.%22.

Millar, Katherine M. 2015. "Death Does Not Become Her: An Examination of the Public Construction of Female American Soldiers as Liminal Figures." *Review of International Studies* 41 (4): 757–79.

Mitchell, Brian. 1997. *Women in the Military: Flirting With Disaster.* 1st ed. Washington, DC: Regnery Publishing.

Mohanty, Chandra Talpade. 1988. "Under Western Eyes: Feminist Scholarship and Colonial Discourses." *Feminist Review* 30: 61–88.

Morral, Andrew R., Kristie Gore, Terry L. Schell, Barbara Bicksler, Coreen Farris, Madhumita Ghosh Dastidar, Lisa H. Jaycox, Dean Kilpatrick, Steve Kistler, Amy Street, Terri Tanielian, and Kayla M. Williams. 2015. *Sexual Assault and Sexual Harassment in the U.S. Military.* Rand Corporation Technical Reports. www.rand.org/pubs/research_briefs/RB9841.html.

Montegary, Liz. 2015. "Militarizing US Homonormativities: The Making of 'Ready, Willing, and Able' Gay Citizens." *Signs: Journal of Women in Culture & Society* 40 (4): 891–915.

Moussawi, Ghassan. 2020. *Disruptive Situations: Fractal Orientalism and Queer Strategies in Beirut*. 1st ed. Philadelphia: Temple University Press.
Muñoz, Jose Esteban. 2009. *Cruising Utopia: The Then and There of Queer Futurity*. New York: NYU Press.
Nagel, Joane. 1998. "Masculinity and Nationalism: Gender and Sexuality in the Making of Nations." *Ethnic and Racial Studies* 21 (2): 242–69.
Nash, Catherine Jean, and Kath Browne. 2020. *Heteroactivism: Resisting Lesbian, Gay, Bisexual and Trans Rights and Equalities*. London: Zed Books.
#NatSecGirlSquad. n.d. "About." www.natsecgirlsquad.com/about.
Neff, Christopher L., and Luke R. Edgell. 2013. "The Rise of Repeal: Policy Entrepreneurship and Don't Ask, Don't Tell." *Journal of Homosexuality* 60 (2–3): 232–49.
Negin, Elliott. 2020. "Time to Rein in Inflated Military Budgets." *Scientific American*, September 14. www.scientificamerican.com/article/its-time-to-rein-in-inflated-military-budgets/.
New York Times. 1989. "Transcript of Reagan's Farewell Address to American People." January 12. www.nytimes.com/1989/01/12/news/transcript-of-reagan-s-farewell-address-to-american-people.html.
O'Brien, Jodi. 2009. "Sociology as an Epistemology of Contradiction." *Sociological Perspectives* 52 (1): 5–22.
Office of the Secretary of Defense. 1962. *Hearings Before the Subcommittee on Constitutional Rights of the Senate Committee on the Judiciary*. 87th Cong., 2nd Sess.
Okros, Alan, and Denise Scott. 2014. "Gender Identity in the Canadian Forces: A Review of Possible Impacts on Operational Effectiveness." *Armed Forces & Society* 41 (2): 243–56.
Parco, James E., and David A. Levy. 2013. "Policy and Paradox: Grounded Theory at the Moment of DADT Repeal." *Journal of Homosexuality* 60 (2–3): 356–80.
Parco, James E., David A. Levy, and Sarah R. Spears. 2015. "Transgender Military Personnel in the Post-DADT Repeal Era: A Phenomenological Study." *Armed Forces & Society* 41 (2): 221–42.
Parker, Kathleen. 2015. "Women in Combat Will Put Men at Greater Risk." *Washington Post*, December 11.
Pascoe, C. J. 2011. *Dude, You're a Fag: Masculinity and Sexuality in High School*. Berkeley: University of California Press.
———. 2013. "Notes on a Sociology of Bullying: Young Men's Homophobia as Gender Socialization." *QED: A Journal in GLBTQ Worldmaking* (Fall): 87–104.
Patil, Vrushali. 2013. "From Patriarchy to Intersectionality: A Transnational Feminist Assessment of How Far We've Really Come." *Signs* 38 (4): 847–67.
———. 2018. "The Heterosexual Matrix as Imperial Effect." *Sociological Theory* 36 (1): 1–26.

Pauw, Linda Grant De. 1981. "Women in Combat: The Revolutionary War Experience." *Armed Forces & Society* 7 (2): 209–26.

Peterson, V. Spike. 1999. "Political Identities/Nationalism as Heterosexism." *International Feminist Journal of Politics* 1 (1): 34–65.

Puar, Jasbir. 2007. *Terrorist Assemblages: Homonationalism in Queer Times*. Durham, NC: Duke University Press.

Puar, Jasbir K. 2017a. *The Right to Maim: Debility, Capacity, Disability*. Durham, NC: Duke University Press.

Puar, Jasbir K. 2017b. "The Right to Maim: A Reply." *The Disorder of Things*, https://thedisorderofthings.com/2018/12/15/the-right-to-maim-a-reply/.

Puar, Jasbir K., and Amit Rai. 2002. "Monster, Terrorist, Fag: The War on Terrorism and the Production of Docile Patriots." *Social Text* 20 (3): 117–48.

Puri, Jyoti. 2016. *Sexual States*. Durham, NC: Duke University Press.

Ray, Victor. 2018. "Diversity of Thought." *Inside Higher Ed*, June 8. www.insidehighered.com/advice/2018/06/08/three-faulty-premises-many-conservatives-believe-about-diversity-thought-opinion.

Razavi, Negar. 2021. "NatSec Feminism: Women Security Experts and the US Counterterror State." *Signs: Journal of Women in Culture and Society* 46 (2): 361–86.

Reddy, Chandan. 2008. "Time for Rights? Loving, Gay Marriage, and the Limits of Legal Justice." *Fordham Law Review* 76 (6): 2849.

———. 2011. *Freedom with Violence: Race, Sexuality, and the US State*. Durham, NC: Duke University Press.

Rich, Adrienne. 1980. "Compulsory Heterosexuality and Lesbian Existence." *Signs: Journal of Women in Culture & Society* 5 (4): 631–60.

Rich, Craig, Julie Kalil Schutten, and Richard A. Rogers. 2012. "'Don't Drop the Soap': Organizing Sexualities in the Repeal of the US Military's 'Don't Ask, Don't Tell' Policy." *Communication Monographs* 79 (3): 269–91.

Rimalt, Noya. 2003. "When a Feminist Struggle Becomes a Symbol of the Agenda as a Whole: The Example of Women in the Military." *Nashim: A Journal of Jewish Women's Studies & Gender Issues*, no. 6, 148–64.

Robinson, Brandon Andrew. 2020. *Coming Out to the Streets: LGBTQ Youth Experiencing Homelessness*. Oakland: University of California Press.

Rollins, Angela. 2011. "Act Like a Lady: Reconsidering Gender Stereotypes & the Exclusion of Women from Combat in Light of Challenges to Don't Ask, Don't Tell." *Southern Illinois University School of Law Journal* 36: 355–82.

Rosen, Leora N., Kathryn H. Knudson, and Peggy Fancher. 2003. "Cohesion and the Culture of Hypermasculinity in U.S. Army Units." *Armed Forces & Society* 29 (3): 325–51.

Rosenberg, Matthew, and Dave Philipps. 2015. "All Combat Roles Now Open to Women, Defense Secretary Says." *New York Times*, December 3.

Rostker, Bernard D., Scott A. Harris, James P. Kahan, Erik J. Frinking, C. Neil Fulcher, Lawrence M. Hanser, Paul Koegel, John D. Winkler, Brent A.

Boultinghouse, Joanna Heilbrunn, Janet Lever, Robert J. MacCoun, Peter Tiemeyer, Gail L. Zellman, Sandra H. Berry, Jennifer Hawes-Dawson, Samantha Ravich, Steven L. Schlossman, Timothy Haggarty, Tanjam Jacobson, Ancella Livers, Sherie Mershon, Andrew Cornell, Mark A. Schuster, David E. Kanouse, Raynard Kington, Mark Litwin, Conrad Peter Schmidt, Carl H. Builder, Peter Jacobson, Stephen A. Saltzburg, Roger Allen Brown, William Fedorochko, Marilyn Fisher Freemon, John F. Peterson, and James A. Dewar. 1993. *Sexual Orientation and U.S. Military Personnel Policy*. Boston: RAND.

Rubin, Gayle. 1975. "The Traffic in Women." In *Toward an Anthropology of Women*, edited y R. R. Reiter, 157–210. New York: Monthly Review Press.

Rumens, Nick, and Deborah Kerfoot. 2009. "Gay Men at Work: (Re)Constructing the Self as Professional." *Human Relations* 62 (5): 763–86.

Sandoval, Chela. 1991. "U.S. Third World Feminism: The Theory and Method of Oppositional Consciousness in the Postmodern World." *Genders* 10: 1–24.

Schaefer, Agnes Gereben, Jennie W. Wenger, Jennifer Kavanagh, Jonathan P. Wong, Gillian S. Oak, Thomas E. Trail, and Todd Nichols. 2015. *Implications of Integrating Women into the Marine Corps Infantry*. Boston: RAND.

Schaefer, Agnes Gereben, Radha Iyengar, Srikanth Kadiyala, Jennifer Kavanagh, Charles C. Engel, Kayla M. Williams, and Amii M. Kress. 2016. *Assessing the Implications of Allowing Transgender Personnel to Serve Openly*. Boston: RAND.

Schilt, Kristen, and Laurel Westbrook. 2015. "Bathroom Battlegrounds and Penis Panics." *Contexts* 14 (3): 26–31.

Schulman, Sarah. 2011. "Isreal and Pinkwashing." *New York Times*, November 22.

Scrivener, Laurie. 1999. "U.S. Military Women in World War II: The SPAR, WAC, WAVES, WASP, and Women Marines in U.S Government Publications." *Journal of Government Information* 26 (4): 361–83.

Sedgwick, Eve Kosofsky. 1990. *Epistemology of the Closet*. Berkeley: University of California Press.

———. 1993. *Tendencies*. Durham, NC: Duke University Press.

Seidman, Steven. 2002. *Beyond the Closet: The Transformation of Gay and Lesbian Life*. Reprint ed. New York: Routledge.

Serlin, David Harley. 2003. "Crippling Masculinity: Queerness and Disability in U.S. Military Culture, 1800–1945." *GLQ: A Journal of Lesbian and Gay Studies* 9 (1): 149–79.

Shawver, Lois. 1995. *And the Flag Was Still There: Straight People, Gay People, and Sexuality in the U.S. Military*. London: Psychology Press.

Shilts, Randy. 1994. *Conduct Unbecoming: Gays and Lesbians in the U.S. Military*. New York: St. Martin's Griffin.

Shipherd, Jillian C., Lauren Mizock, Shira Maguen, and Kelly E. Green. 2012. "Male-to-Female Transgender Veterans and VA Health Care Utilization." *International Journal of Sexual Health* 24 (1): 78–87.

shuster, stef M. 2021. *Trans Medicine: The Emergence and Practice of Treating Gender.* New York: NYU Press.

Skidmore, Emily. 2011. "Constructing the 'Good Transsexual': Christine Jorgensen, Whiteness, and Heteronormativity in the Mid-Twentieth-Century Press." *Feminist Studies* 37 (2): 270–300.

Snorton, C. Riley. 2017. *Black on Both Sides: A Racial History of Trans Identity.* Minneapolis: University of Minnesota Press.

Snorton, C. Riley, and Jin Haritaworn. 2013. "Trans Necropolitics: A Transnational Reflection on Violence, Death, and the Trans of Color Afterlife." In *Transgender Studies Reader*, edited by S. Stryker and A. Z. Aizura, 66–76. New York: Routledge.

SOFREP. 2015. "How It Really Went Down in the First Class to Graduate Female Rangers." August 21. https://sofrep.com/news/really-happened-women-ranger-school-class-06-15/.

Somerville, Siobhan B. 2000. *Queering the Color Line: Race and the Invention of Homosexuality in American Culture.* Durham, NC: Duke University Press Books.

——. 2005. "Queer Loving." *GLQ: A Journal of Lesbian and Gay Studies* 11 (3): 335–70.

Spade, Dean. 2011. *Normal Life: Administrative Violence, Critical Trans Politics and the Limits of Law.* Brooklyn, NY: South End Press.

——. 2020. *Mutual Aid: Building Solidarity During This Crisis.* New York: Verso.

Spade, Dean, and Aaron Belkin. 2021. "Queer Militarism?! The Politics of Military Inclusion Advocacy in Authoritarian Times." *GLQ: A Journal of Lesbian and Gay Studies* 27 (2): 281–307.

Spade, Dean, and Craig Willse. 2014. "Sex, Gender, and War in an Age of Multicultural Imperialism." *QED: A Journal in GLBTQ Worldmaking* 1 (1): 5–29.

Sparta. n.d. "Who We Are." Accessed May 8, 2022. https://spartapride.org/about-us/.

Spivak, Gayatri Chakravorty. 1985. "Can the Subaltern Speak? Speculations on Widow Sacrifice." *Wedge* 7 (8): 120–30.

Stacey, Judith. 1988. "Can There Be a Feminist Ethnography?" *Women's Studies International Forum* 11 (1): 21–27.

Street, Amy E., Dawne Vogt, and Lissa Dutra. 2009. "A New Generation of Women Veterans: Stressors Faced by Women Deployed to Iraq and Afghanistan." *Clinical Psychology Review* 29 (8): 685–94.

Stryker, Susan. 1994. "My Words to Victor Frankenstein Above the Village of Chamounix: Performing Transgender Rage." *GLQ* 1 (3): 237–54.

——. 2008. "Transgender History, Homonormativity, and Disciplinarity." *Radical History Review* 2008 (100): 145–57.

Stryker, Susan, and Stephen Whittle. 2006. *The Transgender Studies Reader.* New York: Routledge.

Sycamore, Mattilda Bernstein. 2008. *That's Revolting! Queer Strategies for Resisting Assimilation*. Brooklyn, NY: Soft Skull Press.

———. 2013. "An L.G.B.T. Movement Should Be More Radical." *New York Times*, October 15. www.nytimes.com/roomfordebate/2013/10/15/are-trans-rights-and-gay-rights-still-allies/an-lgbt-movement-should-be-more-radical.

Szitanyi, Stephanie. 2020. *Gender Trouble in the U.S. Military—Challenges to Regimes of Male Privilege*. New York: Palgrave Macmillan.

Taber, Nancy. 2011. "'You Better Not Get Pregnant While You're Here': Tensions Between Masculinities and Femininities in Military Communities of Practice." *International Journal of Lifelong Education* 30 (3): 331–48.

Taylor, Verta, and Nella Van Dyke. 2008. "'Get Up, Stand Up': Tactical Repertoires of Social Movements." In *The Blackwell Companion to Social Movements*, edited by D. Snow, S. A. Soule, and H. Kriesi, 262–93. Malden, MA: Blackwell.

Terry, Jennifer. 1999. *An American Obsession: Science, Medicine, and Homosexuality in Modern Society*. Chicago: University of Chicago Press.

Thompson, Cooper. 2001. "A New Vision of Masculinity." In *Race, Class, and Gender*, edited by M. L. Andersen and P. H. Collins, 205–22. Belmont, CA: Wadsworth Thomson Learning.

Timmermans, Stefan, and Iddo Tavory. 2012. "Theory Construction in Qualitative Research: From Grounded Theory to Abductive Analysis." *Sociological Theory* 30 (3): 167–86.

Trivette, Shawn A. 2010. "Secret Handshakes and Decoder Rings: The Queer Space of Don't Ask/Don't Tell." *Sexuality Research & Social Policy* 7 (3): 214–28.

Trobaugh, Elizabeth. 2018. "Women, Regardless: Understanding Gender Bias in U.S. Military Integration." *Joint Force Quarterly* 88. https://ndupress.ndu.edu/Media/News/News-Article-View/Article/1411860/women-regardless-understanding-gender-bias-in-us-military-integration/.

"TS Discharged from Naval Reserve." 1978. *Drag* 7 (26). https://archive.org/details/drag726unse/page/6/mode/2up.

Turchik, Jessica A., and Susan M. Wilson. 2010. "Sexual Assault in the U.S. Military: A Review of the Literature and Recommendations for the Future." *Aggression and Violent Behavior* 15 (4): 267–77.

Turley, Jonathan. 2010. "Gay Barracks? Marine Commandant Promises to Force Gay to Live in Separate Housing." March 28. https://jonathanturley.org/2010/03/28/separate-equal-and-fabulous-barracks-marine-commandant-promises-to-force-gay-to-live-in-separate-housing/.

Valentine, David. 2007. *Imagining Transgender: An Ethnography of a Category*. Durham, NC: Duke University Press.

Walters, Suzanna Danuta. 2014. *The Tolerance Trap: How God, Genes, and Good Intentions Are Sabotaging Gay Equality*. New York: NYU Press.

Ward, Jane. 2008. *Respectably Queer: Diversity Culture in LGBT Activist Organizations*. Nashville, TN: Vanderbilt University Press.
———. 2015. *Not Gay: Sex Between Straight White Men*. New York: NYU Press.
———. 2020. *The Tragedy of Heterosexuality*. New York: NYU Press.
West, Candace, and Don H. Zimmerman. 1987. "Doing Gender." *Gender & Society* 1 (2): 125–51.
Westbrook, Laurel. 2020. *Unlivable Lives: Violence and Identity in Transgender Activism*. Oakland: University of California Press.
Westbrook, Lauren, and Kristen Schilt. 2014. "Doing Gender, Determining Gender: Transgender People, Gender Panics, and the Maintenance of the Sex/Gender/Sexuality System." *Gender & Society* 28(1): 32–57.
Wilder, Heather, and Jami Wilder. 2012. "In the Wake of Don't Ask Don't Tell: Suicide Prevention and Outreach for LGB Service Members." *Military Psychology* 24 (6): 624–42.
Williams, Christine L., and Catherine Connell. 2010. "'Looking Good and Sounding Right' Aesthetic Labor and Social Inequality in the Retail Industry." *Work and Occupations* 37 (3): 349–77.
Williams, Christine L., Patti A. Giuffre, and Kirsten Dellinger. 2009. "The Gay-Friendly Closet." *Sexuality Research & Social Policy* 6 (1): 29–45.
Wittig, Monique. 1992. *The Straight Mind and Other Essays*. Boston: Beacon Press.
Yerke, Adam F., and Valory Mitchell. 2013. "Transgender People in the Military: Don't Ask? Don't Tell? Don't Enlist!" *Journal of Homosexuality* 60 (2–3): 436–57.
Yoshino, Kenji. 1998. "Assimilationist Bias in Equal Protection: The Visibility Presumption and the Case of 'Don't Ask, Don't Tell.'" *Yale Law Journal* 108 (3): 485–571.
———. 2006. *Covering: The Hidden Assault on Our Civil Rights*. Reprint ed. New York: Random House Trade Paperbacks.
Young, Iris Marion. 1980. "Throwing Like a Girl: A Phenomenology of Feminine Body Comportment Motility and Spatiality." *Human Studies* 3 (1): 137–56.
Zeeland, Steven. 1995. *Sailors and Sexual Identity: Crossing the Line Between "Straight" and "Gay" in the U.S. Navy*. New York: Harrington Park Press.
Zopf, Bradley J. 2018. "A Different Kind of Brown: Arabs and Middle Easterners as Anti-American Muslims." *Sociology of Race and Ethnicity* 4 (2): 178–91.

Index

Founded in 1893,
UNIVERSITY OF CALIFORNIA PRESS
publishes bold, progressive books and journals on topics in the arts, humanities, social sciences, and natural sciences—with a focus on social justice issues—that inspire thought and action among readers worldwide.

The UC PRESS FOUNDATION
raises funds to uphold the press's vital role as an independent, nonprofit publisher, and receives philanthropic support from a wide range of individuals and institutions—and from committed readers like you. To learn more, visit ucpress.edu/supportus.